CHEFS & COMPANY

75 TOP CHEFS SHARE MORE THAN 180 RECIPES TO WOW LAST-MINUTE GUESTS

MARIA ISABELLA

TESTER FOR AMERICA'S TEST KITCHEN AND *BON APPÉTIT*

FOREWORD BY TED ALLEN

PHOTOGRAPHY BY KEN GOODMAN

PAGE STREET
PUBLISHING CO.

PAGE STREET
PUBLISHING CO.

Distributed by Macmillan, sales in Canada by The Canadian Manda Group.

21 20 19 18 17   1 2 3 4 5

ISBN-13: 978-1-62414-455-4

ISBN-10: 1-62414-455-4

Library of Congress Control Number: 2017930480

Cover and book design by Page Street Publishing Co.

Photography by Ken Goodman

Photos of Guy Savoy (page 8) by Laurence Mouton

Photo of Daniel Boulud (page 142) by Thomas Schauer

Author photo (page 459) by Heidi Campany

Printed and bound in China

C424
I

**FOR MY BEAUTIFUL MOTHER,
MADDALENA TIJANICH**

who always added one extra secret ingredient to every
special dish she ever made for me: her undying love.

AND FOR MY PRECIOUS GRANDCHILDREN

Finley, Harper, Claira, Avery, Ronan, and Baby Christensen—
for whom I also add that very same secret ingredient.

CONTENTS

FOREWORD

When you're in my line of work, reporters often ask you about the latest trends in food. My answer is always the same: I don't care. (Well, sometimes I'll tell them the hot new thing is goat meat, just to see if they'll print it.) But, generally, I'm just not interested in trends, fads, or whatever fleeting sensations are driving the Yelpers to wait 90 minutes for dinner.

But here's a trend I can get behind, because I truly believe it's here to stay, it's cross-generational and touches every demographic, and it's getting stronger by the minute: the improvement in American cooking— everywhere in America. In just the past couple of decades, public interest in and demand for interesting ingredients, culinary classes for all ages, cooking programming on television and online, and, of course, creative, independent restaurants—stationary and motorized—have unmistakably surged in virtually every American city, from Nashville to Asheville, Miami to Minneapolis, from Portland, Oregon, to Portland, Maine. There is jaw-droppingly delicious and creative food in Columbus, Ohio. Indianapolis. Phoenix. Detroit. The White House still has a garden, everybody goes to the farmers' market, and we're eating $7 bunches of ramps as fast as Appalachians can mine them from the side of the road. The butcher shop is back. Charcuterie, brewing, cheesemaking, and distilling are booming.

You know how people keep asking when the "rock-star chef" phenomenon is going to end? Here's your answer: It's not going to.

Which brings me to this book. And, speaking of rock stars, to Maria and Ken. Maria's previous cookbook, presenting 1-hour recipes from top Cleveland chefs, was a hit, not just in Ohio, but across the country. With this collection, however, she takes the concept nationwide. And Ken is to chefs what Danny Clinch is to Springsteen—the go-to, house photographer of the A-list.

Who doesn't want to learn more fast, simple, and delicious recipes? And who couldn't use some great ideas for last-minute guests? (My tip: Keep a bag of cleaned shrimp in the freezer, and cocktail sauce in the fridge— shrimp thaws in minutes under cold water.) But don't take it from me: Instead, go backstage with 75 great American pros, with tips, stories, music suggestions, and more than 180 quick and easy dishes. Care to sit down in Hugh Acheson's Athens, Georgia, kitchen for Chicken Thighs with Kimchi Peas, Shallot & Lemon? Yes, please. A seat at Lidia Bastianich's home table for Veal Scaloppine Saltimbocca with Spinach? What time? Naomi Pomeroy's house in Portland (the one on the left) for Pasta Amatriciana? Sign me up. And what's her address, again?

In *Chefs & Company*, Maria and Ken get you a table that nobody can get—inside the home kitchens of chefs from every corner of our food-obsessed country—and share with you the flavors chefs save for their closest friends and family when the chefs' hats are off, the stereo's on, and they're cracking open beers. It's the best kind of cooking, the relaxed and casually delicious food they pull from the pantry for people close enough to drop by without calling. Get ready for your doorbell to start ringing more often.

—TED ALLEN

INTRODUCTION

The seed of an idea for this book was planted quite a long time ago. More specifically, the fall of 2008, when everything was so unexpectedly—and serendipitously—put into motion.

You see, that was when I flew to New York with one of my twin daughters, who was interviewing at a medical school there at the time (she's now a surgical resident at the Cleveland Clinic!). My oldest daughter, who lives in New York, picked us up at the airport, dropped Monica off at the med school, and then drove to an adorable little coffee shop in upstate New York for some special mother-daughter time. We ordered scones, tea, and hot chocolate, then settled ourselves into a couple of overstuffed armchairs in the back parlor.

As we were sipping and sharing our hopes, dreams, and life goals, one of my long-harbored secrets accidentally spilled out. "I've always wanted to write a book," I blurted. "Really? What kind of book?" asked Nina, looking a little surprised. "A cookbook," I said, almost embarrassed that I sounded so cocksure of myself when, in fact, I had no idea what it entailed—or the journey I was about to embark on.

Four years and countless hours of hard work later, there it was. In my hands. A freshly printed cookbook with my name on the front cover. *In the Kitchen with Cleveland's Favorite Chefs* had finally become a reality. And people from not only Cleveland, but all over the world, bought it. Which is a big reason it's now in its sixth printing. I guess you'd call that a success.

As an encore, I decided to take it a few giant steps further and, this time, reach out to the best chefs in America, not just my hometown. I wanted to create an even bigger, better, and more exciting version than before (i.e., the first book on steroids, if you will). And that, dear reader, is the whole backstory in a nutshell.

However, to continue my tale, what I think is even more important to share is why I chose the topic of last-minute entertaining with star chefs to begin with. Simply put, we all love to eat. We love great food. We love to cook. We love to share with family and friends. And we love to entertain, even if it's at a moment's notice.

Yet we're all busy, busy people. How can we possibly juggle it all and still make a great impression?

Between you and me, even though I've been in the culinary industry a long time (as a cookbook author, editor, reviewer, and judge, as well as a food writer, blogger, recipe tester, instructor, and focus group member), I would still get frazzled whenever I had to prepare an impromptu meal for drop-in guests. "I wonder what so-and-so would make for their guests?" I often found myself muttering under my breath, daydreaming about any one of my all-time favorite chefs.

Finally my curiosity got the best of me, and I decided to simply go out and—gasp!—ask them myself directly. Naturally, and organically, I discovered their secrets, which I'm beyond thrilled to share with you in this comprehensive tome!

I posed the exact same question to each and every chef I approached:

"If you were to entertain last-minute guests at your own home,

what would you prepare for them in one hour or less?"

I reached out to chefs all across the country, from coast to coast to coast.

I reached out to chefs in a multitude of venues, from restaurants and hotels to culinary schools and nonprofits, from food trucks and television shows to national foundations.

I reached out to the best of the best, including Michelin-starred chefs, James Beard award winners, Top Chef judges and contestants, and the handpicked darlings of both *Bon Appétit* and *Food & Wine*.

I reached out to male and female. Younger and older. American born and foreign born. A range of backgrounds and ethnicities. Classically trained and self-taught. And both experienced and up-and-coming.

Speaking of experienced and up-and-coming, there are two chefs in particular who could not have exemplified these extremes any better: the legendary Guy Savoy (of Michelin-starred Restaurant Guy Savoy in Paris and Las Vegas, seen top and middle left) and the wunderkind Flynn McGarry (of the pop-up Eureka in New York City, seen bottom left). They each gave me their take on my question, and I think you'll love both answers equally.

"During one hour," Guy said, "I would offer [my last-minute guests] an apéritif with grilled bread, butter, and sardines, and in the meanwhile I would book a table for dinner in the best restaurant in the neighborhood." (What a wicked sense of humor!)

And Flynn told me, "If some friends called, I would definitely make pasta. Depending on the crowd, it would either be cacio e pepe or one with some roasted vegetables, Meyer lemon, walnuts, and pecorino. I'd also run out and get some bread and cured meat to snack on." (I'm seriously drooling already.)

As you can probably tell, it was really fascinating to see how each chef would answer my question. And although each differed widely, without fail they all blew me away.

Graciously and generously, each chef shared his or her own personal favorite recipes, insights, and advice. They explained what to do—and what not to do. And they finally helped me figure out exactly how to make my own spectacular, company-worthy meal in only an hour. Needless to say, I no longer mutter to myself—and now you're in on the secret, too!

I feel it's also important to note here that I never gave the chefs any direction as to a category or type of meal, but they naturally—and thankfully—covered a really wide range, from meats, poultry, and seafood to pasta, vegetarian/vegan, and even breakfast. There's something for everyone!

And to explain any special techniques and processes mentioned in the recipes that you may not be quite familiar with, there's also a special section at the end to help you with those as well (page 456).

In addition, please keep in mind two things:

1. Although each professional chef in this book can easily create their meal in only one hour or less, anyone who tries these recipes for the first time and/or possesses limited kitchen skills may find it takes longer.

2. All the chefs' titles and affiliations were accurate as of press time. However, due to the ever-changing nature of the food world, some may be different now.

I hope this overview has been helpful to you in learning how this book began, why I decided to write it, and how you, too, can benefit from it.

Now I invite you to start turning the pages. I guarantee you'll love what's in store for you. Enjoy! You're in great company.

MING TSAI

Boston, Massachusetts

Chef/owner of Blue Ginger and Blue Dragon; host/executive producer of Simply Ming; *president, National Advisory Board, of the Family Reach organization; national spokesperson for Food Allergy Research and Education (FARE)*

CHEF SAYS

Items I always keep on hand for unexpected guests are . . .

Chilled sparkling wine/Champagne, frozen dim sum, cooked rice or blanched noodles, marinated protein in the freezer, and cassis or a syrup to make a fancy cocktail. Also cheese.

When hosting a quick get-together, never overlook . . .

Ending with either something sweet or a cheese.

My secret tip for successful last-minute entertaining is . . .

Supply your guests with alcohol.

One fun fact few people know about me is that . . .

I have a bachelor's degree in mechanical engineering.

MENU

Peppercorn Duck with Sweet & Sour Cranberry Chutney and Eight Treasure Rice

CHEF'S PAIRING

Échezeaux Pinot Noir

CHEF'S PLAYLIST

Some classic jazz like Miles Davis or John Coltrane

MAJOR KUDOS

Induction into the James Beard Foundation's "Who's Who in Food & Beverage"; James Beard award for "Best Chef: Northeast"; James Beard nomination for "Best New Restaurant"; named "Best Restaurant" by *Boston Magazine*; "Chef of the Year" award from *Esquire*; "Restaurateur of the Year" award from the Massachusetts Restaurant Association; multiple Zagat awards

HIS STORY

Loyal fans worldwide know Ming as the über popular host and executive producer of the Emmy-nominated public television cooking show called *Simply Ming*—now in its fourteenth season! Many may even remember him earlier as the Emmy Award–winning host of *East Meets West* on Food Network. Or from *Ming's Quest*, also on Food Network.

But did you know he's also a double Ivy Leaguer? And a professional squash player? And one of *People* magazine's "Most Beautiful People"?

Bottom line is, Ming is an all-around talented guy. But he was an all-around talented kid, too. For instance, at only ten years old, he made fried rice for the first time in his life for his parents' drop-by guests. Ironically, we're now asking him to share a recipe for drop-by guests again, this time as a top chef. He chose duck.

"I think it's a shame more people don't cook duck at home," says Ming. "If you can sear a steak, you can cook duck breast."

You heard him. Now enjoy!

Peppercorn Duck with Sweet & Sour Cranberry Chutney and Eight Treasure Rice

SERVES 4

This dish is not only beautiful and delicious, it's also a lot easier to prepare than it looks. "The chutney can be made in advance," says Ming. "And the duck can be scored and prepared while family and friends are gathering. Just don't cook it past medium. Otherwise it can taste livery, which is off-putting to some." As for the fried rice, "It's an easy and quick dish that takes just minutes to come together!"

FOR THE SWEET & SOUR CRANBERRY CHUTNEY

2 tbsp (30 ml) grapeseed or canola oil

1 red onion, cut into ½-inch (12-mm) dice

1 tbsp (3 g) minced fresh lemongrass, white part only

Kosher salt, to taste

Freshly ground black pepper, to taste

1 cup (160 g) dried cranberries, chopped

¼ cup (50 g) sugar

1 cup (240 ml) naturally brewed rice vinegar (preferably Wan Jan Shan)

FOR THE PEPPERCORN DUCK BREAST

4 duck breasts, trimmed of fat, skin side scored

Kosher salt, to taste

½ cup (40 g) coarsely ground peppercorns (preferably black, green, and pink mixed in equal quantities, but just black would also be fine)

FOR THE EIGHT TREASURE RICE

5 tbsp (75 ml) canola oil, divided

4 large eggs, beaten

Kosher salt, to taste

1 tbsp (9 g) minced garlic

1 tbsp (7 g) minced fresh ginger

1 serrano chile, minced

1 large zucchini, diced

1 bunch scallions, white and green parts, thinly sliced, with 1 tbsp (10 g) of the greens reserved for garnish

Kosher salt, to taste

Freshly ground black pepper, to taste

⅓ lb (151 g) shiitake mushrooms, cleaned, stemmed, and cut into ⅛-inch (3-mm) slices

2 tbsp (30 ml) tamari, preferably wheat-free

1 cup (150 g) shelled edamame

7 cups (1.75 kg) 50-50 cooked white and brown rice, cooled

2 tbsp (18 g) white sesame seeds, toasted (page 457), for garnish

To make the sweet and sour cranberry chutney, set a sauté pan over medium-high heat. Add the oil and swirl to coat the pan. Add the onion and lemongrass. Sauté until soft, about 5 minutes. Season with salt and pepper.

Stir in the cranberries and sugar, then add the rice vinegar and cook, scraping the pan, until the vinegar bubbles and the sugar is dissolved. Let cook, uncovered, until the liquid is absorbed, about 6 to 8 minutes (a good time to get started on the duck breasts). Remove the chutney pan from the heat, adjust the seasoning, and set aside.

To prepare the peppercorn duck breast, season the duck breasts on both sides with salt and ground peppercorns.

Set a sauté pan over medium-low heat and add the breasts skin side down. Let them cook, rendering the fat away, until the skin is brown and crispy, about 15 minutes.

Flip the breasts skin side up and sear for 3 to 5 minutes for medium rare, flipping onto the skin sides just to recrisp at the end. Transfer to a cutting board, skin side up, and let rest 5 to 7 minutes. While the duck is resting, get started on the fried rice.

Line a large plate with paper towels. Set a wok over medium-high heat and add 4 tablespoons (60 ml) of the oil, swirling to coat. When the oil is hot, add the eggs and season with salt. When the eggs puff, stir vigorously until light and fluffy and cooked through, then transfer the eggs to the paper towels to drain.

Add the remaining 1 tablespoon (15 ml) oil to the wok, swirl to coat, and heat over medium-high heat. When the oil is hot, add the garlic, ginger, and chile and stir-fry until aromatic, about 30 seconds. Add the zucchini and all the scallions except the reserved scallion greens. Stir-fry until the vegetables soften slightly, about 1 minute.

Season with salt and pepper, then add the mushrooms and tamari. Stir-fry until soft, about 2 minutes. Add the edamame and eggs. Stir to break up the eggs. Add the rice and stir until heated through, about 2 minutes. Adjust the seasoning with salt and pepper.

When ready to serve, slice the breast, with the breast laid horizontal, into ⅓-inch (8-mm) thick slices. Spoon a bed of rice over each plate and top with the sliced meat of one duck breast, then top the duck with a large spoonful of the cranberry chutney. Garnish with the reserved scallion greens and the toasted sesame seeds to serve.

CHEF'S TIP
Leftover chutney can be transferred to a container, covered, and stored in the fridge for up to 2 weeks.

CURTIS STONE

Beverly Hills, California

Chef/owner of Maude (Beverly Hills) and Gwen (Hollywood)

CHEF SAYS

Items I always keep on hand for unexpected guests are . . .

Good wine and Champagne (a couple of bottles in the fridge at all times), incredible cheese and chocolate, a good-quality extra virgin olive oil that's like liquid gold, some sort of seasonal fruit, and a selection of homemade pickles.

When hosting a quick get-together, never overlook . . .

The fact that your guests came to spend time with you, so don't get so caught up making dishes that prevent you from spending time with them. Also, a golden rule when cooking for guests, cook something you've made before so you are confident and familiar with it.

My secret tip for successful last-minute entertaining is . . .

Remember that nobody is reading a menu when they arrive, so you can totally make it up with whatever you have on hand. And you should always surround yourself with foods you love. If you love what's around you, chances are you're able to put together a delicious meal from it.

One fun fact few people know about me is that . . .

My affinity for seasonal eating and cooking was inspired by my mother, Lorraine. She's a gardener and the president of the Herb Society in Australia!

MENU

Charcuterie with Pickled Onions, Cauliflower & Mustard Seeds

Charcoal-Grilled Rib Eye Steaks & Broccolini

Roasted Anjou Pears with Greek Yogurt & Honeycomb

CHEF'S PAIRING

With the charcuterie: either a Pinot Gris from Alsace, France, or an orange wine (skin-fermented white wine) from northeastern Italy

With the rib eye: either a good-quality Sangiovese from Chianti, Italy, or a cool-climate Syrah from Victoria, Australia

With the pears: either a late harvest Riesling like Auslese from Mosel, Germany, or a sweet wine like a Vouvray Moelleux from Loire Valley, France

CHEF'S PLAYLIST

A "hipster dinner party" playlist on Spotify featuring Frank Sinatra, Jack Johnson, The Lumineers, Chet Faker, and more

MAJOR KUDOS

Editor's and Reader's Choice for "Chef of the Year" and "Restaurant of the Year" by Los Angeles Eater; one of "The World's Top 40 Best New Restaurants" by *Travel + Leisure*; "Best Restaurant Los Angeles" and "Best New Restaurant" awards from *LA Weekly*; James Beard award semifinalist for "Best New Restaurant"; "Most Beautiful Restaurant in the Country" by Eater National; one of *Sunset*'s "10 Best New Restaurants in SoCal"

HIS STORY

The little four-year-old tot whose first food memory was making Yorkshire fudge alongside his beloved granny, Maude, back home in Australia would have had no way of knowing he would someday become an internationally renowned chef.

But after training in Australia and Europe for twelve years, including eight years under legendary chef Marco Pierre White, Curtis now heads two world-class restaurants and is making a real difference with his commitment to using seasonal ingredients.

"To me, this is the perfect casual, three-course meat lover's meal to serve up at a moment's notice in the fall or winter," says Curtis. "Each course is delicious, and together they make for a well-balanced, satisfying meal your guests will rave about!"

As the perfect host, Curtis goes on to add, "I like to keep things casual and be able to spend time with my guests. If they're relaxed and having a good time, and I'm able to hang out with them, then it's a fun party for all of us."

Are we invited, too?

Charcuterie with Pickled Onions, Cauliflower & Mustard Seeds

SERVES 4

"I think it's nice to begin a meal with a platter to share," says Curtis. "If you can get your hands on great-quality charcuterie sliced to order at your local deli or butcher shop, then most of the work with the starter is done for you." He also includes a uniquely creative garnish on his platter: pickled onions with purple cauliflower and mustard seeds. As a bonus, this mixture can be made up to five days ahead and refrigerated, covered.

1 cup (240 ml) Champagne vinegar (can substitute white wine vinegar)

½ cup (120 ml) water

2 tbsp (26 g) sugar

1 tsp kosher salt

2 fresh tarragon sprigs

2 fresh thyme sprigs

¼ cup (32 g) yellow mustard seeds

5 oz (140 g) red or white pearl onions, peeled

1½ cups (225 g) small purple cauliflower florets

8–12 oz (224–336 g) assorted charcuterie (shown here: blackstrap ham, duck speck, country style pâté, leek ash and porcini salami, and Calabrese salami)

1 French baguette, thinly sliced

To make the pickling liquid, combine the vinegar, water, sugar, salt, tarragon, and thyme in a heavy saucepan. Bring to a boil over high heat. Add the mustard seeds, reduce the heat to medium, and simmer for about 25 minutes, or until the mustard seeds are plump. Transfer the mixture to a bowl and set aside.

Prepare a bowl of ice water and set it beside the stove.

Meanwhile, to a large pot of boiling salted water add the pearl onions. Cook until the onions are just tender, about 5 minutes, then drain and transfer the onions to the ice bath. When the onions are cool, drain well and then cut them in half, separating each layer into petals.

Stir the onions and cauliflower into the warm mustard-seed mixture and refrigerate until cold.

Arrange the charcuterie on a platter. Serve with the baguette slices and pickled cauliflower mixture.

CHEF'S TIP

To help make sure this meal can be prepared in 1 hour, here's the prep plan I recommend:

FIRST 25 MINUTES

1. Make pickling liquid and blanch onions for the charcuterie platter.

2. Make wine syrup and, meanwhile, make/cool honeycomb for dessert.

NEXT 35 MINUTES

1. Roast pears for dessert. (These are served warm, so there is no cooling time required.)

2. Grill steaks. Meanwhile, prep and then grill broccolini.

3. Assemble charcuterie on platter. Transfer pickles to serving bowl at end of the hour.

Charcoal-Grilled Rib Eye Steaks & Broccolini

SERVES 4

Curtis enjoys a great steak as much as anyone else—and for good reason. "This course is substantial and requires minimal prep," he says. "I buy big, thick steaks to achieve that juicy, rosy, medium-rare doneness." Be sure to buy the best quality you can afford. You'll also appreciate knowing that the broccolini can marinate in the oil mixture for up to eight hours, covered and refrigerated—a really helpful, do-ahead trick when time is of the essence.

2 (1½-lb [680-g]) dry-aged bone-in rib eye steaks, about 2 inches (5 cm) thick, outer part of meat (spinalis) attached

Regular olive oil, for brushing

2 tsp (10 g) kosher salt, plus additional to taste

1 tsp freshly ground black pepper, plus additional to taste

2 tbsp (30 ml) extra virgin olive oil

2 tsp (5 g) finely chopped fresh thyme

1 clove garlic, finely chopped

¼ tsp red chili flakes (crushed red pepper)

2 (½-lb [224-g]) bunches fresh broccolini, stalks trimmed

Prepare the grill for indirect high heat. If using a charcoal grill (preferred), fill a chimney starter with hardwood lump charcoal and ignite. When the coals are covered with white ash, dump them in an even layer on one half of the grill, leaving the other half of the grill empty. Place the grill grate in position. Preheat the grill grate for 5 minutes. If using a gas grill, preheat all the burners to high heat. Before grilling, turn half the burners off.

Pat the steaks dry with paper towels. Lightly brush each steak with the olive oil and season liberally with the salt and pepper.

Place the steaks on the unlit side of the grill and cover the grill. Cook, flipping over halfway through the cooking, for about 30 minutes, or until the centers of the steaks register 110°F (43°C) on an instant-read thermometer.

Move the steaks directly over the lit coals. Cook, turning as needed, for about 5 minutes, or until both steaks have a charred crust and an internal temperature of 125°F to 130°F (52°C to 54°C) for medium-rare. Set the steaks aside to rest for 10 minutes.

Meanwhile, in a large bowl whisk the extra virgin olive oil, thyme, garlic, and chili flakes to mix well. Add the broccolini and toss to coat. Season with salt and pepper to taste.

Grill the broccolini on the direct heat, turning as needed, until tender and lightly charred, about 8 minutes. Set aside.

Cut the meat from the bone and separate the eye of the rib eye (the center piece of meat) from the spinalis (the outer piece of meat) by cutting through the fat that separates the two pieces. Carve each separate piece against the grain and serve with the broccolini.

Roasted Anjou Pears with Greek Yogurt & Honeycomb

SERVES 4

"After a meaty dinner," explains Curtis, "I think a light seasonal fruit dessert is the best way to finish on a sweet note, and the homemade honeycomb brings an extra touch of elegance." The honeycomb candy can be made and stored in an airtight container at room temperature for up to 3 days.

2 cups (480 ml) dry rosé wine

1¼ cups (300 ml) water, divided

1¾ cups (350 g) sugar, divided

1 small lemon, divided

2 large, ripe but firm red pears, such as Anjou, unpeeled, halved, and cored

¼ cup (84 g) organic honey

1 tbsp (14 g) baking soda

1 cup (245 g) good-quality Greek yogurt

Preheat the oven to 350°F (177°C).

In small heavy saucepan, bring the wine, 1 cup (240 ml) of the water, and ¼ cup (50 g) of the sugar to a boil over medium-high heat. Cook the mixture until reduced by half, about 5 minutes. Take off the heat.

Using a vegetable peeler, shave 4 strips of lemon peel from the lemon. Add the lemon strips to the wine mixture. Reserve the remaining lemon.

Let the lemon syrup stand for 10 minutes, or until only slightly warm. Discard the lemon strips.

In an 8-inch (20-cm) square baking dish, arrange the pears cut side down. Pour the lemon syrup over the pears and roast in the oven, basting every 10 minutes, until the pears are tender, about 30 minutes.

Meanwhile, to make the honeycomb, lightly coat a rimmed 13 × 9-inch (33 × 23-cm) baking sheet with nonstick spray. Set aside.

In a large, heavy saucepan, bring the honey, remaining ¼ cup (60 ml) water, and remaining 1½ cups (300 g) sugar to a boil over high heat, stirring constantly. Reduce the heat to medium high and cook, without stirring, until a candy thermometer reaches 305°F (152°C).

Remove the saucepan from the heat, and whisk in the baking soda just until blended and the mixture begins to bubble. Gently pour the hot mixture onto the prepared baking sheet. Allow the honeycomb to cool completely.

When cool, chop about one-fourth of the honeycomb into bite-size pieces. Reserve the rest for another use.

To serve, evenly spoon the yogurt into 4 bowls. Top each with half a warm roasted pear. Spoon the warm syrup over the pears, then sprinkle with the honeycomb pieces. Using a microplane, finely grate zest from the reserved lemon over the pears. Serve immediately.

STEPHANIE IZARD

Chicago, Illinois

Chef/owner of Girl & the Goat, Little Goat, and Duck Duck Goat

CHEF SAYS

Items I always keep on hand for unexpected guests are . . .

Cheese, crackers, cured meats, wine, and beer.

When hosting a quick get-together, never overlook . . .

Making sure the guests attending will all have fun things in common. A quiet dinner table can make for an uncomfortable (and long) night.

My secret tip for successful last-minute entertaining is . . .

Always have a pre-batched welcome cocktail. It takes the stress off of getting a tasty beverage in people's hands when they walk in the door and you're in the height of prepping for the meal. Plus, it's a great way to set the tone for the theme/vibe of the evening.

One fun fact few people know about me is that . . .

I'm an excellent skipper! I can skip faster than many people can run and can often be found skipping across the street between my two restaurants: Girl & the Goat and Little Goat.

MENU

Fish Fillet with Vanilla Herb Yogurt & Szechuan Chili Sauce

Stir-Fried Eggplant

Sesame Cucumber Salad

Ice Cream Sundaes with Sautéed Pineapple, Sesame Whipped Cream & Pie Crust Crumble

CHEF'S PAIRING

A nice, crisp local lager beer

CHEF'S PLAYLIST

Pharrell

MAJOR KUDOS

James Beard award for "Best Chef: Great Lakes"; nomination for James Beard "Best New Restaurant" Award; winner of and guest judge on Bravo's *Top Chef*; winner of *Iron Chef*; named "America's Best Restaurant" by *Saveur* and as "Best New Chef" by *Food & Wine*; listed as one of "Best New Restaurants" by *Chicago Magazine*; named one of "10 Best Small U.S. Restaurants" by *Bon Appétit*

HER STORY

She's sweet. She's tough. And she's super-über talented. Which is why Stephanie broke ground as the first female to ever win Bravo's *Top Chef*. But first things first.

In a nutshell, Stephanie grew up in Connecticut. Got a degree from the University of Michigan. Went to Scottsdale Culinary Institute. Worked for some of the best in Chicago. Opened her first restaurant in Bucktown. Sold it. Then made her mark in food show history.

She eventually opened another restaurant, this time a nose-to-tail concept featuring goat. Why goat? As it turns out, her last name is actually a type of goat found in the Pyrenees. We figure that's reason enough.

As for this meal: "With the array of textures and flavors, your guests will never know you didn't spend hours in the kitchen working on it," says Stephanie. "This Szechuan chili sauce is one of my favorite go-tos. I can pretty much put it on top of anything, and the dish gets some Chinese flair without being over the top."

Fish Fillet with Vanilla Herb Yogurt & Szechuan Chili Sauce

SERVES 4

The fish is prepared simply. But the sauces, my god, the sauces! "While in Chengdu, China," explains Stephanie, "we came across a little stand selling dumplings. They were so good we went back there for breakfast three days in a row! The sauce from those dumplings became the inspiration for this Szechuan chili sauce." In fact, the Szechuan chili sauce recipe serves triple duty in this meal. You make it only once but divide/incorporate it three ways: in the Fish Fillet recipe (with garlic chives added), in the Stir-Fried Eggplant recipe (again, with garlic chives added), and in the Sesame Cucumber Salad (in its virgin form without any other additions).

FOR THE VANILLA HERB YOGURT

½ cup (120 ml) heavy cream

¼ cup (10 g) fresh mint

¼ cup (10 g) fresh basil

Seeds scraped from 1 vanilla bean

1 cup (245 g) Greek yogurt

¼ tsp salt

FOR THE SZECHUAN CHILI SAUCE

⅓ cup (80 g) broad bean chili paste

⅓ cup (80 ml) fish sauce

¾ cup (180 ml) malt vinegar

¼ cup (60 ml) sesame oil

¼ cup (60 ml) chili oil

2 tbsp (18 g) white sesame seeds, toasted (page 457)

1 tbsp (8 g) Szechuan peppercorns (found in Asian stores and online), toasted (page 457) and ground

½ cup (25 g) sliced (¼ inch [6 mm]) garlic chives (can substitute regular chives or scallions)

FOR THE FISH FILLET

2 large fillets meagre, corvina, black bass, wild striped bass, or snapper (¾–1 lb [336–450 g] total weight), with skin on

Salt, to taste

Rice bran oil or canola oil, for grilling

4 oz (115 g, 1 stick) butter

To make the vanilla herb yogurt, purée the cream, mint, basil, and vanilla seeds in a blender or food processor. Place in a bowl and add the yogurt. Season with the salt, then whisk together well. Smear a healthy amount on a large serving platter. Set aside.

To make the Szechuan chili sauce, mix together all the ingredients except the garlic chives in a bowl. Remove 1¼ cups (300 g) to another bowl for use in the Stir-Fried Eggplant and Cucumber Sesame recipes that follow; set aside. Mix the garlic chives into the remaining ¾ cup (180 g) sauce and set aside.

Place a heavy pancake griddle or large flat griddle pan on the stovetop over medium-high heat. Allow it to heat until just smoking.

While the pan is heating, score the skin of the fish in ½ x ½ inch (12 x 12 mm) squares. Season the flesh side with salt.

Heat a small amount of cooking oil on the griddle, then add the fish, skin side down, and cook for 5 to 7 minutes. Add the butter to the griddle, and as it melts, begin to baste the fish with it. Move the butter to the edges of the fish so it seeps under and helps crisp the skin. The fish will not flip until skin is very crispy and has released from the pan. Do not attempt to flip until this point; then, once the skin is crispy, about 6 to 8 minutes, carefully flip the fillets. Add a little extra oil to help release cleanly, if needed. Cook for another 2 to 3 minutes.

Transfer the fish, skin side up, to your serving platter. Drizzle the ¾ cup (180 g) Szechuan chili sauce over the fish and serve immediately.

Stir-Fried Eggplant

SERVES 4

A luscious side dish, this eggplant recipe is made even more aromatic and flavorful with the addition of ground pork. Stephanie kicks it up one more notch with the addition of her fabulous Szechuan Chili Sauce and some Shaoxing wine—commonly aged for at least 10 years, similar in taste to dry sherry, and named after a famous wine-making city in China of the same name.

¾ cup (180 g) Szechuan Chili Sauce (page 24)

½ cup (25 g) sliced (¼ inch [6 mm]) garlic chives (can substitute regular chives or scallions)

½ cup (120 ml) rice bran oil or canola oil, divided

1 lb (450 g) ground pork

3 Japanese eggplants, sliced lengthwise and cut into ½-inch (12-mm) thick half moons, divided

1 small sweet onion, thinly sliced, divided

Salt, to taste

½ cup (120 ml) Shaoxing rice wine (can substitute dry sherry), divided

Mix the Szechuan Chili Sauce and garlic chives together. Set aside.

Heat a small amount of the oil in a nonstick sauté pan over medium-high heat. When hot, add the ground pork. When the pork is almost cooked, about 5 to 6 minutes, drain off the fat and reserve it for cooking the eggplant. Continue cooking until the pork is cooked through, about 8 to 10 minutes. Remove the pork to a bowl and set aside.

Return half the pork fat along with ¼ cup (60 ml) of the cooking oil to the sauté pan and set over medium-high heat. Allow to heat for a few seconds, then add half the eggplant slices; they should cover the bottom of the pan but not crowd it. Allow the slices to brown for at least 3 minutes, then turn the slices. You may need to add a little bit more oil to brown, but you don't want the eggplant to be greasy.

Brown the eggplant until it begins to get tender. Add half the onion and toss to combine. Season well with salt. Cook for another 5 to 7 minutes before adding half the rice wine. Toss and allow it to cook off before adding half the cooked ground pork to the pan.

Cook for 3 minutes and add half the Szechuan sauce. Turn off the heat, toss once more to evenly coat, and transfer to a serving platter. Keep warm.

Clean your pan and repeat this process all over again, starting with the remaining ¼ cup (60 ml) oil and then the rest of the eggplants, onion, salt, rice wine, and Szechuan sauce. Add to the platter and serve warm.

Sesame Cucumber Salad

SERVES 4

Simple. Quick. Delicious. That's the best way to describe this refreshing side salad, which will elevate any dinner, casual or elegant. It gets top scores as a winning recipe for any last-minute entertainment.

2 seedless English cucumbers

½ cup (120 ml) Szechuan Chili Sauce (page 24)

2 tbsp (5 g) fresh mint, torn, for garnish

2 tbsp (5 g) Thai or regular basil leaves, torn, for garnish

2 tbsp (18 g) white sesame seeds, toasted (page 457), for garnish

Using a Japanese mandolin or a very sharp knife, slice the cucumbers into very thin rounds. When all the cucumbers are sliced, you should have 3 to 4 cups (685 to 915 g). Place in a bowl and toss with the Szechuan chili sauce. Garnish with the mint, basil, and toasted sesame seeds.

*See photo on page 22.

Ice Cream Sundaes with Sautéed Pineapple, Sesame Whipped Cream & Pie Crust Crumble

SERVES 4

If you think all ice cream sundaes are alike, you've never tried this version by Stephanie. It's at once exotic, tropical, and utterly delectable. She achieves this by combining the deep sweetness of sautéed pineapple with the nutty deliciousness of sesame-flavored whipped cream (who would have thought!), plus a crumble that's made of crispy baked pie crust. Pure genius.

FOR THE PIE CRUST CRUMBLE

¾ cup (94 g) all-purpose flour

¼ tsp kosher salt

1 tbsp (13 g) sugar

8 oz (230 g, 2 sticks) unsalted butter, cubed and chilled

⅓ cup (75 g) lard, chilled

½ tsp fresh lemon juice

¼ cup (60 ml) ice water, or as needed

FOR THE SAUTÉED PINEAPPLE

2 tbsp (28 g) unsalted butter

2 cups (400 g) diced pineapple

¼ cup (55 g) dark brown sugar, firmly packed

¼ tsp kosher salt

¼ tsp red chili flakes (crushed red pepper)

FOR THE SESAME WHIPPED CREAM

2 cups (480 ml) heavy cream, chilled

¼ cup (60 g) sweetened condensed milk

1 tsp sesame oil

2 pints (960 g) of your favorite ice cream

To make the pie crust crumble, place the flour, salt, and sugar in a food processor. Pulse in the butter and lard until pea-sized balls form. Add the lemon juice and pulse to combine. Add the ice water, a teaspoon at a time, until a somewhat dry dough ball begins to form. The dough should not look sandy but should not be overly wet, either. You may not need all the water.

Turn the dough out onto a lightly floured surface and bring all the pieces together. Wrap in plastic wrap and refrigerate until cold, at least 25 minutes.

Preheat the oven to 425°F (218°C).

On a piece of parchment paper or wax paper, roll the dough out to a ¼-inch (6-mm) thick square. Use a fork to prick holes at random throughout the sheet of dough.

Transfer the dough to a parchment-lined baking sheet. Bake until golden brown and crispy, about 20 to 25 minutes. Remove from the oven and let cool, then break into shards and set aside.

To make the sautéed pineapple, set a nonstick sauté pan over medium heat. Melt the butter and add the pineapple. Allow the pineapple to release a bit of juice before adding the brown sugar, salt, and red chili flakes. Toss to coat, then cook for 3 to 5 minutes, or until the sugar is bubbly and coats the pineapple in syrup. Remove to a bowl and let cool for a few minutes while you make the sesame whipped cream.

Add all the ingredients for the whipped cream to a chilled metal bowl and beat until medium-stiff peaks form.

Scoop even amounts of the ice cream into 4 dishes. Top each with ½ cup (100 g) of the sautéed pineapple, a large dollop of the sesame whipped cream, and a handful of the pie crust crumble. Serve immediately.

NAOMI POMEROY

Portland, Oregon

Chef/owner of Beast and Expatriate

CHEF SAYS

Items I always keep on hand for unexpected guests are . . .

A bottle of rosé, a wedge of Parmigiano-Reggiano, house-made pickles, fifteen kinds of mustard, and twelve bottles of hot sauce. Plus, a huge jar of Best Foods mayo!

When hosting a quick get-together, never overlook . . .

Beverages.

My secret tip for successful last-minute entertaining is . . .

Have good music and the willingness to order delivery.

One fun fact few people know about me is that . . .

I lived in India for a year during college.

MENU

Pan-Seared Hanger Steak

Pasta Amatriciana

Broccoli Rabe Salad with Anchovy, Lemon & Garlic

CHEF'S PAIRING

Red Mastroberardino, Campania Aglianico Mastro wine

CHEF'S PLAYLIST

Prince

MAJOR KUDOS

James Beard award for "Best Chef: Northwest"; numerous James Beard award finalist nominations; recognition as one of "10 Best New Chefs in America" by *Food & Wine*; contestant on Bravo's *Top Chef Masters*; judge on Esquire Network's *Knife Fight*; "Chef of the Year" award from *Portland Monthly*; "Restaurant of the Year" award from *The Oregonian*

HER STORY

No, she didn't go to culinary school. She didn't do any stages overseas. And she didn't work under any big names. But as a self-made, multi-award-winning chef, Naomi proudly wears her background as a badge of honor.

"When I launched my catering business," explains Naomi, "everything came from books. Richard Olney, Larousse, Harold McGee . . . Alice Waters." She devoured each recipe. Duplicated them. Tweaked them. And perhaps even eventually outdid them.

And yet, even though she's now recognized as one of the best, she still enjoys the simple pleasures in life.

"I chose this dish because it's honestly what I had around," explains Naomi, "and I *do* have a friend coming over for dinner tonight!"

She adds, "This meal is really fast and easy, it's fairly seasonless, and it has only a few basic ingredients that you (a) probably already have, or (b) can quickly get, all from the same store."

Another bonus? Naomi says this meal can also be adapted to be gluten free by serving fresh tomatoes with mayo instead of the pasta.

Ahhh . . . fabulous in every way.

Pan-Seared Hanger Steak

SERVES 4

"People often want to know about hanger steaks," says Naomi. "Actually, another name for them is 'butcher's cut,' because that was the cut the butcher often saved for himself." She goes on to say, "It's a really delicious cut of beef with a rich and intense flavor. But it can be hard to tell when it's cooked properly. That's why I chose it for this book. Not only is it so delicious, but I also wanted to share with home cooks my method for testing its doneness." See below for Naomi's unique technique.

4 (4–5-oz [112–140-g]) hanger steaks, at room temperature (out of the fridge at least 1 hour)

4 tsp (21 g) good-quality sea salt, divided

1 tsp freshly cracked black pepper, divided

1 tbsp (15 ml) olive oil

Fleur de sel (can substitute sea salt), for finishing

Preheat the oven to 400°F (204°C), preferably a convection oven.

Season each steak with 1 teaspoon of the salt and ¼ teaspoon of the pepper.

Set a black steel or cast-iron pan over medium-high heat until hot. Add the olive oil. Place the steaks in the pan, weighed down with a heatproof plate, and sear for 1½ minutes on each side, or until crisp and deep golden brown. Hanger is a "round" cut, but try to get a really nice sear on as many "sides" as possible.

Remove the plate. Using oven mitts, place the pan in the oven for 3 to 4 minutes, or until the steaks feel firm on the edges but still are quite soft in the very centers, where the temperature should register about 115°F (46°C) if checking with a thermometer. Otherwise, another way to test them is to insert a thin metal skewer or cake tester into the center of the meat and touch it to the outer edge of your bottom lip. If the skewer is warm, not cool, the meat is done.

Place the steaks on a large piece of foil set on top of a platter. Very loosely tent the meat with the foil by pulling up the sides of the foil and closing them several inches above the meat. Don't seal tightly or the meat will continue to cook.

Allow the steaks to rest for 10 to 15 minutes before slicing across the grain on a strong bias. Taste one slice and finish with a little crunchy fleur de sel as needed.

Pasta Amatriciana

SERVES 4

"I wanted to make something that was very similar to the everyday meals I make at home," says Naomi. "My husband is a total pasta fanatic . . . any noodles, really." So, this simple, classic, spicy pasta dish—named for the town of Amatrice, about an hour east of Rome—was a no-brainer. *Buon appetito!*

4 oz (112 g) bacon scraps, roughly chopped

4 tbsp (60 ml) olive oil

1 small yellow onion, diced

4–5 cloves garlic, sliced

2 tbsp (30 g) tomato paste

¼ tsp Espelette pepper (can substitute Aleppo pepper), optional

¼ tsp red chili flakes (crushed red pepper)

3–4 plum (Roma) tomatoes, seeded and cut into large dice (can substitute a 6-oz [168-g] can chopped tomatoes)

Small pinch of sugar

Salt, to taste

Pepper, to taste

1 lb (450 g) bucatini pasta (fresh, if possible)

½ bunch scallions, thinly sliced

2 oz (56 g) Parmigiano-Reggiano cheese, shaved with a vegetable peeler

Cook the bacon in a 10- to 12-inch (25- to 30-cm) stainless steel or nonreactive saucepan over medium heat until the fat is rendered out and the bacon pieces are beginning to brown on the edges and curl slightly, about 3 to 4 minutes. Add the olive oil and raise the heat to medium high. Add the onion and sauté for about 1 to 2 minutes, or until translucent. Add the garlic and sauté for 1 more minute. Add the tomato paste and "fry-out"—meaning, allow it to cook until it becomes one shade darker and looks slightly "scrambled," about 1 to 2 minutes.

Add the Espelette pepper, if using, chili flakes, and tomatoes. Cook for about 2 to 3 minutes, or until the flavors have melded and the sauce tastes cooked but still slightly "fresh." Season with the sugar and any additional salt or pepper as desired. Turn off the heat but leave the sauce in the pan.

To cook the pasta, bring 1 gallon (3.8 L) of water and 2 tablespoons (32 g) of salt to a boil in a 6-quart stockpot over high heat. Add the bucatini and cook for 8 minutes, if dried, or as directed on the package. If using fresh pasta, cook for about 4 minutes or until al dente.

Before draining the pasta, scoop out about 1½ cups (360 ml) of the starchy water and keep to the side. When the pasta is cooked, drain and rinse under cold water.

When ready to serve the pasta, heat the sauce in the sauté pan over medium-high heat. Add the cooked pasta and reserved pasta water. Stir rapidly with tongs to combine and emulsify. The sauce should be smooth and juicy over the cooked pasta.

Remove the pasta and sauce to a bowl. At the last second before serving, toss with the scallions and cheese.

Broccoli Rabe Salad with Anchovy, Lemon & Garlic

SERVES 4

This super-easy side dish centers around the earthy, pungent, nutty, slightly bitter vegetable called "broccoli rabe" (aka broccoli raab, broccoli rape, or rapini). Widely regarded as a powerful superfood, it gets tossed here with a rich mixture of olive oil, anchovy paste, lemon, and garlic. Feel free to give this same delicious treatment to other bold veggies as well, including kale, Swiss chard, and spinach.

1 tbsp (16 g) salt, plus additional to taste, if needed

1 lb (450 g) broccoli rabe, trimmed, divided

FOR THE DRESSING

1 clove garlic

½ tsp salt

2 tbsp (30 ml) olive oil

1 tbsp (15 ml) fresh lemon juice

1 tsp lemon zest

1 tsp sherry vinegar (can substitute red wine vinegar)

½ tsp anchovy paste

¼ tsp freshly ground black pepper, plus additional to taste, if needed

Prepare a large bowl of ice water. Set near the stove.

Bring 2 quarts (1.9 L) of water and the salt to a full rolling boil in a large pot. Add half the stalks of broccoli rabe and blanch for 3 minutes, or until the stems are tender. Scoop out of the water and immediately place in the ice bath to shock. Drain, then pat dry with paper towels. Repeat with the second half of the broccoli rabe. Set aside.

To make the dressing, mash well the garlic with the salt in a mortar with a pestle or in a bowl with a spoon. Transfer the purée to a jar with a lid, then add the olive oil, lemon juice, lemon zest, sherry vinegar, anchovy paste, and pepper. Shake well to blend.

No more than 5 minutes before serving, or else the acids in the vinaigrette will discolor the broccoli rabe, toss the vinaigrette in a large bowl with the stalks of broccoli rabe. Taste for salt and pepper and serve immediately.

HUGH ACHESON

Athens, Georgia

Chef/partner of 5&10 and The National (Athens), Empire State South and Spiller Park Coffee (Atlanta), and The Florence (Savannah); founder of Seed Life Skills

CHEF SAYS

Items I always keep on hand for unexpected guests are . . .

Some pecans and cheese for snacks, chocolate bars for a quick dessert, old Calvados, a movie picked out for such an occasion, and Cards Against Humanity.

When hosting a quick get-together, never overlook . . .

The fact that people need to drink water. More than we think.

My secret tip for successful last-minute entertaining is . . .

Don't freak out. Enjoy yourself by making something that is in your arsenal.

One fun fact few people know about me is that . . .

I like American Pickers a bit too much.

MENU

Chicken Thighs with Kimchi Peas, Shallot & Lemon

Farro Risotto with Pea Shoots & Almonds

Chopped Salad with Chickpeas, Feta, Garlicky Croutons & Red Wine Vinaigrette

CHEF'S PAIRING

A rosé with the salad, then a full-bodied white like a German Riesling (a Kabinett with some real nuance, maybe something from Dönnhoff)

CHEF'S PLAYLIST

Fun garage, punky stuff like "You Will Always Bring Me Flowers" by Shannon and the Clams

MAJOR KUDOS

James Beard award for "Best Chef: Southeast"; *Food & Wine's* "Best New Chef" award; "Restaurant of the Year" award from the *Atlanta Journal Constitution*; numerous James Beard award nominations; contestant on Bravo's *Top Chef Masters*; judge on multiple episodes of the *Top Chef* series

HIS STORY

Canadian by birth, Hugh knew from a young age that he was meant to be a chef. So he humbly began his ascent at age fifteen—as a dishwasher.

He quickly climbed the ladder with positions at prestigious restaurants throughout Ottawa (his hometown), Montréal, San Francisco, and Athens, Georgia—where he finally put down roots and opened his own place.

Today Hugh walks the talk as he maintains his commitment to preparing fresh, wholesome, fulfilling meals from scratch.

"If we have last-minute guests, I have to cook what I have around," says Hugh. "Thus, this meal is pretty much going to show off my pantry. We always have some chicken in the fridge. We have peas in the freezer, and most all of everything else is just pretty straightforward. It has to be food that plays to the soul and plays to a healthy life, hence a salad and a main. Nothing complex, nothing too rich, just clean flavors that are contemporary and achievable."

We couldn't have said it better ourselves, Hugh.

Chicken Thighs with Kimchi Peas, Shallot & Lemon

SERVES 8

"The interplay of kimchi with the peas begets a chat about how American palates now yearn for amped-up flavors," says Hugh about this dish. "As for the chicken you buy, I implore you to go with the best you can afford. Most chicken thighs weigh about five to six ounces (140 to 168 g) , so you can get away with one per person. Amp up the size of everything else if you want to make it a bigger meal."

8 skin-on, bone-in chicken thighs

1 tsp salt

1 tbsp (16 ml) vegetable oil

1 large shallot, cut into thin rings

2 cups (300 g) frozen English peas, thawed

½ cup (150 g) cabbage kimchi, chopped

½ tsp lemon zest

1 tbsp (14 g) butter

2 cups (80 g) fresh pea shoots (can substitute watercress), for garnish

Preheat the oven to 400°F (204°C).

Pat the chicken dry and place on a plate. Season the pieces all over with the salt.

Place a large, ovenproof frying pan over medium heat. When the pan is hot, add the oil, then put in the chicken, skin side down. Lower the heat to medium-low and let the thighs cook, without fiddling with them, for about 12 minutes, then turn them over and place the pan in the oven to roast for about 15 minutes. The thighs should have an internal temperature of 160°F (71°C) when they are done.

Remove the pan from the oven. Transfer the thighs to a wire rack and put the pan, as is, on the burner. Turn the burner to medium heat and add the shallot. Cook for 2 minutes, then add the peas and kimchi. Stir well and cook for 1 minute, until the peas are warmed through. Add the lemon zest and butter and stir until the butter is melted and thoroughly mixed in, then remove from the heat.

Spoon the kimchi peas onto a platter, arrange the thighs on top, then garnish with the pea shoots to serve.

CHEF'S TIP

There's a cadence to cooking, and that cadence is up to you. But to really enjoy yourself, you need a plan to follow. You have an hour; let's make it work. For this meal, I would get the chicken going first, then start the vegetable work for the salad. Make the vinaigrette, then get the farro going, and then make the croutons. Back to the chicken and finish that up. Dress that salad and get the farro up and done. This is not rocket science, merely good clock management.

Farro Risotto with Pea Shoots & Almonds

SERVES 8

Farro, an ancient grain found in tombs of Egyptian kings, has actually been a mainstay of Italian cuisine for centuries. With its nutty flavor, high fiber content, and great nutritional value, it's now finally gaining popularity in the U.S. as well. Hugh uses it in place of Arborio rice in this decidedly decadent version of risotto, made even more resplendent with the addition of almonds and the tender, sweet tendrils of young pea plants.

4 cups (946 ml) chicken stock

1 tbsp (16 ml) extra virgin olive oil

1 large shallot, minced

1 cup (148 g) semi-pearled farro

1 bay leaf

2 cups (80 g) finely chopped pea shoots (can substitute watercress)

½ cup (90 g) almonds, toasted (page 457) and chopped

¼ cup (45 g) grated Parmigiano-Reggiano cheese

2 tbsp (28 g) butter

Kosher salt, to taste

Pour the chicken stock into a small saucepan and set it on a back burner over low heat.

Heat the olive oil in a medium-size saucepan over medium heat and add the shallot. Cook for 3 minutes, or until very aromatic. Add the farro, stir well to coat, and lightly toast for about 5 minutes. Add the bay leaf, then start gradually adding the warm chicken stock, about 1 cup (236 ml) every 5 minutes or so. Stir frequently. As each addition cooks down and the stock is almost fully incorporated, add more stock. Taste after 20 to 25 minutes. The farro should be just tender and quite wet (wetter than a risotto would be if it came to your table at an Italian restaurant).

Add the pea shoots and toasted almonds to the risotto. Stir to incorporate, then remove the bay leaf and vigorously stir in the cheese and butter. Season with salt.

Remove from the heat and serve warm.

Chopped Salad with Chickpeas, Feta, Garlicky Croutons & Red Wine Vinaigrette

SERVES 8

A chopped salad is just that: A wonderful variety of chopped vegetables combined to form one beautiful dish. Juicy, crunchy, and bright. What a delightful way to start this meal. But wait! Throw in some unexpected surprises in the form of chickpeas, feta, and croutons, and suddenly this salad is elevated to a whole new level of deliciousness.

FOR THE RED WINE VINAIGRETTE

½ cup (120 ml) olive oil

3 tbsp (45 ml) red wine vinegar

1 clove garlic, minced

½ tsp mustard

¼ tsp kosher salt

FOR THE SALAD

¼ cup (60 ml) olive oil

2 thick slices of sourdough bread

1 clove garlic, halved

1 large ripe tomato, diced (½ inch [12 mm])

1 English cucumber, diced (½ inch [12 mm])

1 cup (120 g) diced celery (½ inch [12 mm])

1 cup (120 g) diced fresh fennel bulb (½ inch [12 mm])

1 head radicchio, cored and chopped

1 cup (152 g) canned chickpeas

¼ cup (10 g) chopped fresh flat-leaf parsley

¼ cup (60 g) capers

¾ cup (115 g) crumbled feta cheese

½ tsp fine sea salt

To make the red wine vinaigrette, combine the oil, vinegar, garlic, mustard, and salt in a jar with a lid and shake vigorously. Set aside.

To make the salad, pour the oil into a large, heavy sauté pan over medium-high heat. When the oil is hot but before it's smoking, add the bread. Fry for 2 minutes per side, or until golden brown. Remove and place on a wire rack. Rub the garlic, cut side down, aggressively on both sides of each slice. Cut the bread into large cubes and set aside as you build your salad.

In a large salad bowl, combine the tomato, cucumber, celery, fennel, radicchio, chickpeas, parsley, capers, and feta. Season with sea salt.

When ready to serve, shake the vinaigrette well. Dress the salad liberally with the vinaigrette, then add the croutons and toss lightly to serve.

LIDIA BASTIANICH

New York, New York

Chef/owner of Felidia, Becco, Esca, and Del Posto (New York), Lidia's Pittsburgh (Pittsburgh), and Lidia's Kansas City (Kansas City, Missouri); founder/president of Tavola Productions; co-owner of Eataly (New York, Chicago, Boston, and São Paolo, Brazil); co-owner of Nonna Foods; co-owner of Bastianich and La Mozza Vineyards; host of American Public Television's Lidia's Kitchen

CHEF SAYS

Items I always keep on hand for unexpected guests are . . .

Dry pasta, frozen shrimp, anchovies, canned San Marzano tomatoes, and a chunk of Grana Padano.

When hosting a quick get-together, never overlook . . .

Having some good chilled wine and crusty bread on hand.

My secret tip for successful last-minute entertaining is . . .

Be calm, have fun, have a drink, and enjoy your guests. They will truly appreciate anything that you do.

One fun fact few people know about me is that . . .

I love playing chess. I was on my high school chess team.

MENU

Veal Scaloppine Saltimbocca with Spinach

Barolo-Flavored Zabaglione

CHEF'S PAIRING

Morellino di Scanzano La Mozza (a medium-bodied Tuscan red from Maremma)

CHEF'S PLAYLIST

Old Roman songs like "Quanto Sei Bella Roma" or "Three Coins in the Fountain"

MAJOR KUDOS

James Beard awards for "Best Broadcast Media Special," "Best Television Food Show," "Outstanding Chef," "Best Chef: New York City," and "Who's Who of Food and Beverage in America"; multiple James Beard award nominations; Daytime Emmy award for "Outstanding Culinary Host"; induction into the Culinary Hall of Fame; "Humanitarian of the Year" award by the National Italian American Foundation; inclusion in "New York's Most Influential Businesswomen" list by *Crain's New York*; and invited chef for both Pope Benedict XVI's and Pope Francis's visits to America

HER STORY

Although known the world over as a legendary chef, famous TV personality, award-winning author, noted food historian, and grand doyenne of Italian cuisine, Lidia is entirely down to earth when it comes to entertaining.

"Food is the essence of life," she says. "And when it comes to the best recipes, they are the ones that are simple and straightforward." Just like the two recipes she shares with us here, both featured in her latest cookbook, *Lidia's Mastering the Art of Italian Cuisine.*

"I chose these recipes because they are very flavorful and easy to make—a quick, balanced meal," says Lidia.

"It is a minimalistic approach to using ingredients and equipment," she continues. "There are only three main ingredients for the main course and three for the dessert. And there is just one sauté pan for the veal, one pot for the spinach, and one bowl for the zabaglione. It's so easy and quick, allowing the host to have time with their guests."

Now, as Lidia loves to say, "*Tutti a tavola a mangiare!*" (Everyone to the table to eat!)

Veal Scaloppine Saltimbocca with Spinach

SERVES 4

In Italian, *saltimbocca* means "jumps in mouth"—which is exactly what happens when you taste all the wonderful flavors in this classic veal dish, which is traditionally topped with prosciutto and sage. For even more ease, ask your butcher to pound the scaloppine for you. Who says sensational and impressive can't be simple, too?

FOR THE SPINACH

1 bunch spinach (about 1 lb [450 g]), stemmed

2 tbsp (30 ml) extra virgin olive oil

3 cloves garlic, crushed

Kosher salt, to taste

Freshly ground black pepper, to taste

FOR THE SCALOPPINE

8 slices (about 1½ lb [680 g]) veal scaloppine

Kosher salt, to taste

Freshly ground black pepper, to taste

4 slices (about 2 oz [56 g]) imported Italian prosciutto, halved crosswise

8 large fresh sage leaves

All-purpose flour, for dredging

3 tbsp (45 ml) extra virgin olive oil, or additional as needed

6 tbsp (86 g, ¾ stick) butter, divided

¼ cup (60 ml) dry white wine

1 cup (240 ml) chicken stock

First wash the spinach, but don't dry it completely. The water that clings to the leaves will steam the spinach as it cooks.

Heat the olive oil in a large skillet over medium heat. Add the garlic and cook, shaking the pan, until it is golden, about 2 minutes. Scatter the spinach into the pan, a large handful at a time. Season lightly with salt and pepper, cover, and cook until the spinach begins to release its liquid. Uncover the pan, and cook, stirring, until the spinach is wilted and its water has evaporated, about 1 to 3 minutes. Taste, and season it with additional salt and pepper if necessary. Remove it from the heat, cover, and keep it warm while you make the veal.

To make the scaloppine, season each piece of veal with salt and pepper. Cover each with a half slice of the prosciutto. Tap the prosciutto with the back of a knife so it adheres well to the meat. Center a sage leaf over the prosciutto, and fasten it in place with a toothpick, weaving the toothpick in and out as if you were taking a stitch.

Spread the flour on a rimmed plate or sheet pan. Dredge the scaloppine in the flour to coat both sides lightly, then shake off excess flour.

Heat the olive oil and 2 tablespoons (28 g) of the butter in a large skillet over medium heat until the butter is foaming. Slip as many of the scaloppine, prosciutto side down, into the pan as will fit without touching. Cook just until the prosciutto is light golden, about 2 minutes. Turn, and cook until the second side is slightly browned, about 2 minutes. Remove the scoloppine and drain on paper towels. Repeat with the remaining scaloppine, adding more oil if necessary.

Remove all the scaloppine from the skillet and pour off the oil and butter. Return the pan to the heat and pour in the wine. Add the remaining 4 tablespoons (58 g) butter and cook until the wine is reduced by about half. Pour in the chicken stock and bring it to a vigorous boil. Tuck the scaloppine into the sauce. Simmer until the sauce is reduced and slightly thickened, about 3 to 4 minutes. Taste, and season with salt and pepper, if necessary.

To serve, spoon the hot spinach in a mound in the center of each of 4 plates. Arrange 2 pieces of the saltimbocca over each serving of spinach, remove the toothpicks, then spoon some of the pan sauce over the scaloppine and serve immediately.

Barolo-Flavored Zabaglione

SERVES 4

"Certainly the making of zabaglione is always a fun show to watch," says Lidia with a smile. "It could be whipped up in front of your guests. It's a demonstration that will surely lead to a conversation and will yield a delicious warm dessert upon completion." Just be sure to use a great-quality wine like Barolo, which is made from the Nebbiolo grape and is often described as one of Italy's greatest wines.

6 large egg yolks

¾ cup (180 ml) superior Barolo

6 tbsp (78 g) sugar

Mixed fresh berries, for garnish, optional

In a large copper or stainless-steel bowl, whisk together the egg yolks, Barolo, and sugar. Set the bowl over a pan of simmering water and whisk constantly until the mixture is light and frothy and forms a ribbon figure-eight when you draw your whisk out.

Serve the zabaglione immediately in parfait glasses. Garnish with berries if desired.

RICK BAYLESS

Chicago, Illinois

Chef/owner of Frontera Grill, Topolobampo, Xoco River North, and Xoco Wicker Park (Chicago), Frontera Fresco (Chicago, Skokie, and Evanston, Illinois), and Tortas Frontera (Chicago and Philadelphia); co-founder of Frontera Farmer Foundation and Frontera Scholarship

CHEF SAYS

Items I always keep on hand for unexpected guests are . . .

A green chile adobo (a spicy relative of pesto), a bright red chile adobo, a slow-roasted garlic mojo (a pungent type of garlicky oil with sweet garlic solids), a sweet-and-spicy, tangy-and-smoky chipotle sauce, and a nice bottle of mezcal from Oaxaca to start or end the meal.

When hosting a quick get-together, never overlook . . .

Serving hot food on warm plates, no matter how simple the meal, so that your food doesn't cool to room temperature too quickly. A stack of 4 plates will take 2 minutes in the microwave.

My secret tip for successful last-minute entertaining is . . .

Keep the dish simple and keep laser-focused on the task of cooking. That also means having a solid understanding of your kitchen equipment—how it works and when to use it.

One fun fact few people know about me is that . . .

I'm crazy for live theater. People usually assume that I'm eating out during my free time, but the truth is that my wife, Deann, and I love to spend time taking in plays and performances.

MENU

Pork Tenderloin with Roasted Tomatillos, Poblanos & Potatoes

CHEF'S PAIRING

A dry white Riesling from Germany, Austria, or Alsace; or a fruit-forward red California Syrah or Australian Shiraz

CHEF'S PLAYLIST

Anything by Lila Downs

MAJOR KUDOS

James Beard awards for "Outstanding Restaurant," "Best International Cookbook," "Best Chef: Midwest," "National Chef of the Year," "Humanitarian of the Year," "Who's Who of American Food and Drink," and "Best Podcast"; Julia Child Award; International Association of Culinary Professionals Awards for "Humanitarian of the Year," "Cookbook of the Year," and "Chef of the Year"; winner of *Top Chef Masters*; Daytime Emmy nomination for "Best Culinary Host"; Order of the Aztec Eagle Award from the Government of Mexico (the highest order awarded to foreigners in the country)

HIS STORY

With several long-running PBS series, a half-dozen restaurants, nine cookbooks, and too many awards to mention, Rick still finds time to teach Mexican cooking classes and lead cultural tours to Mexico.

So what do you think he serves when he's entertaining at home? You guessed it: an elegant-but-rustic Mexican dish! More specifically, *lomo de puerco en salsa verde con papas* (pork tenderloin with roasted tomatillos, poblanos, and potatoes).

"This meal is just a soulful, satisfying, and uniquely Mexican take on meat and potatoes," says Rick. "The browned pork in the classic tanginess of roasted tomatillo sauce—rich with green chiles—is a perfect, comforting match for the waxy potatoes. It's a real crowd pleaser."

Rick adds, "This dish utilizes roasted tomatillo sauce that you could make ahead, which makes the rest of the cooking pretty easy. However, a jar of roasted tomatillo salsa, thinned with some broth, would make for an even easier, last-minute sauce base."

So, there you have it, folks. *¡Olé!*

Pork Tenderloin with Roasted Tomatillos, Poblanos & Potatoes

SERVES 4 (GENEROUSLY)

"With some minor tweaks in preparation," says Rick, "this dish can be made with a well-trimmed pork loin roast, cubes of pork shoulder, chicken breast, or even chicken thighs. All will be delicious and worthy of company!"

FOR THE ROASTED TOMATILLO SAUCE BASE

1 lb (450 g, 6 to 8 medium) tomatillos, husked and rinsed

4 unpeeled cloves garlic

1–2 fresh serrano chiles

1 small white onion, sliced ½-inch (12-mm) thick

Salt

FOR THE PORK TENDERLOIN

1 large fresh poblano chile

1½ lb (680 g, about 10) small red- or white-skinned boiling potatoes (preferably about 1-inch [2.5-cm] across; if any larger, cut them in halves or quarters), peeled if you wish

Vegetable oil, olive oil, bacon drippings, or freshly rendered pork lard

1½ lb (680 g, usually 1 large or 2 very small) pork tenderloins, silver skin removed

Salt

1 cup (240 ml) chicken broth, pork broth, vegetable broth, or water

3–4 tbsp (5–7 g) chopped epazote or cilantro leaves, plus additional for garnish

1 lime, quartered, for drizzling

To make the roasted tomatillo sauce base, on a rimmed baking sheet spread out the tomatillos, garlic, serrano, and onion. Slide the baking sheet as close up under a preheated broiler as possible. After 4 or 5 minutes, when everything is blotchy-black and softening, turn the vegetables and roast the other side. Look for everything to cook through (they should be soft), while taking on an attractive bit of rustic char. Remove from the broiler until cool enough to handle.

Slip the skins off the garlic and pull the stem off the chiles. In a blender, combine the tomatillos and any juice on the baking sheet, garlic, chiles, onion, and a scant teaspoon of salt. Blend everything to a coarse purée. Set aside.

To make the pork tenderloin, roast the chile directly over high heat of a gas flame or charcoal fire until the tough skin blisters and blackens, about 5 minutes. If only an electric stove is available, heat the broiler, adjust the shelf as high as it will go, and roast, turning, until the chile is uniformly charred, about 10 minutes. While the chile is roasting, place the potatoes in a microwavable bowl, sprinkle with 1 tablespoon (15 ml) of water, cover with plastic, poke a few holes in the top, and microwave at 100% for 4 minutes.

Place the blackened chile in a bowl and cover it with a kitchen towel to trap a little steam and loosen the charred skin. When the chile has cooled enough to be handled, rub off the charred skin and remove the seed pod by pulling firmly on the stem, then rinse the peeled, seeded flesh briefly under cool water.

In a very large (12-inch [30-cm]) heavy skillet set over medium-high, heat the vegetable oil (or one of its stand-ins) to coat the bottom. When hot, dry off the meat with paper towels, sprinkle it generously with salt, and lay it in an uncrowded single layer in the pan. When brown on all sides—this takes 5 to 10 minutes—remove the meat to a plate and add the roasted tomatillo sauce base to the pan. Let the sauce simmer and reduce, stirring frequently, for about 4 minutes. Roughly chop the chile and add it to the pan along with the potatoes. Finally, stir in the chicken broth and chopped epazote or cilantro leaves.

Nestle the meat into the pan, immediately reduce the heat to medium-low, cover it, and let the meat coast slowly toward doneness, about 20 minutes.

When the meat is done, remove the pork to a cutting board. Bring the sauce to a full boil, then taste and season it with salt, usually about 1 teaspoon. Cut the tenderloin into thick oval slices on the diagonal and lay them overlapping on each of 4 plates. Drizzle with a light squeeze of lime. The sauce and potatoes get spooned over and around the meat before the plates are carried to the table. Cilantro leaves add freshness to the finished dish.

MICHELLE BERNSTEIN

Miami, Florida

Chef/owner of Crumb on Parchment and MBC Catering; host of SoFlo Taste *and PBS's* Check, Please! South Florida

MENU

Braised Halibut with Clams, Chorizo & Fregula

Torrejas

CHEF'S PAIRING

San Salvatore Falanghina Campania 2013 with the entrée
El Maestro Sierra Pedro Ximénez with the dessert

CHEF'S PLAYLIST

Upbeat flamenco or salsa

MAJOR KUDOS

James Beard award for "Best Chef: South"; co-host of Food Network's *Melting Pot*; winner on *Iron Chef America*; *Food & Wine*'s award for "Best New Restaurant"; named one of "Top 50 Restaurants in the U.S." by *Gourmet*; named one of the "Best New Restaurants in America" by *Esquire*

HER STORY

She was born and raised in Miami—of Jewish and Latin descent—to a mom who loved to cook. And since little Michelle showed so much interest in the kitchen, her mom taught her all the "basics": escargot when she was seven, osso buco at eight, and *arroz con pollo* by nine. Whew!

But there's also so much more to her story.

Michelle was actually aspiring to become a professional ballerina. In fact, she was so talented, she got a scholarship to study with the world-renowned Alvin Ailey American Dance Theater in New York when she was only seventeen. But four years—and one unfortunate injury—later, she packed her pointe shoes, wiped her tears, and headed to Johnson and Wales University in North Miami instead. Soon she was happy again.

"I chose these recipes because they're one-pan picks," says Michelle. "Simple to make, yet complex in their flavor. They're also very consistent. It's hard to mess them up because they're so straightforward."

We're all ready to give it a try!

Braised Halibut with Clams, Chorizo & Fregula

SERVES 4

"In this dish, I combine the flavors from the rendering of the chorizo to infuse into one of my favorite pastas, fregula, which is from Sardinia," says Michelle. "My mother taught me how to cook fish like this when I was very young, and there's no better way to ensure such a moist and juicy fish dish with so much flavor and color!"

4 tbsp (60 ml) olive oil, divided

1 tbsp (14 g) butter

8 oz (224 g) fresh halibut or your favorite local white fish, cut into 2-oz (56-g) pieces

2 cloves garlic, sliced very thin

4 oz (112 g) fregula (can substitute Israeli couscous)

2–3 oz (56–84 g) Spanish chorizo, casings removed, in ¼-inch (6-mm) dice

¼ cup (60 ml) dry Spanish sherry, preferably amontillado (can substitute dry white wine)

2½ cups (600 ml) clam juice or fish broth, divided

½ cup (120 g) canned tomatoes, chopped very fine

¼ tsp crushed red chili flakes (crushed red pepper)

1 lb (450 g) fresh littleneck clams, placed in ice water for about 30 minutes, then drained

¼ cup (10 g) fresh parsley leaves, chopped fine

2 tbsp (5 g) fresh cilantro leaves, chopped fine

2 tbsp (30 ml) high-quality extra virgin olive oil

Kosher salt, to taste

Freshly ground black pepper, to taste

Preheat the oven to 250°F (121°C).

Set a large sauté pan over medium-high heat with 2 tablespoons (30 ml) of the oil and the butter. When the butter begins to foam, add the halibut. Cook, turning the fish until golden on all sides, about 4 to 5 minutes. Remove the halibut from the pan with a spatula and set aside on a plate. Pour off the fat from the pan and discard.

Return the pan to medium heat. Add the remaining 2 tablespoons (30 ml) of oil and the garlic. Cook until the garlic is just golden, about 2 to 3 minutes. Remove the garlic quickly with a slotted spoon, keeping the oil in the pan.

Add the fregula and chorizo, stirring for 1 to 2 minutes. Add the sherry and reduce by half, about 4 minutes.

Add 2 cups (480 ml) of the clam juice, the tomatoes, and chili flakes. Increase the heat to high and bring to a boil, then lower to medium and add the clams. When they all open, add the parsley, cilantro, and oil, shaking and stirring the pan. If there is not too much liquid, add the remaining ½ cup (120 ml) clam juice. The sauce should be juicy but thick enough to coat the back of a spoon. Add the cooked halibut to the pan and warm through. Season with salt and pepper.

Place the halibut on a serving platter. Spoon the clams, fregula, and remaining juices all over the fish to serve.

Torrejas

SERVES 4

Think of these as the Cuban/Spanish/Guatemalan/Salvadorian version of French toast. Only maybe better.
That's probably because they're usually only made once a year for Easter as a traditional Latin American dessert.
You, on the other hand, can make it any time you want, as often as you want!

2 cups (480 ml) whole milk

¾ cup (150 g) sugar, divided

1 tsp pure vanilla extract

⅜ tsp ground cinnamon, divided

Zest of 1 orange

Zest of 1 lemon

1 French baguette (not too slender),
sliced into 1-inch (2.5-cm) thick slices

¼ cup (60 ml) olive oil

3 large eggs

Vanilla ice cream, for serving

Marmalade, preferably fig, for serving

Combine the milk, ½ cup (100 g) of the sugar, vanilla, ⅛ teaspoon of the cinnamon, orange zest, and lemon zest in a saucepan. Bring to a simmer. Remove from the heat and cool to room temperature.

Place the bread slices in a shallow pan. Pour the cooled milk mixture over the bread and allow to soak for a few minutes.

Heat the olive oil in a medium-size sauté pan over medium-high heat.

Meanwhile, beat the eggs in a medium-size bowl. Working with a few slices at a time (enough to fit in one layer in the sauté pan), dip the soaked bread slices into the eggs, making sure to fully coat both sides. Allow excess egg to drip off, then place the bread in the hot pan. Cook, turning once, until golden on both sides and cooked through, about 6 to 8 minutes. Remove the bread from the pan and place on paper towels to drain. Repeat the dipping procedure and the frying with the remaining bread slices.

Mix together the remaining ¼ cup (50 g) sugar and remaining ¼ teaspoon cinnamon in a small bowl. Dust the torrejas with the cinnamon-sugar mixture and serve warm with a scoop of ice cream and your favorite marmalade.

JOHN BESH

New Orleans, Louisiana

Chef/owner of August, Besh Steak, Domenica, Borgne, La Provence, Lüke, Pizza Domenica, Johnny Sánchez New Orleans, Shaya, and Willa Jean (New Orleans); Lüke San Antonio (San Antonio), and Johnny Sánchez Baltimore (Baltimore); founder of the John Besh Foundation

CHEF SAYS

Items I always keep on hand for unexpected guests are . . .

Eggs, arugula, lots of vegetables, cheese, and good pasta (both frozen and dried).

When hosting a quick get-together, never overlook . . .

Your stress level. Just enjoy. Cook a little bit, eat a little bit, and know that it's all going to be just fine.

My secret tip for successful last-minute entertaining is . . .

Be calm, have fun, have a drink, and enjoy your guests. They will truly appreciate anything that you do.

One fun fact few people know about me is that . . .

I'm just as happy having a simple meal with good friends as I would be dining in the fanciest restaurants.

MENU

Creamy Fennel Soup

Zucchini & Mozzarella Frittata

Arugula Salad with Toasted Pecans

Warm Fig Crumble

CHEF'S PAIRING

Côtes du Rhône red wine

CHEF'S PLAYLIST

Dave Matthews

MAJOR KUDOS

Induction into the James Beard Foundation's "Who's Who in Food & Beverage"; James Beard award for "Best Chef: Southeast"; multiple James Beard nominations for "Outstanding National Restaurant" and "Outstanding Service"; one of *Food & Wine*'s "Top 10 Best New Chefs in America"

HIS STORY

A native son of southern Louisiana, John takes zealous pride in the culinary riches of the Big Easy.

For instance, when not cooking a favorite regional dish at one of his many restaurants, he's assisting local Gulf Coast farmers to obtain micro-loans . . . or providing both fully paid culinary scholarships and individualized mentorships to minority residents of the Greater New Orleans area . . . or hosting a charity event through his foundation that works to "protect and preserve the culinary heritage and foodways of New Orleans." Which amazes us that he has any time left to entertain at all.

But as John puts it, "Easy execution is so important when entertaining. These featured recipes are ones any home cook of any level of experience can conquer."

He goes on to add, "Eggs are too often overlooked as a viable dinner option. I love the idea of using whatever you have in the fridge for a quick and delicious frittata. Add a salad and soup, and you've got yourself a real soul-warming meal."

We couldn't agree more.

Creamy Fennel Soup

SERVES 8

This flavorful, velvety soup is perfect any time of year. If you'd like, give it a try with other vegetables, too. Just replace the fennel with either a cup (230 g) of chopped carrots, corn off the cob, chopped broccoli, or diced turnips. The method is always the same: Soften the vegetables, add the broth and a bit of cream, simmer, and purée. If you choose to omit vegetables altogether, serve it chilled as a great vichyssoise!

¼ cup (60 ml) olive oil

1 leek, light green and white parts, cleaned and trimmed (page 456), chopped

½ fennel bulb, trimmed and chopped, tops reserved for garnish

2 cloves garlic, minced

1 potato, peeled and roughly chopped

4 cups (946 ml) chicken broth

½ cup (120 ml) heavy cream

Salt

Freshly ground black pepper

Chive blossoms, for garnish, optional

Heat the oil in a large heavy-bottomed pot over medium-high heat and sweat the leeks and fennel, stirring, for about 2 minutes. Add the garlic and cook 2 minutes.

Add the potato, chicken broth, and cream. Bring to a boil, then reduce immediately to a simmer. Cook until the potato is soft, about 20 minutes.

Transfer the soup to a blender and purée. Season with salt and pepper and garnish with the chopped fennel fronds and chive blossoms, if desired.

Zucchini & Mozzarella Frittata

SERVES 8

John considers the frittata (basically an open-face omelet) his go-to instant meal. And it's so versatile! Try adding some cooked diced potatoes and cooked sausage. Or a little corn and crabmeat. Or even some Spanish chorizo, olives, and tomatoes. "One trick," says John, "is to flash the pan into the oven for just a few minutes to heat the cheese."

4 large eggs

2½ tsp (12 ml) canola oil

⅓ cup (50 g) chopped onion

⅓ cup (40 g) diced zucchini

4 slices fresh mozzarella, in pieces

Salt, to taste

Freshly ground black pepper, to taste

Preheat the oven to 400°F (204°C).

In a small bowl, vigorously beat the eggs until frothy.

Heat the oil in an 8-inch (20-cm) ovenproof nonstick skillet over medium-high heat. Add the onion and zucchini. Sauté until softened and slightly golden, about 3 minutes. Add the eggs and swirl around the pan, using a spatula. Gently lift the edges of the eggs to evenly disperse the liquid. Once the eggs have begun to firm up, scatter the mozzarella over the top.

Put the pan in the oven for 4 to 5 minutes, or until the eggs are just set. Hold a large plate over the skillet and invert the skillet so the frittata drops onto the plate. Slice into wedges, season with salt and pepper, and serve it up!

Arugula Salad with Toasted Pecans

SERVES 8

This salad is deceptively simple and distinctly delicious. The bonus? You can make the vinaigrette up to 2 days ahead and refrigerate in an airtight container. Just let it stand at room temperature for 20 minutes before assembling the salad. Nothing could be easier!

¼ cup (60 ml) balsamic vinegar

Salt, to taste

Freshly ground black pepper, to taste

1 cup (240 ml) olive oil

8 oz (224 g) arugula

2 cups (240 g) pecan halves, toasted (page 457)

In a small bowl, whisk together the balsamic vinegar, salt, and pepper. Gradually drizzle in the olive oil, whisking until emulsified.

Place the arugula in a large serving bowl and toss with just enough vinaigrette to coat. Sprinkle with the toasted pecans.

Warm Fig Crumble

SERVES 8

It's hard to imagine a more satisfying dessert. Feel free to assemble well in advance and cook when you're ready. For other delicious variations, try using 3 cups (480 g) of any fruit or berries of your choice for an almost-instant dessert.

FOR THE FRUIT FILLING

3 cups (480 g) chopped figs, stems removed (can substitute any other fruit or berries)

1 large egg, lightly beaten

3 tbsp (42 g) brown sugar, firmly packed

2 tbsp (16 g) all-purpose flour

2 tbsp (28 g) unsalted butter, melted

Pinch of ground cinnamon

FOR THE TOPPING

⅔ cup (84 g) all-purpose flour

⅓ cup (74 g) brown sugar, firmly packed

¼ cup (50 g) granulated sugar

½ tsp ground cinnamon

Pinch of salt

6 tbsp (86 g) unsalted butter, cut into ½-inch (12-mm) pieces

Ice cream, for serving, optional

Preheat the oven to 400°F (204°C).

To make the fruit filling, toss the figs in a bowl with the egg, brown sugar, flour, melted butter, and cinnamon to coat. Spoon the fruit mixture into individual ramekins or into one big baking dish.

To make the topping, combine the flour, brown sugar, granulated sugar, cinnamon, and salt in a medium-size bowl. Cut the butter into the mixture until the topping is crumbly. Sprinkle over the fruit.

Bake until the figs are bubbly and the topping turns a lovely golden brown, about 25 to 30 minutes. Serve warm with the ice cream if desired.

SUSAN FENIGER

Los Angeles, California

Co-chef/owner of Border Grill Restaurants (Los Angeles and Las Vegas) and Border Grill Truck and Blue Window (Los Angeles); co-host of Food Network's series Too Hot Tamales *and* Tamales World Tour

CHEF SAYS

Items I always keep on hand for unexpected guests are . . .

Crackers, great cheese, olives, avocados, and daal of some sort. Plus rice.

When hosting a quick get-together, never overlook . . .

Planning your menu, no matter how simple. Write down all the prep for it. Set up in the kitchen area so you can hang out with your guests when they arrive. Enjoy!

My secret tip for successful last-minute entertaining is . . .

Stock your dry storage area so you can cook up something with very little you have to go out of the house for.

One fun fact few people know about me is that . . .

I love to stay up late, watch Rachel Maddow, and eat a bowl of salted, buttered popcorn. Then get up early before the sun rises, have a cup of tea, and watch the sun come up.

MENU

Goat Cheese Avocado Mash

Rib Eye Steaks with Chimichurri

Okinawa Sweet Potatoes with Pink Peppercorn Sour Cream

CHEF'S PAIRING

12-year-old Scotch on the rocks with a tiny bit of Fever-Tree Ginger Ale, then shift to a yummy Cabernet

CHEF'S PLAYLIST

Jazz (begin with Benny Goodman, then move to Bill Evans during dinner)

MAJOR KUDOS

Elizabeth Burns Lifetime Achievement Award from the California Restaurant Association; induction into the Menu Masters Hall of Fame; participant on Bravo's *Top Chef Masters*

HER STORY

She grew up in Toledo, Ohio. Trained in Hyde Park, New York. Worked on the French Riviera. And then ended up right where she felt most comfortable: Los Angeles. Hippie vibes and all.

Susan quickly embraced her new city, and it returned the favor. In fact, Susan is credited with forever changing the culinary landscape of LA. And she did that by offering the locals authentic, eclectic dishes from all over the world. This is clearly reflected in the delicious meal she is so graciously sharing with all of us in this book.

"This is an easy go-to meal for me," says Susan. "My mom and dad used to marinate steak all the time, so I have vivid memories of them when I do this. I'm a Midwest gal, so what can I say!"

Any other great reason for choosing this dish?

"Everything—or almost everything—can be done ahead," she explains.

Now that, we love!

Goat Cheese Avocado Mash

SERVES 4

If you know anything about Susan, it's that one of her absolute most favorite things on this planet is Hass avocados. So it goes without saying she would somehow find a way to include them in her featured meal. But rather than turn to the ever-traditional guacamole, she fuses it with goat cheese in this marvelous appetizer. Clever!

2 oz (56 g) mild, soft goat cheese, such as Montrachet

¼ cup (60 ml) olive oil

2 ripe avocados, halved, seeded, and peeled

Juice of ½ lemon

2 dashes of Tabasco

Pinch of freshly ground white pepper

Salt, to taste

Thick tomato slices, for garnish

Thick cucumber slices, for garnish

Freshly ground black pepper, for finishing

Thin rounds of French baguette, toasted (page 457), for garnish

Place the goat cheese and olive oil in a small container with a cover and marinate at room temperature for up to 45 minutes.

Just before serving, lift the cheese out of the oil. Place in a large bowl with the avocados, lemon juice, Tabasco, and white pepper. Mash with a fork until the mixture is slightly lumpy, not a smooth purée. Season sparingly with salt since goat cheese can be very salty.

To serve, place a scoop in the center of each small serving plate. Garnish with the tomato and cucumber slices. Finish the slices with the pepper and add the French baguette to the plate.

CHEF'S TIPS

If you wish to flavor the cheese, just add fresh herbs and spices such as basil, thyme, rosemary, or peppercorns.

The goat cheese can marinate indefinitely as long as it's completely covered with oil.

Rib Eye Steaks with Chimichurri

SERVES 4

This meal clearly evokes happy thoughts of childhood for Susan, when her parents would grill steaks all the time. To add her own twist, she pairs the steaks with the Latin flavor of delicious homemade chimichurri and 24 (yes, 24!) cloves of garlic. Quick. Simple. And absolutely perfect.

FOR THE CHIMICHURRI

½ bunch fresh mint, chopped

¼ bunch fresh Italian parsley, chopped

¼ bunch fresh chives, chopped

¼ bunch fresh cilantro, chopped

½ cup (120 ml) extra virgin olive oil

2 tbsp (30 ml) red wine vinegar

Juice of 1 lime

2 cloves garlic, minced

⅛ tsp red chili flakes (crushed red pepper)

Salt, to taste

FOR THE RIB EYE STEAKS

¼ cup (60 ml) extra virgin olive oil

6 jalapeño chiles, stemmed and seeded, optional

24 cloves garlic, peeled

4 (10–12-oz [280–340-g]) rib eye steaks, at least 1-inch (2.5-cm) thick

Salt, to taste

Freshly ground black pepper, to taste

If grilling, preheat the grill to high heat.

To make the chimichurri, whisk together all the ingredients in a medium-size bowl. Let sit at least 30 minutes, allowing the flavors to combine.

To prepare the rib eye steaks, heat the oil in a heavy-bottomed skillet over moderate heat. If using jalapeños, add them to the skillet and sauté until they soften and their skins start to brown, about 3 to 4 minutes. Remove with a slotted spoon and drain on paper towels. When cooled, slice each jalapeño into 4 slices, for a total of 24 slices.

Add the garlic to the skillet and cook, stirring occasionally, over low heat until soft and lightly browned, about 4 to 6 minutes. Transfer to paper towels and let cool.

With a paring knife, make six 1-inch (2.5-cm) horizontal slits around the edges of each steak. Stuff each slit with 1 clove of garlic and 1 slice of jalapeño, if using. Season the steaks generously with salt and pepper.

Grill the steaks on the grill or sauté in a lightly oiled cast-iron pan over medium-high heat, about 3 to 5 minutes per side, depending on the thickness and desired doneness.

Top the steak with a generous spoonful of chimichurri and serve warm.

Okinawa Sweet Potatoes with Pink Peppercorn Sour Cream

SERVES 4

Recently designated as a superfood, Okinawa sweet potatoes are a popular staple of both Japanese and Hawaiian cuisines. With their light brown skin and unusual purple flesh, they're richly nutritious (featuring 150% more antioxidants than blueberries!) and surprisingly sweet, with a naturally creamy flavor. Look for them at your local Asian market. (You can substitute regular sweet potatoes, but, Susan says, the flavor just won't be the same.)

1 tbsp (15 ml) canola oil

1 lb (450 g) Okinawa sweet potatoes (can substitute regular sweet potatoes), peeled and cut into large pieces

½ tsp kosher salt

1 cup (240 ml) sour cream

3 scallions, cut thinly on the bias, reserving a few slices for garnish

1 tbsp (5 g) pink peppercorns, slightly crushed but mostly whole

1 tsp Maldon smoked sea salt or other smoked sea salt

Preheat the oven to 350°F (177°C).

Heat the oil in a large ovenproof sauté pan over medium-high heat. Add the potatoes, sprinkle with the kosher salt, and cook, stirring, until browned, about 3 to 4 minutes. Place in the oven and finish cooking for another 15 to 20 minutes, stirring every so often to ensure even cooking.

While the potatoes are in the oven, mix together the sour cream, scallions, peppercorns, and smoked sea salt in a small bowl until well combined.

When the potatoes are ready, serve while still warm, topped with the pink peppercorn sour cream. Garnish with the reserved scallions.

ANDY HUSBANDS

Boston, Massachusetts

Cheflowner of Tremont 647, Sister Sorel, and Smoke Shop

CHEF SAYS

Items I always keep on hand for unexpected guests are . . .

Smoked rack of ribs, eggs, chicken thighs, edamame, and fresh herbs growing in my windows.

When hosting a quick get-together, never overlook . . .

That it's about having fun.

My secret tip for successful last-minute entertaining is . . .

Have a Boulevardier before the guests show up.

One fun fact few people know about me is that . . .

I'm a huge George Jones fan.

MENU

Quinoa Stir Fry with Pork, Herbs & Eggs

CHEF'S PAIRING

Anything from Hill Farmstead Brewery

(Sake works, too)

CHEF'S PLAYLIST

Anything by Kinny, funky and raw

MAJOR KUDOS

Semifinalist for multiple James Beard "Best Chef" awards; "Best of Boston" award from *Boston Magazine*; first-place team member (out of 510 teams) in the Brisket category of the Kansas City Royal BBQ Championship; participant in the sixth season of *Hell's Kitchen* hosted by Gordon Ramsay

HIS STORY

Andy loves to surprise people.

Like when he rode his motorcycle cross country in his early twenties to live on an organic farm in New Mexico. Like when he took his life's savings and turned a boarded-up storefront into a trendy, high-end eatery. Like when the barbecue team cleverly named IQUE BBQ, of which he is a founding member, became world champions at the Jack Daniel's World Championship Invitational Barbecue.

And like when he shared this recipe with me.

"It's my go-to comfort food," he says. "It has so much flexibility and really wows people. It's quick, easy, sexy, and tasty, too."

It's no wonder this dish is such a hit. It not only includes any leftover meat you happen to have in your fridge (making it turn out different every time), but it's also infused with a secret ingredient.

"I love the use of mint in savory items," he confesses.

We confess it's perfect.

Quinoa Stir Fry with Pork, Herbs & Eggs

SERVES 4 AS AN ENTRÉE

This Thai-style dish is not only easy to throw together, it also makes a beautiful presentation! Yes, of course you can use fresh veggies if you prefer. Just make sure to adjust the cooking time. Want nuts, too? Oh, yeah. Cashews or peanuts would be rockin'. And as a bonus, this is all gluten free as long as you use the tamari. Score!

1 tbsp (15 ml) sesame oil, divided

2 tbsp (30 ml) olive or canola oil, divided

1 cup (225 g) diced or roughly chopped leftover grilled pork, chicken, or steak

1 tbsp (7 g) minced fresh ginger

2 large cloves garlic, minced

1 red jalapeño chile, sliced super thin

2 ribs celery, cut ⅛-inch (3-mm) thick on the bias

1½ cups (225 g) frozen edamame (can substitute frozen mixed vegetables such as peas and carrots), warmed in the microwave for 3 minutes

1 tbsp (15 ml) tamari (can substitute soy sauce)

2 tbsp (30 ml) fish sauce

3 cups (555 g) hot cooked quinoa (made from 1 cup [170 g] dry quinoa)

1–2 tbsp (15–30 ml) Sriracha hot sauce, to taste

1 cup (40 g) roughly chopped fresh mint, cilantro, and basil leaves

2 large eggs

3 fresh cilantro sprigs

In a large heavy-bottomed sauté pan or cast-iron skillet (the latter is Andy's favorite), over medium-high heat, add half the sesame oil and half the olive oil. Heat until smoking.

Add the leftover pork and cook, stirring occasionally, for 2 minutes, or until it starts to brown. Add the ginger, garlic, jalapeño, and celery, then continue to cook and stir for 1 minute.

Add the edamame and continue to cook and stir until everything is hot. Add the tamari and fish sauce, stirring to combine for 1 minute. Set aside.

Place the hot quinoa in a large bowl. Pour the meat mixture over the quinoa. Add the Sriracha and most of the chopped herbs (set some aside for garnish). Mix well, turn out onto a serving platter, and set aside, keeping it warm.

Place a nonstick sauté pan over medium-high heat. Add the remaining sesame and olive oils, then break the eggs in gently and fry both over easy; the yolks should be hot but not cooked. Remove from the heat and slide the eggs on top of the quinoa. Garnish with the cilantro sprigs and reserved chopped mint and basil. Serve immediately.

CHEF'S NOTE

Upon serving, stir the eggs in. The yolks will cook and give the dish a killer richness. Eat hot.

SEAN BROCK

Charleston, South Carolina

Chef/partner of McCrady's and McCrady's Tavern (Charleston), Husk (Charleston and Greenville, South Carolina; Nashville; and Savannah), and Minero (Charleston and Atlanta)

CHEF SAYS

Items I always keep on hand for unexpected guests are . . .

A country ham on a carving stand for guests to help themselves; an open bottle (or four) of Antique Bourbon from the Stitzel Weller Distillery; pimento cheese and benne wafers; a drawer full of fine Southern cheeses in my fridge; and a huge bowl of GooGoo Clusters.

When hosting a quick get-together, never overlook . . .

Anticipating the guests' needs before they even realize they need anything at all. This is the same mantra we have at my restaurants, and I carry it over to entertaining at home. Also, I always make it a point to send guests home with a takeaway gift. Even if it's as simple as an antique spoon or a GooGoo Cluster, it shows them that you are glad they came to hang.

My secret tip for successful last-minute entertaining is . . .

While the food, drink, and music are all very, very important, having great flatware and china can really add to the party. I love thrifting for antique pieces from old cruise ships and the great hotels of the nineteenth century.

One fun fact few people know about me is that . . .

My apartment is essentially a Southern folk art museum. I am obsessed with collecting the work of two artists: Jimmy Lee Sudduth and Mose Tolliver.

MENU

Shrimp & Okra Purloo

CHEF'S PAIRING

Blackberry Farm's "Classic Saison" farmhouse ale

CHEF'S PLAYLIST

Hill Country Blues (specifically Junior Kimbrough, T-Model Ford, and R. L. Burnside)

MAJOR KUDOS

James Beard award for "Best Chef: Southeast"; several James Beard award finalist nominations; "Best New Restaurant" award from *Bon Appétit*; host of PBS's *The Mind of a Chef*; Daytime Emmy Award nomination; contestant on *Iron Chef America*; named one of the "12 Most Outstanding Restaurants of the Year" by *GQ*; named one of the "Best New Restaurants in America" by *Esquire*

HIS STORY

You'd think anyone born and raised in a small, rural coal-mining town with no restaurants would learn a thing or two about self-sustainability.

Well, Sean did. But he also took it many steps further.

You see, he eventually left Virginia to attend Johnson and Wales University in Charleston, South Carolina. After graduation and several high-level restaurant posts, he opened his own place. Plus, he cultivated a 2.5-acre farm. And he got into seed saving, heirloom crops, and heritage breeds of livestock. And he started in-house canning, preserving, pickling, and fermenting. And he got passionate about wood-fire cooking. And . . .

Well, you get the idea. So, when Sean was asked to submit a recipe for this book, his answer was swift and enthusiastic.

"Purloo is an iconic dish in the Low Country," says Sean. "It's one of my favorite dishes to make at home. It's quick, easy, and insanely delicious. It also tells the story of the Carolina Rice Kitchen, from its troubled past to the current repatriation of the rice pantry. All of these stories teach us lessons along the way and remind us how powerful a bowl of food can be."

We tend to agree.

Shrimp & Okra Purloo

SERVES 4 TO 6

Purloo, for those of you who never heard of it, is a classic rice stew and close relative of both jambalaya and paella. It's also a simple comfort dish of economy, diversity, and family history. "This one is always my go-to in a pinch," says Sean, "and can be made with any protein you have on hand. I love switching out deeply roasted vegetables like eggplant for the shrimp and ham sometimes. It also requires minimal cleanup. The last thing you want to do when you have guests over is scrub a sink full of pots and pans." One-pot wonder. Gotcha!

4 cups (946 ml) stock, preferably shrimp stock

4 tbsp (58 g) butter, divided

½ cup (70 g) crumbled, deboned smoked herring

2 cups (370 g) uncooked rice, preferably Carolina Gold

1 cup (230 g) small-diced country ham

1 cup (150 g) medium-diced sweet onion

1 clove garlic, finely chopped

½ cup (60 g) small-diced celery

½ cup (60 g) medium-diced green bell pepper

3 cups (720 g) crushed tomatoes

2 cups (256 g) peeled and deveined shrimp, cut into small pieces

1 cup (60 g) okra slices (½-inch [12-mm] thick)

¼ cup (10 g) chopped fresh Italian parsley

1 tsp Worcestershire sauce

Hot sauce, to taste

Espelette pepper (can substitute Aleppo pepper), to taste

Fresh lemon juice, to taste

3 scallions, sliced, for garnish

Bring the stock to a simmer. Meanwhile, place a medium-size saucepot over medium-high heat. Add 2 tablespoons (28 g) of the butter. When the butter gets frothy, add the herring and stir. Add the rice and stir to coat. Add the warm stock and bring to a simmer. Cover and cook for 15 minutes on low, or until the rice is tender. Strain and reserve the stock for the stew. Keep the rice warm.

In a large Dutch oven over medium-high heat, add the remaining 2 tablespoons (28 g) of butter and the ham. Cook for 5 minutes, stirring occasionally. Add the onions and garlic. Sauté until translucent, about 2 minutes. Add the celery and pepper and cook for about 2 minutes. Add the tomatoes and the reserved stock and simmer for 30 minutes. Add the shrimp and okra and simmer for 5 minutes. Remove from the heat, then season with the parsley, Worcestershire sauce, hot sauce, Espelette pepper, and lemon juice. Serve over the rice and garnish with the scallions.

EDWARD LEE

Louisville, Kentucky

Chef/owner of 610 Magnolia and MilkWood

CHEF SAYS

Items I always keep on hand for unexpected guests are . . .

Gochujang, ssamjang, Kentucky country ham, homemade persimmon vinegar, and lots of bourbon.

When hosting a quick get-together, never overlook . . .

The beverages. Don't just serve whatever is lying around. Put some thought into it, and it will elevate the dinner.

My secret tip for successful last-minute entertaining is . . .

Use great ingredients because you don't have time to build flavor with long-cooking techniques.

One fun fact few people know about me is that . . .

I mostly eat vegetarian at home.

MENU

Spicy Pimento Fundido with Corn Relish & Crackers

Quick Ramen with Ssamjang Carbonara Sauce

Quick Cucumber Kimchi

CHEF'S PAIRING

Jefferson's Reserve Very Old Bourbon on the rocks to start

Virtue Apple Cider with the meal

CHEF'S PLAYLIST

Johnny Cash

MAJOR KUDOS

Multiple James Beard award nominations for "Best Chef: Southeast"; winner of Food Network's *Iron Chef America*; host of PBS's *Mind of a Chef*, season three; guest judge on *Master Chef*; contestant on *Top Chef: Texas*

HIS STORY

Take a first-generation Korean kid who was raised in Brooklyn. Send him to NYU for a degree in English lit. Have him graduate magna cum laude. Let him dabble (actually quite seriously) in the culinary arts at high-profile restaurants throughout France and New York. Even have him open up his own successful chichi restaurant in Manhattan. Then get him to attend the Kentucky Derby in Louisville. Only once. And what do you think happens next?

If we're talking about Edward, he ends up permanently moving to Louisville and joining the area's most forward-thinking chefs—making way for lots and lots of personal accolades.

Today Edward continues to enjoy Southern hospitality, both at work and at home.

"This is my go-to meal," says Edward. "It's quick and easy to make, but it doesn't taste like a last-minute meal. It's comforting but still exciting. I always have Korean ingredients on hand in my house, but traditional Korean food is too time-consuming. This is a great way to enjoy the bold flavors without the hours of back-breaking work."

Sounds intriguing, does it not?

Spicy Pimento Fundido with Corn Relish & Crackers

"Guests always ask about gochujang and ssamjang [featured in the Quick Ramen recipe]," says Edward, "which are two staples of Korean cooking that have a lot of versatility. I like to show how they can add umami flavor to dishes as different as pimento cheese and carbonara sauce." His take on *fundido*—meaning "melted"—has a little kick and is altogether marvelous. Just add your favorite brand of corn relish and crackers or crispy lavash, and you're all good to go.

FOR THE PIMENTO CHEESE

4 oz (112 g) sharp yellow Cheddar cheese, grated

2 oz (56 g) white Cheddar cheese, grated

1 oz (28 g) cream cheese

1 tbsp (15 g) gochujang paste (found in Asian markets and some supermarkets)

½ clove garlic

2 dashes of Worcestershire sauce

6 tbsp (85 g) mayonnaise, preferably Duke's

½ (4-oz [112-g]) jar pimentos, drained and reserved if needed

Salt, to taste

Pepper, to taste

FOR THE FUNDIDO

8 oz (224 g) sharp yellow Cheddar cheese, grated

8 oz (224 g) white Cheddar cheese, grated

8 oz (224 g) Jack cheese, grated

FOR THE GARNISH AND SERVING

Jarred corn relish

1 tsp chopped fresh parsley

Crackers or crispy lavash

To make the pimento cheese, combine the two Cheddar cheeses, the cream cheese, gochujang, garlic, Worcestershire sauce, and mayonnaise in a food processor. Pulse until mixed but still crumbly. Or you can mix together in a bowl with a wooden spoon.

With the cheese mixture in a bowl, add the pimentos. If it needs it, add a little pimento juice to make the mixture creamy. Season with salt and pepper. Set aside.

To make the fundido, combine the two Cheddar cheeses and the Jack cheese in a bowl. Mix well.

Heat a cast-iron skillet over medium-high heat. Add the cheese and heat until melted and bubbling around the edges, about 3 minutes. Remove from the heat.

Immediately add the pimento cheese in a large dollop over the fundido. Top with the corn relish and parsley. Serve piping hot, in the skillet, with the crackers, making sure the skillet is resting on a trivet or a folded towel, and *not* directly on the table.

Quick Ramen with Ssamjang Carbonara Sauce

SERVES 4

Speaking of fusion food, here's a classic example. Take a traditional Italian carbonara sauce. Swap some traditional Asian condiments. And you've got yourself one wonderful hybrid of a dish! Two specialized ingredients in this recipe—ssamjang and furikake—can be found at Asian markets or in the Asian section of many supermarkets.

8 oz (224 g) applewood smoked bacon, diced small

8 large egg yolks

1 tbsp (15 ml) toasted sesame oil

¾ cup (135 g) grated Parmigiano-Reggiano cheese, plus additional for garnish

¼ cup (60 g) ssamjang

4 packages instant ramen, spice packets removed and discarded

1 tbsp (3 g) chopped fresh parsley

1 tbsp (5 g) furikake

Freshly ground black pepper, to taste

Zest of 1 lemon, for garnish

Set a skillet over medium heat and add the bacon. Cook for about 5 minutes, or until the fat is rendered and the bacon bits are crispy. Remove the bits and reserve on a paper towel–lined plate. Discard all but 1 tablespoon (14 g) of the bacon fat.

Bring 1 gallon (3.8 L) of water to a boil in a large pot.

Meanwhile, combine the egg yolks, oil, ¾ cup (135 g) Parmigiano-Reggiano, and ssamjang in a large bowl that has been lightly prewarmed in the oven. Whisk until combined, then set aside.

To the boiling water add the ramen noodles only and cook for about 3 to 4 minutes, depending on the brand you use. Drain and immediately transfer the noodles to the bowl with the egg sauce. Start whisking the mixture vigorously and add the reserved bacon fat to the noodles while whisking. Add the crispy bacon, parsley, and furikake.

Stir once more and divide into warmed bowls. Top the ramen with a little pepper, lemon zest, and extra Parmigiano-Reggiano. Serve immediately.

Quick Cucumber Kimchi

SERVES 4

Although traditional Korean kimchi is usually associated with fermented cabbage, there are still loads of other versions featuring many other vegetables. To produce this tasty delight, Edward makes full use of fresh cucumbers that are quickly pickled.

1 lb (450 g) cucumbers, with peel, halved lengthwise and sliced ¼-inch (6-mm) thick

1 tbsp (16 g) sea salt

2 tbsp (30 ml) toasted sesame oil

½ tbsp Korean chili powder or red chili flakes (crushed red pepper)

2 tsp (10 ml) persimmon vinegar (can substitute rice vinegar)

1 tbsp (5 g) chopped scallions

1½ tsp (4 g) grated fresh ginger

½ tsp fish sauce, preferably Red Boat

Toss the sliced cucumbers with the salt and let stand for 20 minutes, then rinse and squeeze out any excess liquid with your hands. Place in a serving bowl.

In a separate bowl, whisk together the remaining ingredients. Toss with the cucumbers and leave out at room temperature until ready to serve.

*See photo on page 86.

ANITA LO

New York, New York

Cheffowner of Annisa

CHEF SAYS

Items I always keep on hand for unexpected guests are . . .

Chilled sparkling or still white and rosé wines, Parmigiano-Reggiano, pasta, frozen head-on shrimp, and a full bar (gotta keep 'em boozed up!).

When hosting a quick get-together, never overlook . . .

Tasting everything.

My secret tip for successful last-minute entertaining is . . .

Keep it simple!

One fun fact few people know about me is that . . .

I can ride a five-foot unicycle.

MENU

Shrimp Stew with Tomatoes, Calabrian Chilis & Capers

Arugula Salad with Toasted Pistachios & Parmesan

Yogurt Panna Cotta with Dates & Pedro Ximénez

CHEF'S PAIRING

White wine (a full-bodied Viognier would be nice)

CHEF'S PLAYLIST

Macy Gray

MAJOR KUDOS

"Best New Chef" award from *Food & Wine*; "Best New Restaurant Chef" award from *The Village Voice*; 3-star review from the *New York Times*; contestant on the first season of *Iron Chef America* and on *Chopped*; fourth place (out of twenty-four) on first season of *Top Chef Masters*; first female guest chef invited to cook for a state dinner at the White House

HER STORY

Anita is a second-generation Malaysian American who grew up in Birmingham, Michigan. She's also an Ivy Leaguer with a degree in French literature from Columbia, as well as a graduate of the prestigious École Ritz Escoffier in Paris (where she interned with legendary icons Guy Savoy and Michel Rostang).

So what does this gifted chef like to do in her spare time? Travel. Around the world. And back. Which is our luck when it comes to the meal she chose for this book.

"I've collected specialty dry goods from around the planet," says Anita. "And I have these little capers kept in salt from Pantelleria Island that are supposedly the best in the world."

So what better ingredient for her to showcase than these little pickled flower buds from the caper plant grown in rich Sicilian volcanic soil? (Psst, you and I don't have to travel so far to get them today. They are readily available on the Internet, thank goodness. Unless, that is, you've always wanted to visit Sicily.)

"This meal couldn't be easier," admits Anita. "I generally keep many of the ingredients at my house, and there's very little cleanup."

Now that, we love.

Shrimp Stew with Tomatoes, Calabrian Chilis & Capers

SERVES 4

This exotic, aromatic stew packs plenty of flavorful punch. And to be quite honest, most of it comes from the Calabrian chiles (pepperoncini). These complex, mildly fruity, yet spicy peppers with bright red wrinkled skin are aged on the vine to produce a score of 25,000 to 40,000 on the Scoville Heat Scale. So yeah, they're pretty hot. But also so damn good!

3 tbsp (45 ml) olive oil

1 small onion, sliced

2 cloves garlic, finely chopped

1 fresh thyme sprig (or a small pinch of dried thyme)

1 bay leaf

4 Calabrian chiles, sliced (can substitute 1 cherry pepper)

1½ cups (360 ml) white wine

1 cup (240 g) chopped ripe tomatoes

2 tbsp (30 g) capers, drained if in brine, rinsed

2 (8-oz [240-ml]) bottles clam juice

20 uncooked jumbo gulf shrimp, peeled and deveined, heads left on

Salt, to taste

Freshly ground black pepper, to taste

Fresh lemon juice, to taste

12 slices French baguette, toasted (page 457) and rubbed with a garlic clove

Extra virgin olive oil, for drizzling

1 tbsp (3 g) chopped fresh chives or parsley, for garnish, optional

Set a large pot over medium-high heat. Add the olive oil, then stir in the onion slices. Reduce the heat to medium and cook, stirring often, until onions are soft and translucent but not browned.

Add the garlic, thyme, bay leaf, and chiles. Cook 1 more minute, then add the white wine and cook until the wine is reduced by two-thirds to three-fourths.

Add the tomatoes and capers and simmer until tomatoes start to break up, then add the clam juice and bring to a boil. Reduce the heat to a simmer, then add the shrimp and cook only until the shrimp curl but the very center of the thickest part of the tails near the heads are still translucent.

Remove from the heat and season with salt, pepper, and lemon juice. Remove the bay leaf, then divide the stew among 4 bowls. Place 3 baguette slices in each bowl. Drizzle with the extra virgin olive oil.

Serve garnished with the chives, if desired.

Arugula Salad with Toasted Pistachios & Parmesan

SERVES 4

Also known as rocket salad, arugula adds a zippy, peppery flavor that balances perfectly with this simple dressing. A cinch to throw together, it's the perfect accompaniment to any meal in your repertoire.

8 oz (224 g) arugula

4 slices red onion

Juice of ½ large lemon

2–3 tbsp (30–45 ml) extra virgin olive oil

Salt, to taste

Freshly ground black pepper, to taste

3 tbsp (28 g) shelled pistachios, toasted (page 457), for garnish

Shaved Parmigiano-Reggiano cheese, for garnish

Combine the arugula, onion, lemon juice, and olive oil in a bowl and toss to mix. Add the salt and pepper. Divide among 4 plates, then garnish with the toasted pistachios and cheese to serve.

*See photo on page 95.

Yogurt Panna Cotta with Dates & Pedro Ximénez

SERVES 4

Who else would think to blend a creamy, oh-so-slightly-salty panna cotta with a sauce that's basically made up of sherry-drenched date strips? Only Anita. And she doesn't choose just any sherry. She calls for Pedro Ximénez, also known as PX. This Spanish varietal wine is dark and intensely sweet with a strong taste of raisins and molasses. Ahhh . . .

¾ tsp powdered unflavored gelatin

1 cup (245 g) labne kefir yogurt (can substitute full-fat Greek yogurt)

1⅓ cups (320 ml) heavy cream

¼ cup (50 g) sugar

1 cup (150 g) pitted dates, cut into strips

1½ cups (360 ml) Pedro Ximénez sherry (can substitute another good-quality sweet dessert sherry), or as needed

Rock candy crystals, for garnish, optional

To make the panna cotta, bloom the gelatin by mixing it with 1 tablespoon (15 ml) tepid water in a small bowl. Allow to sit for 3 minutes.

Heat the yogurt, cream, and sugar in a saucepan until piping hot, then remove from the heat and whisk in the gelatin to dissolve. Put through a fine-mesh sieve, then divide the mixture among 4 (4-ounce) molds and refrigerate.

To make the date sauce, place the dates in a small saucepan and cover liberally with sherry. Simmer until the alcohol is cooked off and the mixture is juicy and syrupy. Remove from the heat and let cool.

To serve, unmold each panna cotta in the center of a dessert plate. Surround with the date mixture and garnish with the rock candy, if desired.

JENN LOUIS

Portland, Oregon

Chef/owner of RAY

CHEF SAYS

Items I always keep on hand for unexpected guests are . . .

Unbaked, scooped cookie dough in the freezer; homemade cordials; really good olives; Marcona almonds with the skin on; and pickles and jam that go well with charcuterie.

When hosting a quick get-together, never overlook . . .

Setting a simple but nice table. Simple is quick, but candles or pretty glasses make the table look lovely to sit around.

My secret tip for successful last-minute entertaining is . . .

Relax, enjoy your guests. They would rather enjoy your company than have you worry about random unnecessary details.

One fun fact few people know about me is that . . .

In my early twenties I was an Outward Bound instructor. I slept on the ground two hundred nights each year for two years. I never go camping now.

MENU

Charcuterie 101, On the Fly

Strozzapreti

Chocolate Cookies with Cocoa Nibs & Almond

CHEF'S PAIRING

A northern Italian white wine. Rich, but still clean.

Or Champagne. It goes with everything.

CHEF'S PLAYLIST

M.I.A. or Santigold

MAJOR KUDOS

Multiple James Beard "Best Chef" nominations; "Best New Chef" award from *Food & Wine*; competitor on Bravo's *Top Chef Masters*; *Condé Nast Traveler*'s "Hot List"

HER STORY

Jenn Louis didn't always love to cook. But as an avid and curious traveler, worldwide detours (including stopovers in Europe, North and South America, and Israel) plus a bit of serendipity ended up playing a role in her future career choice.

"I learned of a job opening from a close friend cooking for an Outward Bound base camp deep in the North Carolina woods," she says. A few weeks after landing the job, she had an epiphany that cooking was her passion.

While her style is considered at once soul-satisfying, comforting, and unfussy using only the highest-quality ingredients available, it's no surprise she decided to share this menu with us.

"This is a super quick meal," says Jenn, "but it's still so unique—not average fare—and so interesting and delicious. I'm hard pressed to imagine many people would think to make this in an hour!"

But you should. You most certainly should.

Charcuterie 101, On the Fly

SERVES 6

When putting together this impressive antipasto spread, Jenn says, "Use whatever you have at home. There are always so many options in an average fridge." Here are just some of her tantalizing suggestions.

QUINCE MOSTARDA

2 lb (907 g) quinces, peeled, cored, and cut into 1-inch (2.5-cm) pieces (can substitute pears or apples)

½ cup (120 ml) white wine

½ cup (120 ml) fresh orange juice

½ cup (120 ml) water

⅓ cup (112 g) honey

½ dropperful mustard oil (found in Indian specialty stores) (can substitute some powdered mustard, but won't be quite the same)

Salt, to taste

A VARIETY OF SELECTIONS

1 thick (5-oz [140-g]) slice pork terrine

1 thick (5-oz [140-g]) slice pheasant terrine

4 oz (112 g) soppressata, sliced

3 oz (84 g) good beef jerky

1 (4-oz [112-g]) ball fior di latte mozzarella

4 oz (112 g) Crottin (fresh goat cheese)

1 wedge Cotswold blue cheese

½ cup (86 g) Marcona almonds, with skin

½ cup (75 g) corn nuts (the fancy Spanish kind!)

¾ cup (135 g) Castelvetrano olives

⅓ cup (55 g) cornichon pickles

⅓ cup (55 g) pepperoncini

2 pretty tangerines

1 French baguette

1 package crackers

8 shortbread cookies

To make the quince mostarda, combine the quinces, wine, juice, water, and honey in a large saucepot. Simmer until the quinces are soft, about 5 to 10 minutes. Remove the quinces with a slotted spoon, leaving the remaining liquid behind.

Simmer the remaining liquid until reduced to a syrup, about 3 to 4 minutes.

Put the quinces through a food mill or process in a food processor until smooth and cool. Remove to a bowl, then thin to the desired consistency using the reduced syrup. Add the mustard oil and salt, then store in the refrigerator.

On the largest platter or board you have, place a selection of the meats, cheeses, garnishes, and breads. Make sure to leave some breathing room around the edges of the platter and each ingredient. Serve with the Quince Mostarda.

Strozzapreti

SERVES 6

In most of Italy, these delicate dumplings are called *gnocchi verdi* ("gnocchi with greens") or *ravioli gnudi* ("naked ravioli"). In Florence, however, they're cleverly called *strozzapreti*—pronounced stroh-zah-PRAY-tee and literally meaning "priest stranglers." The story goes that a gluttonous priest, who loved these dumplings, ate so many so fast that he strangled himself by swallowing them whole. An urban legend? Who knows. But a word to the wise: Chew them slowly and you'll be fine.

Kosher salt, plus additional, to taste

12 oz (336 g) lacinato kale or white chard, ribs removed

2 large eggs

1 cup plus 2 tbsp (255 g) ricotta

1 cup plus 1 tbsp (190 g) finely grated Parmigiano-Reggiano cheese, plus additional for serving

5 tbsp (6 g) fresh bread crumbs, finely ground in blender or food processor

Pepper, to taste

Few swipes of freshly grated nutmeg, to taste

All-purpose flour, for dusting

Melted butter, for serving

Fill a large bowl with ice water and set near the stove.

Fill a large pot with water, generously salt it, and bring to a boil. Add the kale and simmer until tender, about 3 minutes.

Remove the greens with tongs to the ice water to cool. When cool, drain the greens in a colander, then place in a kitchen towel and wring until mostly dry.

Chop the kale fine and add to the bowl of a food processor, along with the eggs, ricotta, Parmigiano-Reggiano, bread crumbs, salt, pepper, and nutmeg. Process until the ingredients are blended and smooth but not completely puréed; they should still have some texture. Scrape the batter into a bowl.

Line one or two baking sheets with parchment and dust well with flour. Using 2 teaspoons, scoop up a heaping spoonful of ricotta mixture with one spoon, then push it onto a prepared baking sheet with the back of the second spoon. With lightly floured hands, gently roll the dumpling around in the flour on the baking sheet to coat.

Repeat the procedure with the remaining dough, then refrigerate, uncovered, on the prepared baking sheets until ready to cook (up to 1 hour ahead). Make sure the dumplings don't touch, or they will stick together. Do not freeze.

To cook the strozzapreti, bring a large pot of generously salted water to a simmer.

Add the strozzapreti, enough that they can swim around as they cook, but not so many that they sit on each other. Let simmer, watching carefully. As soon as the dumplings float to the surface, remove immediately with a slotted spoon to a serving platter. Make sure to keep the cooking water at a medium simmer, as a rapid boil can break your dumplings apart.

Serve topped with melted butter and grated Parmigiano-Reggiano.

Chocolate Cookies with Cocoa Nibs & Almond

MAKES ABOUT 2 DOZEN COOKIES

Quiz: How much chocolate is too much? Answer: Is there even such a thing? Not with these soft, cakey, and thrice chocolate-flavored delights! You'll enjoy the bold undertones of cocoa powder, the fragrant crunch of cocoa nibs, and the velvet silkiness of chocolate chips in each and every bite. Ahhh . . . heaven. Chocolatey heaven.

1½ cups (188 g) all-purpose flour

1 cup (114 g) powdered sugar

⅓ cup (27 g) cocoa powder

½ tsp salt

¼ tsp baking soda

8 oz (230 g, 2 sticks) unsalted butter, cut into 1-inch (2.5-cm) cubes, at room temperature

1 tsp pure vanilla extract

½ tsp almond extract

¼ cup (38 g) cocoa (cacao) nibs

¾ cup (112 g) chocolate chips

1 cup (200 g) granulated sugar, for rolling the cookies

Preheat the oven to 350°F (177°C). Line two baking sheets with parchment paper.

Sift the flour, powdered sugar, cocoa powder, salt, and baking soda into a bowl. Set aside.

In the bowl of a stand mixer fitted with the paddle attachment, cream the butter until broken up. Add the flour mixture, a cupful at a time, and beat on low until starting to combine. Mix in the vanilla and almond extracts, then the cocoa nibs and chocolate chips. Beat at low speed until a dough is formed.

Remove the bowl from the mixer and chill the dough, in the bowl, for 30 minutes.

Spread the granulated sugar on a plate.

Scoop the chilled dough by heaping tablespoons into rounds (preferably with a #40 ice cream scoop, packing lightly), then roll each cookie as it is made in the granulated sugar and place on a parchment-lined baking sheet. Space the cookies about 1 inch (2.5 cm) apart. Do not flatten.

Place in the oven and bake for 12 to 15 minutes, rotating the pans after 6 to 8 minutes, or until the cookies start to crackle on top.

Using a spatula, remove the cookies to wire racks to cool.

TIM LOVE

Fort Worth, Texas

Chef/owner of Lonesome Dove Western Bistro (Fort Worth and Austin, Texas; Knoxville, Tennessee), Woodshed Smokehouse and White Elephant Saloon (Fort Worth), Queenie's Steakhouse (Denton, Texas), and Love Shack (Fort Worth and Dallas/Fort Worth Airport); co-founder of the Austin Food & Wine Festival, Music City Food & Wine Festival, and Chicago Food & Wine Festival; official chef for Austin City Limits; founder of the Burgers 4 Babies charity

CHEF SAYS

Items I always keep on hand for unexpected guests are . . .

Tequila, Champagne, cured ham, caviar, and good bread.

When hosting a quick get-together, never overlook . . .

Having enough ice.

My secret tip for successful last-minute entertaining is . . .

Have some bites around that can keep your guests busy while they wait. Good crackers, cheese, sausage, and/or some good dips always bridge the gap while you get organized and start cooking. I always keep these snacks in my fridge in case of any emergencies.

One fun fact few people know about me is that . . .

I thought I was going to be a professional soccer player the first eighteen years of my life. Look at me now!

MENU

Chili-Marinated Shrimp

Burnt Carrots

Individual Ancho Chile Chocolate Cakes

CHEF'S PAIRING

Start with a French Sauvignon blanc.

Finish with Amaro on the rocks.

CHEF'S PLAYLIST

Billy Joel

MAJOR KUDOS

James Beard award nomination; one of *Bon Appétit*'s "America's 50 Best New Restaurants"; champion of *Iron Chef America*; contestant on both *Top Chef Masters* and *Top Chef: The Cruise*

HIS STORY

As a true-blue, born-and-bred, native Texan (even though he did cross state lines to get his degree in finance and marketing from the University of Tennessee), Tim is widely regarded as a de facto ambassador for Texas. He also happens to be pretty well known for his signature "urban Western cuisine"—which features lots of meat.

"The meal I happened to choose for this book doesn't contain any meat," says Tim, laughing, "which people would normally expect from me. But it's delicious with very pungent flavors, and all of the ingredients are readily available almost anywhere."

Every one of his chosen dishes also happens to have chili in it, but they are distinctly different in flavor. "I think the use of all the chilies in very different ways is really fun!" he says. "It specifically shows the versatility in using different levels of heat."

As for what makes this particular meal perfect for last-minute entertaining, Tim explains, "These recipes take very familiar ingredients and change them into something very interesting."

We love interesting! And you can bet your cowboy boots they're all super delicious, too.

Chili-Marinated Shrimp

SERVES 8

It just doesn't get any easier than this! Start by buying the freshest-looking shrimp you can find. Prepare the simple marinade. Let them enjoy each other's company for a while. Then sear. Voilà, y'all! One of the best renditions of shrimp ever. (Humble brag.)

2 red onions, diced

2 cups (80 g) fresh cilantro leaves, chopped

Juice of 4 limes

6 cloves garlic, roasted (page 457) and minced

¼ cup (20 g) chili powder

2 cups (480 ml) blended oil (75/25 canola/olive oil), plus additional as needed

4 lb (1.8 kg) shrimp, peeled and deveined

Combine the onions, cilantro, lime juice, roasted garlic, chili powder, and 2 cups (480 ml) of the oil in a large bowl and mix well. Add the shrimp and toss, then add more oil until the shrimp is just covered. Refrigerate for at least 30 minutes.

Fifteen minutes before planning to serve, preheat the grill, if using. Otherwise, set a large sauté pan over medium-high heat.

When ready to serve, drain the shrimp, and working in batches, sear for 2 to 3 minutes on each side either on the grill or in the pan. Remove the shrimp as they are done to a platter.

Burnt Carrots

SERVES 8

Okay, so maybe think of them as beautifully charred instead of burnt. But toss these babies with a little honey, Brie, and chili flakes for kicks, and you've got yourself something sweet, spicy, smoky, cheesy, and tangy—all in one very happy bite.

15 whole jumbo carrots, unpeeled, divided

¾ cup (180 ml) peanut oil, plus additional, as needed

⅓ cup (112 g) honey

5 oz (140 g) Brie cheese, crumbled or diced

1 tbsp (5 g) red chili flakes (crushed red pepper), or to taste

Salt, to taste

Freshly ground black pepper, to taste

Bring a large pot of water to a boil. Trim off the ends of the carrots and cut into approximately 4-inch (10-cm) lengths. Add to the boiling water, reduce the heat, and simmer until the carrots are knife tender, about 15 to 20 minutes. Drain and let cool completely.

Preheat a large skillet over medium-high heat. Add the oil and wait until it just starts to smoke. Gently add half the carrots to the pan. Do not stir or shake the pan.

Once the carrots have charred on one side, rotate in the pan and char the remaining sides.

Meanwhile, combine the honey, Brie, and chili flakes in a large stainless-steel bowl.

When the carrots are seared on all sides, remove from the pan and add to the bowl with the honey mixture. Toss well, then season with salt and pepper. Set aside while you repeat the searing procedure with the remaining carrots, adding more oil as necessary.

Individual Ancho Chile Chocolate Cakes

SERVES 8

Ancho (a dried poblano chile and the sweetest of all dried chiles) is the secret ingredient that gives these luscious chocolate cakes the slightest bit of oomph. Just wait and watch the surprised-yet-delighted look on your guests' faces! It's the perfect ending for any meal of your choice.

FOR THE ANCHO PURÉE

2 qt (720 g) ancho chiles (stemmed and deseeded)

⅓ cup (67 g) sugar

FOR THE CHILE CHOCOLATE CAKES

1 lb (450 g) bittersweet chocolate, chopped

Pinch of salt

6 oz (345 g, 1½ sticks) unsalted butter

1 cup (200 g) sugar

¼ cup (60 ml) orange juice

4 large eggs

¼ cup (31 g) all-purpose flour

Almond brittle crumbs, for garnish, optional

Vanilla ice cream, for serving

Chocolate curls, for garnish, optional

Preheat the oven to 350°F (177°C). Grease 8 (5-ounce [140-g]) ramekins with baking spray.

To make the ancho purée, place the anchos and sugar in a medium saucepan. Add just enough water to cover the anchos. Over medium heat, cook until soft. Remove from the heat. Using a measuring cup, remove most of the liquid in the pan, reserving the liquid. Using an immersion blender, purée the anchos in the pan to a smooth consistency, adding some of the reserved liquid to achieve a mayonnaise-like texture. Remove the purée to a bowl and set aside.

To make the chile chocolate cakes, combine the chocolate and salt in the bowl of a stand mixer. Set aside.

In a saucepan, combine ½ cup (120 g) of the ancho purée, the butter, sugar, and orange juice. Bring to a scalding boil, stirring to melt the butter and sugar and combine with the other ingredients. Remove from the heat and pour immediately over the chocolate in the mixer bowl.

Using the paddle attachment, beat the chocolate mixture to a smooth purée. Add the eggs, two at a time, and beat until fully incorporated. Scrape the sides of the bowl, then, on low speed, add in the flour. Mix until just combined.

Divide the batter evenly among the prepared ramekins, then bake for 16 to 18 minutes.

Remove from the oven and let the cakes cool, in the ramekins, on a wire rack.

At serving time, unmold the ramekins on individual serving plates. Decorate the plates with almond brittle crumbs, if desired, and serve the cakes topped with vanilla ice cream and optional chocolate curls.

CHEF'S TIPS

Refrigerate the unused ancho purée, tightly covered, for a future use.

For easiest removal, let the ramekins chill in the fridge, then use a knife to loosen the sides of each cake. Tap the bottom of the ramekins on the kitchen counter to loosen the cakes so they can be removed.

JONATHAN WAXMAN

New York, New York

Chef/owner of Barbuto and Jams (New York), Brezza Cucina (Atlanta), and Waxman's (San Francisco); chef/co-owner of Adele's and Bajo Sexto (Nashville); founding partner of Nashville's Music City Food & Wine Festival

CHEF SAYS

Items I always keep on hand for unexpected guests are . . .

Tortillas, smoked salmon, potatoes, greens, and tequila.

When hosting a quick get-together, never overlook . . .

A well-set table.

My secret tip for successful last-minute entertaining is . . .

Improvise.

One fun fact few people know about me is that . . .

I love Persian rugs, especially Serapi.

MENU

Cast-Iron Seared Sea Scallops with Pea Shoots & Kale Salad

CHEF'S PAIRING

A really young, non-oaked Chablis

CHEF'S PLAYLIST

Mendelssohn's Symphony No. 3

MAJOR KUDOS

James Beard award for "Best Chef: New York City" and "Who's Who of Food & Beverage in America"; numerous James Beard award nominations; named "One of the Most Influential Americans" by *Esquire*; judge on Bravo's *Recipe for Deception*; two-time *Top Chef Masters* contestant

HIS STORY

What do trombones, Ferraris, and the "California cuisine" revolution all have in common? Quite simply, Jonathan Waxman.

Confused? Don't be. It all began after Jonathan, a native Californian, graduated from college and started traveling as a professional trombonist. To make ends meet, he sold vintage cars for a Ferrari dealer in Berkeley . . . who introduced him to Tante Marie's Cooking School in San Francisco . . . which led him to the world-famous École de Cuisine La Varenne in Paris . . . where he received the Grand Diplôme. After returning to the U.S., he worked with both Alice Waters and Michael McCarty, and he subsequently created his own version of California (or New American) cuisine.

Jonathan eventually moved to New York City and opened his own restaurant, Jams, which the *New York Times* called a "culinary comet." He later also opened the popular Barbuto (Italian for "bearded"), featuring only the simplest, freshest, most local ingredients—just like in this recipe.

"I chose this meal because my son asked for it last Sunday, and he got his wish," says Jonathan. "It took only twenty-five minutes to cook."

We just got our wish, too.

Cast-Iron Seared Sea Scallops with Pea Shoots & Kale Salad

SERVES 4

This beautiful dish screams springtime—when remarkably sweet pea shoots are in season and at their most delectable peak. A fleeting pleasure, they wilt gracefully and actually intensify in flavor when sautéed, as done here. Paired with succulent sea scallops and nutty, crunchy sunchokes, this is a meal worthy of any company!

4 tbsp (60 ml) olive oil, divided

6 tbsp (86 g) butter, divided

1 lb (450 g) sunchokes (Jerusalem artichokes), peeled and sliced (can substitute carrots, turnips, or fennel)

1 leek, light green and white parts cleaned and trimmed (page 456), julienned

20–24 sea scallops

Kosher salt, to taste

Freshly ground black pepper, to taste

2 shallots, minced

1 pint (60 g) pea shoots (can substitute steamed artichoke hearts or asparagus)

1 tbsp plus 1 tsp (20 ml) fresh lemon juice, preferably from a Meyer lemon, divided

2 cups (60 g) baby kale

Sea salt

1 French baguette, warmed and sliced

Heat 2 tablespoons (30 ml) of the olive oil and 2 tablespoons (28 g) of the butter in a skillet over medium heat. Add the sunchokes and leek. Sauté covered, stirring occasionally, until the sunchokes are cooked through, about 8 minutes. Remove from the heat and set aside.

Preheat a second, cast-iron skillet over medium-high heat.

Remove any connective tissue from the scallops, then rinse and pat the scallops dry. Season with the salt and pepper.

Add the remaining 2 tablespoons (30 ml) oil to the cast-iron skillet. When the oil is smoking, add the scallops, shaking the skillet every 30 seconds until the scallops are golden brown on all sides. Turn off the heat and remove the scallops from the pan.

Immediately add another 2 tablespoons (28 g) of the butter and the shallots to the skillet. Without turning the heat back on again, "cook" the shallots, stirring occasionally, for 2 minutes. Add the pea shoots and the remaining 2 tablespoons (28 g) butter and season with salt and pepper. Add 1 tablespoon (15 ml) of the lemon juice and stir until the additional butter melts.

Divide the sunchoke mixture among 4 plates. Arrange the scallops on the plates and garnish each serving with a small mound of pea shoots.

Toss the kale in a bowl with the remaining 2 tablespoons (30 ml) of olive oil, 1 teaspoon lemon juice, and a pinch of sea salt.

Serve the kale salad and baguette alongside the scallops.

MARC MURPHY

New York, New York

Chef/owner of Benchmarc Restaurants (which includes Landmarc and Ditch Plains) and Benchmarc Events by Marc Murphy

CHEF SAYS

Items I always keep on hand for unexpected guests are . . .

Wine, cheese, frozen loaves of bread, great olives, and Dijon mustard.

When hosting a quick get-together, never overlook . . .

The power of a great roasted nut—perfect for snacking and holding people over.

My secret tip for successful last-minute entertaining is . . .

Choose simple dishes, allowing you to have more time to actually be with your guests.

One fun fact few people know about me is that . . .

Even though my last name is Murphy, I was born in Milan and baptized in the Duomo. I also speak Italian, French, and Spanish.

MENU
Eggs in Purgatory

CHEF'S PAIRING
Prosecco

CHEF'S PLAYLIST
"Good Riddance (Time of Your Life)" by Green Day

MAJOR KUDOS

Judge on Food Network's hit shows *Chopped* and *Chopped Junior*; president of the Manhattan chapter of the New York State Restaurant Association; both a board member and Food Council member of City Harvest; member of the Leadership Council for Share Our Strength's No Kid Hungry campaign; member of the U.S. Department of State's Diplomatic Culinary Partnership

HIS STORY

Born in Milan, Marc also lived in Paris, Villefranche, Rome, and Genoa—all before turning twelve!

After high school graduation, he headed to New York and attended the Institute of Culinary Education. His rationale was that at least if he could learn how to cook, he'd never go hungry.

After graduation, he apprenticed at top-notch restaurants throughout France, Italy, Monte Carlo, and New York. Finally, in 2004, Marc opened his first solo enterprise, Landmarc (in Tribeca). Three years later he opened another Landmarc at the famed Time Warner Center. Ditch Plains in the West Village came later. Marc's restaurants now fall under the Benchmarc Restaurants by Marc Murphy name, where he acts as chef and owner. In addition, Marc also heads up the company's catering division, Benchmarc Events by Marc Murphy. He is the author of *Season with Authority: Confident Home Cooking*.

"I've been using a wood-burning oven for everything, including eggs," says Marc. "This recipe was inspired by the amazing flavors you get from the wood-burning oven that you can also try at home. It's simple, delicious, and impressive!"

Eggs in Purgatory

SERVES 4

"I really like the addition of beef stock to this recipe," explains Marc. "It adds depth of flavor to the sauce." What an extraordinary dish for an elegant breakfast or brunch menu, with plenty of wow factor. For even more pizzazz (if that's even possible), Marc says to serve with a rosemary focaccia.

¼ cup (60 ml) extra virgin olive oil

1 cup (4–6 oz [112–168 g]) guanciale or pancetta, diced

3 cloves garlic, chopped

2 medium-size red onions, quartered lengthwise and sliced crosswise

3 cups (720 ml) beef stock

1 (28-oz [794-g]) can chopped tomatoes

6 fresh thyme sprigs, leaves only

1 tsp red chili flakes (crushed red pepper)

8 large eggs

Kosher salt, to taste

Freshly cracked black pepper, to taste

¼ cup (45 g) grated Parmigiano-Reggiano cheese

5–6 fresh basil leaves, torn, for garnish

In a large skillet with high sides, heat the olive oil over medium heat until it shimmers, about 2 to 3 minutes.

Add the guanciale and cook, stirring, about 6 to 7 minutes. Add the garlic and onions and cook until the onion pieces are translucent, about 5 minutes. Add the beef stock and cook until the stock is reduced by half, about 6 to 8 minutes, scraping the pan with a wooden spoon to loosen the browned meat bits. Add the chopped tomatoes, thyme, and red chili flakes. Simmer for 15 to 20 minutes, stirring occasionally, until the sauce is reduced and slightly thick.

Using the back of a large serving spoon, make 8 small wells in the thickened sauce. Crack an egg into each well. Cook over low heat for about 7 minutes, or until the whites are set but the yolks are still runny. You can use your fork to carefully break up the whites so they cook more quickly.

When the eggs are cooked, season with salt and pepper, sprinkle with the grated cheese, and garnish with the basil. Serve directly from the pan.

CHARLIE PALMER

New York, New York

Cheflowner of Aureole (New York and Las Vegas); Liberty Room at Aureole, Upper Story by Charlie Palmer, Crimson & Rye, Jake's at The Knick, Charlie Palmer at The Knick, and St. Cloud (New York); Charlie Palmer Steak (New York, Washington, D.C., Las Vegas, and Reno); Briscola (Reno); Harvest Table (St. Helena, California); Dry Creek Kitchen and Spirit Bar (Sonoma County, California); and Burritt Room & Tavern (San Francisco). Also, partner in Hotel Healdsburg (Sonoma County); owner of Harvest Inn by Charlie Palmer (St. Helena) and Mystic Hotel by Charlie Palmer (San Francisco)

CHEF SAYS

Items I always keep on hand for unexpected guests are . . .

Wine, cheese, good fresh bread, my famous oatmeal cookies, and probably some local craft brews like Lagunitas.

When hosting a quick get-together, never overlook . . .

That presentation makes a big difference, as do good-quality ingredients. Just because you're rushed doesn't mean you shouldn't have great olive oil with your bread.

My secret tip for successful last-minute entertaining is . . .

Always have a game plan and be organized. If you have to cook dinner at the last minute or the group grows in size, get your mise en place in order and make sure you know the plan.

One fun fact few people know about me is that . . .

I grew up on a farm in Upstate New York, and my love for cooking started in my high school's home economics program with my teacher, Sharon Crane. She still gets a Christmas card from me every year!

MENU

Chicken Paillard with Kale & Blood Orange Salad

CHEF'S PAIRING

Étienne Sauzet White Burgundy

CHEF'S PLAYLIST

John Legend

MAJOR KUDOS

One Michelin Star; James Beard awards for "Best Chef: New York" and "Who's Who of Food & Beverage in America"; multiple *Wine Spectator* "Best of Awards of Excellence" and "Grand Awards"; "Relais Gourmand Award" from Relais & Chateaux; Robert Mondavi "Culinary Award of Excellence"; induction into the AAC Culinary Hall of Fame

HIS STORY

During his teenage years, Charlie worked several after-school restaurant jobs. He also started dabbling at home with recipes out of *Larousse Gastronomique*. He even hosted a formal dinner party for his football buddies, serving coulibiac of salmon. ("They had no idea what they were even eating!" says Charlie, half joking, half serious.) Back then, he was just enjoying himself.

Today, Charlie's still enjoying himself—but now as a preeminent culinarian who's known worldwide for his signature "Progressive American" cuisine, a style that reinterprets classic European cooking using regional American ingredients.

Which perfectly explains his meal of choice for this book.

"This is an incredibly approachable recipe and something I often cook at home for my own family," says Charlie. "I don't know anyone who doesn't like fried or breaded chicken, and it's so easy to make. You don't even have to have the salad ingredients on hand. You can just sub anything you've got in your fridge or garden."

Progressive American? Yep! Easy? Yep! Delicious, too? Absolutely.

Chicken Paillard with Kale & Blood Orange Salad

SERVES 6

Paillard is an older French culinary term for a thin piece of meat that's quickly cooked. Charlie still likes to use the term since, as he playfully puts it, "Chicken paillard sounds a whole lot fancier than fried chicken cutlets!" He also isn't shy about admitting that the secret to this recipe is using Wondra flour, which is much lighter and airier than regular flour. "It gives the chicken a better texture and consistency on the outside," explains Charlie. So, Wondra it is!

2 blood oranges

1 bunch kale, tough stems removed

½ cup (25 g) bias-cut scallions

6 boneless, skinless chicken breast halves

¾ cup (90 g) Wondra flour

Salt, to taste

Freshly ground black pepper, to taste

¼ cup (60 ml) olive oil, plus additional 3 tbsp (45 ml), if necessary

2 shallots, minced

½ cup (120 ml) chicken stock or canned nonfat, low-sodium chicken broth

1 tbsp (16 g) Dijon mustard

Grate the zest from the oranges and set the zest aside. Using a sharp paring knife, peel the skin and white pith from one of the oranges, then hold the fruit over a medium-size bowl and cut into segments between the membranes, letting the segments fall into the bowl. After they are in the bowl, squeeze the membranes over them to extract the juice, then discard. Repeat with the remaining orange.

Drain the orange segments in a fine-mesh strainer set over the juice in the bowl, then reserve the juice and the segments separately.

Stack a few kale leaves at a time and roll them up, cigar-fashion. Using a sharp knife, cut the roll crosswise into very thin slices. Pull the slices apart and you should have ribbons of kale. Repeat to slice all the kale and then place in a large salad bowl. Add the reserved orange segments and scallions and toss to coat.

Working with one breast at a time, place the chicken between 2 sheets of plastic wrap. Using a cast-iron skillet or meat mallet, pound the meat until it is about ½-inch (12-mm) thick.

Place the flour in a shallow bowl and season with salt and pepper. Press both sides of each paillard into the seasoned flour, shaking off any excess.

Heat ¼ cup (60 ml) of the oil in a large skillet over medium-high heat. Add the floured chicken and fry, turning once, for about 10 minutes or until golden brown, crisp, and cooked through. Remove to a warm platter and tent lightly with aluminum foil to keep warm.

If most of the oil has been absorbed by the chicken, add the 3 tablespoons (45 ml) oil to the hot pan. Keeping the pan on medium-high heat, add the shallots and cook, stirring and scraping the bottom of the pan to release all the browned bits. Add the chicken stock, along with the reserved orange zest and juice, and bring to a boil. Reduce the heat, whisk in the mustard, season with salt and pepper, and cook for about 3 minutes, or until slightly thickened.

Remove from the heat and pour the dressing over the kale, tossing to coat the kale so that it wilts slightly.

Mound an equal portion of the salad on each of 6 dinner plates. Place a warm paillard on top and serve.

CARLA PELLEGRINO

Las Vegas, Nevada

Chef/owner of Bratalian (Henderson, Nevada)

CHEF SAYS

Items I always keep on hand for unexpected guests are . . .

A variety of European cheeses, bread sticks, wine, grapes, and a box of good-quality spaghetti.

When hosting a quick get-together, never overlook . . .

Sharing your attention equally among your guests. Do not neglect anyone.

My secret tip for successful last-minute entertaining is . . .

Be willing to be in company!

One fun fact few people know about me is that . . .

I'm Brazilian-Italian, therefore I tend to be loud.

MENU

Tortellini in Brodo

Chicken Scaloppine in Beer Sauce

Red Wine–Marinated Mixed Berries with Vanilla Gelato

CHEF'S PAIRING

Plenty of water

A good bottle of La Scolca Gavi dei Gavi white wine

CHEF'S PLAYLIST

Bossa Nova (Tom Jobim, Adriana Rios)

Italian Jazz (Paolo Conte)

Italian pop (Pino Danielle)

MAJOR KUDOS

Winner of Food Network's *Throwdown with Bobby Flay*; contestant on Bravo's *Top Chef*; James Beard Foundation "Women in Food" honoree and VIP member; "Top 10 New Restaurants in Las Vegas" award by Gayot; one of "Top 10 Best Italian Restaurants in Las Vegas" by *USA Today*

HER STORY

Born in Brazil to a Portuguese father and Italian mother, it's no wonder Carla's favorite cuisine hails from these three countries. It's also no wonder those are exactly the types of dishes she helped her mom prepare for her catering business as a young girl.

Eventually Carla moved to Italy, where she opened a small store and conducted daily cooking demonstrations. Later she moved to New York, where she attended the French Culinary Institute, graduating with honors.

Several high-profile gigs later—including the celebrity-magnet Rao's—Carla found her way to Las Vegas, where she now entertains in style.

"These recipes are all delicious, classic northern Italian dishes," says Carla. "And yet they're all so easy and fast to make. They will surprise even the most sophisticated palate for their fulfilling taste and simplicity. They don't look or taste like a 'last-minute' fix up, and they're all very healthy and light. This makes eating at home with friends possible again!"

Tortellini in Brodo

SERVES 4

"This vegetarian dish is served as an appetizer or middle course in Italy," explains Carla, "replacing the pasta course. We can go on about how to make it entirely from scratch, including making your own tortellini. However, I guarantee that products such as Barilla Collezione's three-cheese tortellini will do the job and easily save three hours of labor!"

FOR THE STOCK

1 medium-size onion, peeled and cut into large dice

2 large carrots, peeled, cut into medium-size chunks

5 celery stalks, cut into medium-size chunks

1 bunch leeks, light green and white parts, cleaned and trimmed (page 456), cut into thick slices

½ bunch fresh Italian parsley, roughly chopped

4 fresh thyme sprigs

4 bay leaves, torn in half

1 fresh rosemary sprig

1 tsp white peppercorns

1 (12-oz [336-g]) box of 3-cheese tortellini, preferably Barilla Collezione

Kosher salt, to taste

2 tbsp (24 g) grated Grana Padano cheese

Good-quality extra virgin olive oil, for drizzling

Pour 5 quarts (4.7 L) tepid water into a stockpot. Add the onion, carrots, celery, leeks, parsley, thyme, bay leaves, rosemary, and peppercorns. Bring to a boil over medium-high heat, then reduce the heat and simmer for 30 minutes.

Fifteen minutes before the stock is finished simmering, prepare the tortellini as directed on the box. Drain, but do not shock them in cold water. Set aside.

When the stock is done simmering, strain out the vegetables and herbs, then pour 8 cups (1.9 L) of the liquid back into the pot (refrigerate or freeze the remainder for other uses). Season with salt if needed. Bring to a boil over medium-high heat. Add the cooked tortellini and cheese. Let boil for 2 minutes. Remove from the heat.

Portion the soup into 4 bowls. Drizzle with the oil and serve immediately.

Chicken Scaloppine in Beer Sauce

SERVES 4

Beer lends its own unique and tasty twist to this dish, which is otherwise a very traditional northern Italian recipe. "Be sure to only use Heineken beer," warns Carla. "I find this brand is the most bitter, which gives a much better flavor to the sauce."

12 baby carrots, peeled

8 new potatoes, peeled (and halved if they're big)

1 whole boneless, skinless chicken breast

All-purpose flour, for dredging

Salt, to taste

Freshly ground white pepper, to taste

½ cup (120 ml) corn or vegetable oil, divided

1 medium-size white onion, finely chopped

2 cups (302 g) frozen sweet baby peas

1½ cups (360 ml) chicken stock (can substitute hot water seasoned with chicken bouillon like Knorr)

1½ cups (360 ml) Heineken beer, at room temperature

Prepare a bowl of ice water and set it by the stove. Parboil the carrots by adding them to a saucepan of boiling water. Boil for 2 to 3 minutes, then immediately chill in the ice bath. Set aside.

Parboil the potatoes by adding them to a pot of slightly salted water. Bring to a boil. After 3 minutes, drain and let them air cool. Do not place in the ice bath.

With a sharp chef's or fish knife, cut down the center of the chicken breast, making it into two halves. Then place one hand on top of a chicken breast half, and with the knife held parallel to the cutting board, slice the chicken piece, as evenly as possible, crosswise in half. Repeat with the other chicken breast half. This will give you 4 slices of chicken breast meat about ½-inch (12-mm) thick each. Place each piece between plastic wrap and then, using a meat pounder or the bottom of a heavy skillet, gently pound the chicken slices into scaloppine ¼-inch (6-mm) thick each, being careful not to tear the meat.

Dredge each scaloppine in the flour, shaking off the excess. Season both sides generously with salt and white pepper and set aside on a sheet of wax paper.

Place a large, 14-inch (36-cm), heavy-bottomed sauté pan or skillet over medium-high heat for about 3 minutes, or until it's really hot. Carefully pour in ¼ cup (60 ml) of the oil and swirl to make sure the bottom of the pan is completely coated. Place the scaloppine in the hot pan and sear on both sides without coloring. Remove from the heat and set the scaloppine aside.

Pour the remaining ¼ cup (60 ml) of oil into the same pan and heat over medium heat. Add the onion. Sauté for 3 minutes, or just until crisp but without any color. Add the parboiled carrots, peas, and parboiled potatoes and stir gently. Add the chicken stock and bring to a boil.

Lower the heat, cover, and let simmer for 10 minutes, or until the vegetables are really tender. Season with salt and white pepper, if needed. Stir gently.

Lay the chicken scaloppine over the vegetables. Add the beer, cover, and bring to a boil over medium-high heat. Reduce the heat and simmer for 8 minutes, or until the alcohol is completely evaporated. Remove from the heat.

Arrange the chicken and vegetables on individual serving plates and serve hot.

Red Wine–Marinated Mixed Berries with Vanilla Gelato

SERVES 4

Berries and wine. Who could have thought that such a simple concept could produce such a rich delicacy? Turn summer's sweet bounty into a decadent compote. Note: Carla's signature twist on an otherwise classic dessert is adding just a bit of black pepper, making it unexpected—and totally perfect.

8 oz (224 g) fresh strawberries, stemmed and quartered

4 oz (112 g) fresh raspberries

4 oz (112 g) fresh blackberries

4 oz (112 g) fresh blueberries

1½ tbsp (20 g) sugar

½ tsp freshly ground black pepper

¼ cup plus 2 tbsp (90 ml) fresh lemon juice

1 cup (240 ml) dry red wine (like Chianti or Dolcetto)

4 small scoops vanilla gelato (can substitute ice cream)

Fresh mint leaves, for garnish, optional

Place the berries in a bowl and gently mix together. Add the sugar and pepper and gently mix, then add the lemon juice and wine and gently stir. Cover with plastic wrap and place in the refrigerator for at least 30 minutes, but not more than 2 hours.

Divide the berries and their juices into 4 small dessert bowls or cups. Top with a scoop of the vanilla gelato and garnish with a mint leaf, if desired. Serve immediately.

ERIC RIPERT

New York, New York

Chef/co-owner of Le Bernardin, Aldo Sohm Wine Bar, and Le Bernardin Privé (New York); Culinary Director of Blue by Eric Ripert (The Ritz-Carlton, Grand Cayman); vice board chair, City Harvest

CHEF SAYS

Items I always keep on hand for unexpected guests are . . .

Champagne in the fridge, Scotch on the bar, cheese for an impromptu platter, Bordeaux ready to open, and Le Bernardin's salmon rillettes for a quick canapé.

When hosting a quick get-together, never overlook . . .

A clean kitchen. Everyone always gathers in the kitchen to interact with the host, so it's important to keep your area clean and organized, even when it's tempting to load up the sink with dishes until the guests leave.

My secret tip for successful last-minute entertaining is . . .

Keep everything super simple and super organized. Do not overcomplicate recipes and meals. Great ingredients don't need much added.

One fun fact few people know about me is that . . .

I sometimes dance (and sing—badly!) while I'm cooking.

MENU

Barely Cooked Salmon with Leeks & Red Wine Butter Sauce

Butternut Squash Soup

Raspberry Clafoutis

CHEF'S PAIRING

With the soup, a very nice Chardonnay

With the salmon, a Bordeaux

With the clafoutis, kirsch

CHEF'S PLAYLIST

Classical music

MAJOR KUDOS

3 Michelin stars (2005 to present); winner of numerous James Beard awards, including "Top Chef: New York City" and "Outstanding Chef in the United States"; named number one restaurant in the United States and number two restaurant in the world by La Liste; named one of the "World's 50 Best Restaurants" by S. Pellegrino; rated "Best Food," "Top Service in New York City," and "Most Popular Restaurant in New York City" by Zagat; four-star reviews by the *New York Times* (1986 to present); five-star review and named "#1 Restaurant in the City" by *New York Magazine*; named "Best Restaurant in America" and one of the "Seven Food Temples of the World" by *GQ*; recipient of the Legion d'Honneur (France's highest honor); host of the Emmy-award winning series *Avec Eric*; guest judge on Bravo's *Top Chef*; frequent guest on CNN's *Anthony Bourdain: Parts Unknown*

HIS STORY

Eric was exposed to two cuisines in his early life: that of his birthplace (Antibes, France) and that of the country where he was raised (Andorra, a tiny nation in the eastern Pyrenees mountains between France and Spain). He loved—and savored—them both equally.

And though he dreamed of becoming a mountain climber as a kid, he changed his mind at the tender age of fifteen, when he left home to pursue a culinary career. He studied in Perpignan for two years, then left for Paris to eventually work under the legendary Joël Robuchon.

But one day America came calling, and Eric answered. He first landed in Washington, D.C., at Jean Louis in the Watergate Hotel. Then he made his way to New York, ending up at the world-famous Le Bernardin, which he now co-owns.

"As the weather gets colder, I always think it's the season of soups," says Eric. "Butternut squash, one of my favorite vegetables, makes a rich, warm soup. For me, you don't need many ingredients to make a dish special. All of these dishes are very easy to make, which allows you to spend more time interacting with your guests while you finish cooking."

Barely Cooked Salmon with Leeks & Red Wine Butter Sauce

SERVES 4

"The red wine sauce on this fish makes the dish feel seasonal for the winter months," admits Eric. As for the salmon, cooking it extra slowly on only one side is a technique he employs at Le Bernardin—and one you can easily master at home. The result is a delicate, flaky, ultra-tender, melt-in-your-mouth piece of fish that's just shy of raw and beyond delicious.

½ cup (120 ml) red wine

½ cup (120 ml) red wine vinegar

1 tbsp (5 g) black peppercorns

1 shallot, minced

4 fresh tarragon sprigs, plus additional leaves for garnish

2 leeks, light green and white parts, cleaned and trimmed (page 456)

6 tbsp (86 g) butter, divided

Fine sea salt, to taste

Freshly ground white pepper, to taste

4 (6-oz [168-g]) salmon fillets, skinned

1 tsp freshly cracked black pepper, for garnish

1 tsp finely minced shallots, for garnish

In a small saucepan, combine the wine, vinegar, black peppercorns, shallot, and tarragon. Bring the mixture to a boil and continue cooking for about 8 to 10 minutes, or until reduced to about 6 tablespoons (90 ml). Take off the heat and set aside.

Split the leeks in half lengthwise and cut each half into 3 or 4 lengthwise slices, then cut the slices crosswise into 1½-inch (3.8-cm) pieces. Place in a shallow pot and cover with water. Add 1 tablespoon (14 g) of the butter and bring to a simmer. Lightly season with salt and pepper and continue to cook slowly, uncovered, until the leeks are very tender, about 10 minutes, adding more water as needed.

Finish the red wine butter sauce by whisking in the remaining butter 1 tablespoon (14 g) at a time until fully emulsified. Season with salt and pepper. Strain through a fine-mesh strainer and keep warm.

For the salmon, put about ½ cup (120 ml) of water in a skillet, just enough to cover the surface. Add a little salt and bring to a simmer over medium heat. Season the salmon pieces on both sides with salt and pepper, then place them in the pan. Cook at a bare simmer until the top of the fish is just warm to the touch, about 5 to 7 minutes.

Meanwhile, gently reheat the leeks in their cooking liquid. Drain the leeks, then divide among 4 plates. Carefully remove the salmon from the skillet and drain each fillet on a paper towels. Place 1 salmon fillet on top of each bed of leeks and sprinkle with the tarragon leaves, black pepper, and shallots.

Spoon the sauce around and serve immediately.

Butternut Squash Soup

SERVES 4

"This butternut squash soup is hearty and flavorful," explains Eric, "even though it's made with water instead of the usual chicken stock, which makes it vegetarian friendly as well." Rich, silky smooth, and comforting. What more can you expect from a soup as only Eric can make!

4 cups (946 ml) water

2 cups (480 ml) milk

3 tbsp (43 g) butter

1 large butternut squash, peeled, seeded, and diced

1 tbsp (7 g) grated fresh ginger

Fine sea salt, to taste

Freshly ground black pepper, to taste

¼ cup (28 g) toasted pumpkin seeds (page 457), for garnish

Combine the water, milk, butter, diced butternut squash, and grated ginger in a large pot. Bring to a boil, then reduce the heat to low and simmer until the butternut squash is tender, about 15 to 20 minutes. Season with salt and pepper.

Blend the butternut squash mixture with a hand blender until smooth, or pour carefully into a blender and purée. Be careful when blending hot items as the steam causes the ingredients to expand.

Pour the hot soup into 4 bowls and garnish with the toasted pumpkin seeds to serve.

Raspberry Clafoutis

SERVES 4

This classic French dessert traditionally calls for cherries. But in this version, which is ridiculously easy to make, Eric swaps in fresh raspberries instead, making it "like a thick, moist, fruit-filled crepe," he says.

2 tbsp (28 g) unsalted butter, for greasing

½ cup (100 g) sugar, plus additional for dusting the ramekins

2 large eggs

¾ cup (180 ml) half-and-half

2 tsp (10 ml) pure vanilla extract

6 tbsp (48 g) all-purpose flour

2 cups (246 g) fresh raspberries

Vanilla ice cream, optional

Preheat the oven to 400°F (204°C). Grease 4 (3½-inch [9-cm]) ramekins with butter. Dust with sugar. Set aside.

Whisk the eggs until frothy. Add the ½ cup (100 g) sugar, half-and-half, and vanilla and whisk to combine. Add the flour and whisk very well to blend.

Divide the raspberries among the ramekins. Pour the batter over the raspberries and bake for 8 to 10 minutes, or until golden brown and set in the middle. Remove from the oven and serve immediately with, if desired, a scoop of the ice cream.

AARÓN SÁNCHEZ

New Orleans, Louisiana

Chef/partner of Johnny Sánchez (New Orleans and Baltimore); judge on Food Network's Chopped *and* Chopped Junior*; host of Spanish-language Fox Life series* 3 Minutos con Aarón *and* Motochefs*; chef ambassador for WhyHunger and Food Bank NYC; chef mentor for Chefs Move!*

CHEF SAYS

Items I always keep on hand for unexpected guests are . . .

Good wine (especially rosé), citrus, Cacique cheeses, chicken, and tortillas. Plus, chipotles in adobo.

When hosting a quick get-together, never overlook . . .

Timing! Always make sure you have food ready for when your guests arrive, something to snack on so they aren't waiting and you (as the host) don't feel so pressured to get it all on the table quickly and end up rushing the cooking process.

My secret tip for successful last-minute entertaining is . . .

Do something simple. Some people get so caught up with the cooking that they don't get to enjoy their company.

One fun fact few people know about me is that . . .

I'm a Buddhist and I love to write poetry.

MENU

Chicken with Garlic Chipotle Love & Sautéed Vegetables

CHEF'S PAIRING

Terrazas de los Andes Reserva Malbec from Argentina

CHEF'S PLAYLIST

Kings of Leon and Alabama Shakes

MAJOR KUDOS

James Beard award for "Television Studio Program"; James Beard award nomination for "Rising Star Chef of the Year"; guest chef at the White House

HIS STORY

Aarón couldn't help but become a successful chef. Everything, including his own hard work ethic, was stacked in his favor.

For instance, he was born into culinary royalty (his mom, Zarela Martinez, is one of New York's most celebrated Mexican chefs). He learned to cook from famed chef Paul Prudhomme when he was only sixteen, and he worked under and alongside other bests in the business. He opened restaurants. He appeared on TV. He even cooked for the president. And he now admits, "Cooking is what I was destined to do."

Which is why his meal here is so wonderful.

"This dish is easy to make, delicious, and filling," says Aarón. "It doesn't have a ton of ingredients or a huge list of directions, so you won't be stuck in the kitchen the entire time. You'll have time to hang out and entertain your guests while you're cooking. Plus, if you have leftovers, the chicken makes for a great sandwich the next day!"

Leftovers?! You gotta be kiddin'.

Chicken with Garlic Chipotle Love & Sautéed Vegetables

SERVES 4

From this fun recipe title, you can easily tell that Aarón loves chipotles. "Chipotles have a ton of flavor," he says, "and they have a great shelf life. They're a popular staple in Latin cuisine—and in my home." Pair them with flavorful chicken thighs and deep-roasted vegetables, and you've got yourself one awesome dish!

FOR THE GARLIC CHIPOTLE LOVE

1 cup (240 ml) canola oil

12 cloves garlic

3 tbsp (45 g) chopped canned chipotle chiles in adobo sauce

¼ cup (10 g) chopped fresh cilantro

Grated zest of 1 lime

1 tsp salt

FOR THE CHICKEN

6 skin-on, bone-in chicken thighs

Salt, to taste

Freshly ground black pepper, to taste

2 tbsp (30 ml) vegetable oil

1 clove garlic, sliced

1 cup (240 ml) chicken stock

4 tbsp (115 g) butter

FOR THE SAUTÉED VEGETABLES

8 small red bliss or new potatoes, cut in half

12 Brussels sprouts, cut in half

8 asparagus spears, trimmed and cut into 1-inch (2.5-cm) bias pieces

1 garlic clove, sliced

Salt, to taste

Pepper, to taste

2 fresh thyme sprigs

4 tbsp (115 g) butter

Juice of ½ lemon

Chopped fresh cilantro, for garnish

To make the garlic chipotle love, preheat the oven to 300°F (149°C). Pour the oil into a heavy, medium-size, ovenproof saucepan. Add the garlic. Cover the pot with foil, put it in the oven, and cook until the garlic turns a nutty brown and is really soft (think cream cheese), about 45 minutes. Remove from the oven and let the garlic and oil cool to room temperature. Put the cooled garlic and oil in a food processor or blender. Add the chipotles and sauce, cilantro, lime zest, and salt. Purée until the mixture is very smooth, then set aside.

Preheat the oven to 450°F (232°C).

To make the chicken, pat the chicken thighs dry with paper towels. Season with salt and pepper. Heat the oil in a 12-inch (30-cm) cast-iron or heavy ovenproof nonstick skillet over medium-high heat until hot but not smoking. Add the chicken, skin side down, and cook for 2 minutes. Continue cooking skin side down, occasionally rearranging the thighs and rotating the pan to evenly distribute the heat, until the fat renders out and the skin is golden brown, about 10 minutes. Spoon out and save about ¼ cup (60 ml) of the rendered chicken fat before continuing. Transfer the skillet to the oven and cook for 10 minutes, then flip the chicken and brush the skin with ¼ cup (60 ml) of the garlic chipotle love. Continue cooking until the meat is cooked through, about 5 minutes. Transfer to a plate, and let rest.

While the chicken is resting, make a sauce for it. Set the same skillet on low heat. Add the sliced garlic clove and cook for about 1 minute, just to brown the garlic. Add the chicken stock and 1 tablespoon (15 ml) of the garlic chipotle love. Reduce the pan juices over medium heat until about ½ cup (60 ml) of the liquid remains, about 10 to 12 minutes. Remove from the heat and add the butter, stirring with a wooden spoon while it melts. Cook and stir the pan sauce until it thickens enough to coat the back of the spoon. Season with salt and pepper and set aside.

To make the sautéed vegetables, heat the reserved ¼ cup (60 ml) of chicken fat in a separate pan on medium-high heat. Carefully add the potatoes and cook for about 10 minutes, tossing them only a couple of times. Add the Brussels sprouts and continue to cook for 5 minutes. Add the asparagus and sliced garlic. Cook for 3 minutes. Season with salt and pepper. Add the thyme sprigs and the butter. Reduce the heat to low and cook until the vegetables are tender. Remove from the heat and discard the thyme sprigs.

Arrange the vegetables on one side of each of 4 plates and place a portion of the chicken on the other side. Spoon some of the sauce over the chicken portions and the rest onto the plates, then drizzle the lemon juice over the chicken and garnish with the cilantro.

DANIEL BOULUD

New York, New York

Chef/owner of The Dinex Group, which includes DANIEL, Bar Pleiades, Boulud Sud, Épicerie Boulud, and Feast & Fêtes catering company (New York), Café Boulud (New York, Palm Beach, and Toronto), DBGB Kitchen & Bar (New York and Washington, D.C.), db bistro moderne (New York and Miami), Bar Boulud (New York, Boston, and London), db Brasserie (Las Vegas), Maison Boulud (Montreal), and db Bistro & Oyster Bar (Singapore)

CHEF SAYS

Items I always keep on hand for unexpected guests are . . .

Dry French saucisson from Lyon, olives from Frankies 457, anchovies from Galicia, good Champagne, and confit tuna in olive oil.

When hosting a quick get-together, never overlook . . .

The temperature of the wine, the lighting and music, and a quick snack like a dip with toast.

My secret tip for successful last-minute entertaining is . . .

Stop by Épicerie Boulud and load up for the party—you can order online, too!

One fun fact few people know about me is that . . .

I don't like bananas and I drink my coffee black.

MENU
Moqueca with Coconut-Cashew Rice

CHEF'S PAIRING
Vouvray

CHEF'S PLAYLIST
João Gilberto (it's great party music)

MAJOR KUDOS

Multiple Michelin stars; James Beard awards for "Outstanding Restaurant," "Outstanding Restaurateur," "Best Chef," and "Outstanding Chef of the Year"; "Chef of the Year" awards from the Culinary Institute of America and *Bon Appétit*; member of *Food & Wine*'s first-ever class of "Best New Chefs"; citation as "One of the 10 Best Restaurants in the World" by the *International Herald Tribune*; induction into the Culinary Hall of Fame; Chevalier de la Légion d'Honneur award by the French government

HIS STORY

Daniel. Mention this mononym to anyone who knows anything about the cooking world's true giants, and they will know exactly—exactly—who you're talking about.

And yet, even with nearly twenty restaurants around the world to his name, Daniel is still as humble and down to earth as he was before fame came knocking. So it comes as no surprise that Daniel's choice for his last-minute meal is equal parts pizzazz and simplicity.

"Stews are always good because you can put everything together in a pot, and it cooks itself," says Daniel.

However . . . his fish stew isn't just any fish stew. "Moqueca is a Brazilian fish stew made with dendê oil (from palm) and coconut milk," explains Daniel. "So it has very unique flavors that really transport your guests."

Speaking of guests, Daniel served this very dish at a special event to about seven hundred people, including the Brazilian artist, Vik Muniz. "It was a hit," he says, "so I'm sure your readers will love it, too."

Of course we will.

Moqueca with Coconut-Cashew Rice

SERVES 4

Moqueca is a traditional Brazilian seafood dish dating back at least three hundred years. Firm white fish is a must, as is dendê (palm) oil—a thick, nutty-flavored oil. Look for it in Brazilian and West African grocery stores, as well as online.

FOR THE MOQUECA

12 oz (336 g) shrimp, peeled and deveined

8 oz (224 g) monkfish fillet, cut into 1–2-inch (2.5–5-cm) cubes (can substitute grouper)

2 tbsp (30 ml) dendê oil (same as palm oil), plus additional for drizzling

2 cloves garlic, minced

1 tsp Espelette pepper (can substitute Aleppo pepper)

1-inch (2.5-cm) long piece fresh ginger, peeled and grated

½ bunch fresh cilantro, leaves roughly chopped, divided

2 tbsp (28 g) butter

1 red onion, thinly sliced

1 tbsp (15 ml) white wine vinegar

1 (15-oz [440-ml]) can coconut milk (Sococo brand recommended)

1 cup (240 ml) water

Salt

2 plum (Roma) tomatoes, peeled, quartered lengthwise, seeded, and roughly chopped

2 stalks fresh heart of palm, tender parts cut into ¼-inch (6-mm) thick slices

FOR THE COCONUT-CASHEW RICE

1 cup (185 g) uncooked basmati rice

1½ cups (360 ml) water

½ teaspoon salt, plus additional for seasoning

1 tbsp (15 ml) olive oil

½ cup (69 g) roughly chopped unsalted cashews

½ cup (40 g) unsweetened flaked coconut, toasted (page 457)

Freshly ground white pepper, to taste

1 lime, quartered, optional

To make the moqueca, in a medium-size bowl combine the shrimp, monkfish, dendê oil, minced garlic, Espelette pepper, grated ginger, and half the chopped cilantro. Let marinate in the refrigerator while you prepare the stew. This can also be done overnight with very fresh fish.

Melt the butter in a large saucepot over medium heat. Add the red onion and sauté for 6 to 8 minutes, or until translucent. Add the white wine vinegar, coconut milk, and water. Season with salt. Bring to a simmer.

Add the marinated fish to the pot. Reduce heat to low and cook for 10 to 12 minutes. Add the tomatoes and heart of palm slices. Continue cooking for 5 minutes on low.

In the meantime, to make the coconut-cashew rice, wash the rice in several changes of water until the water is clear, then drain in a sieve.

Place the rice, water, and the ½ teaspoon salt in a 2-quart (1.9-L) saucepan. Bring to a boil, reduce the heat to low, and cook, covered, until the rice is tender and the water is absorbed, about 10 to 12 minutes. Take off the heat and fluff with a fork.

In a large pot, heat the olive oil on medium-high heat. Add the cashews and cook, stirring, until toasted and fragrant. Add the cooked rice and toasted coconut. Stir to combine well. Season with the white pepper, then check the seasoning and add more salt if needed. Keep warm until ready to serve.

To serve, transfer the hot cashew rice to a large serving bowl and spoon the moqueca over the rice, along with the sauce. Garnish with the remaining chopped cilantro and drizzle with dendê oil. If desired, freshly squeeze a quartered lime over each portion after served.

ROBERT DEL GRANDE

Houston, Texas

Chef/owner of Cafe Annie; partner in The Grove and The Lake House

CHEF SAYS

Items I always keep on hand for unexpected guests are . . .

Polenta (which requires no searching for a recipe to prepare), a jar of tomato or pasta sauce, dried salami, ground meat or sausage in the freezer, and wine (both white and red). Plus, a loaf of good bread in the freezer.

When hosting a quick get-together, never overlook . . .

Having plenty of wine glasses. If it's a quick get-together and someone brings a couple of bottles of wine (which I'm sure they would like to taste), it's fun to open bottles and try different ones. You can always serve different foods on the same plate, but different wines in the same glass usually doesn't work.

My secret tip for successful last-minute entertaining is . . .

Have a very small repertoire of quick dishes already in your mind, ones you can do from memory. There will be little time to think at the last minute, which sometimes brings on anxiety. Home cooking should be the cooking that you know the best, the dish you make frequently, that relaxes you the most, and, therefore, made from ingredients you always have on hand.

One fun fact few people know about me is that . . .

When I was very young, I was an altar boy and spoke Latin (but not very well).

MENU

Baked Polenta with Meat Ragù & Spinach

Mushroom & Shaved Fennel Salad with Greens & Balsamic Vinegar

Vanilla Ice Cream with Warm Berries & Cointreau

CHEF'S PAIRING

Pinot Bianco or Arneis from northern Italy with the salad

Rosso di Montalcino or Nebbiolo di Langhe with the polenta

CHEF'S PLAYLIST
String quartets of the Haydn era

MAJOR KUDOS
James Beard award for "Best Chef: Southwest"; induction into the James Beard "Who's Who in Food & Beverage in America"; named one of the "15 Best Restaurants in Houston" by The Daily Meal; named one of "10 Best Foodie Spots" by *USA Today*; the Silver Spoon Award from *Food Arts*; Distinguished Alumni Award from the University of California, Riverside

HIS STORY

Rather than stay in California and do something with his freshly minted PhD degree in biochemistry, Robert followed his heart and wound up in Houston instead, where his then girlfriend (and now wife) was staying with her sister and brother-in-law—who owned Cafe Annie.

Before he knew it, Robert was heading the kitchen as their new executive chef . . . and the rest, as they say, is history.

Thirty-five years later, Robert is still helming this rare gem of a place. But he sure knows how to entertain at home in style, too.

"These recipes represent home cooking as opposed to restaurant cooking," says Robert. "They're quick and simple. Nothing must be done at the last minute, and they don't require a lot of pots and pans. Plus, you can spend time with your guests versus racing around the kitchen. All the work is done *before* your guests arrive!"

He goes on to add, "I like to keep last steps to a minimum so I can be relaxed and know that everything will taste great. It's good to choose a dish that actually improves as it sits or simmers."

Robert's delicious ragù sauce does exactly that.

Baked Polenta with Meat Ragù & Spinach

SERVES 4 TO 6

"My Italian grandmother used to make a dish similar to this," says Robert. "She made it only once a year, and it was my favorite. She would let me stir the pot, which made me feel important. And she always made it with things she had on hand: Swiss chard from the garden and game birds or rabbits my grandfather had hunted. This recipe is a version of that wonderful memory."

FOR THE POLENTA

4 cups (946 ml) water

1 tsp salt

1¼ cups (200 g) coarse polenta or cornmeal

FOR THE MEAT RAGÙ

2 tbsp (30 ml) olive oil, plus additional if needed

4 cloves garlic, minced

½ yellow onion, finely chopped

1 small fennel bulb, chopped

½ tsp fennel seeds

1 lb (450 g) ground beef (can substitute mixture of ground beef and ground sausage)

1 tsp salt

½ tsp freshly ground black pepper

2½ cups (615 g) pasta or tomato sauce, plus additional if needed

½ cup (120 ml) heavy cream

2 oz (56 g) grated or minced Fontina cheese (can substitute 4 tbsp [58 g] butter)

10 oz (280 g) frozen spinach, thawed and squeezed dry

1 cup (180 g) grated Parmigiano-Reggiano cheese, for garnish

Red chili flakes (crushed red pepper), to taste, for garnish

Preheat the oven to 350°F (177°C).

To make the polenta, in a saucepan, bring the water and salt to a boil. Add the polenta in a thin stream, stirring constantly. When all the polenta has been added, lower the heat to a simmer. Cook slowly, stirring frequently, until thick, about 10 minutes.

Meanwhile, to make the ragù, in a large, wide skillet heat the oil until hot. Add the garlic, onion, fennel, and fennel seeds. Sauté until lightly browned and aromatic, about 5 to 8 minutes.

Add the ground beef, salt, and pepper. Sauté, stirring occasionally, until fully cooked, about 5 minutes. Stir in the pasta sauce and simmer for about 5 minutes. The sauce should be thick, but if too thick and dry, add a little water or extra tomato sauce. Set aside.

Stir the cream and Fontina into the prepared polenta. Heat over medium heat and stir until thick and creamy for about 1 minute, or just long enough to melt the cheese. The polenta should be thick but just thin enough to spread easily.

Spread about one third of the hot, creamy polenta over the bottom of a 9 x 9–inch (23 x 23–cm) baking dish, preferably ceramic.

Spoon the hot meat sauce over the polenta, then distribute the spinach over the meat sauce.

Spoon the remaining two thirds of the polenta over the meat sauce and spinach (see Chef's Tip).

Bake for 20 minutes, or until the dish is heated through.

Serve either family style by placing the dish on the table, or spoon onto 4 to 6 individual dinner plates. Garnish with the Parmigiano-Reggiano cheese and chili flakes. (This is also great served with extra warm pasta sauce on the side.)

CHEF'S TIP
The dish can be held at room temperature for an hour or so before baking.

Mushroom & Shaved Fennel Salad with Greens & Balsamic Vinegar

SERVES 4

"I grew up in San Francisco, where I remember playing in fields with fennel growing wild," recalls Robert, "so it's an aroma that always seems to take me back home and makes me feel youthful again. I also love the crisp texture it lends. I happen to make this salad quite often, actually, because it's fast. I assemble it right on the plate and then just add the finishing touches." How's that for easy?

8 oz (224 g) white mushrooms, stemmed, cleaned (page 456), and thinly sliced

1 small fennel bulb

Coarse sea salt

Freshly cracked black pepper

2 cups (60 g) arugula or other greens

½ cup (120 ml) extra virgin olive oil, divided

2 tbsp (30 ml) fresh lemon juice, divided

2 oz (56 g) Parmigiano-Reggiano cheese, grated

Aged balsamic vinegar (or see page 456), for drizzling

Distribute mushroom slices over 4 dinner plates. Set aside.

Remove the green stalks from the fennel. Trim the bulb. On a mandoline or with a sharp knife, shave or slice the fennel bulb as thinly as possible. Divide the shaved fennel over the sliced mushrooms. Season each with salt and pepper. Top with a small cluster of arugula. Sprinkle each serving with 2 tablespoons (30 ml) olive oil and about 1½ teaspoons (7 ml) lemon juice and garnish with the cheese. Drizzle a few drops of balsamic vinegar over each serving.

Vanilla Ice Cream with Warm Berries & Cointreau

SERVES 4

Robert likes to teasingly refer to this recipe as Berries Jubilee-esque because it's basically a variation of Cherries Jubilee, which, in turn, is a variation of an ice cream sundae. "My first job was at a Baskin-Robbins," explains Robert, "so I became an expert at the ice cream sundae. This is simple and good, and it also happens to be a perfect 'quick dessert in a pinch.' We always have ice cream and frozen berries for smoothies in the freezer. Plus, we have a citrus tree in our backyard, so I'll just pull an orange off the tree." We should all be so lucky.

1 orange (can substitute other related citrus fruit)

2 tbsp (28 g) unsalted butter

1 pint (288 g) fresh blueberries, blackberries, or strawberries (can substitute frozen berries, thawed)

2 tbsp (26 g) sugar

1 tsp pure vanilla extract

2 tbsp (30 ml) Cointreau (can substitute other orange liqueur)

1 pint (480 g) vanilla ice cream

Orange zest strips, for garnish, optional

With a potato or vegetable peeler, remove the zest from the orange. Roughly chop the zest and reserve. Juice the orange and reserve.

In a skillet over medium heat, melt the butter. When foaming, add the berries and sauté for 1 minute. Add the orange zest, orange juice, sugar, vanilla, and Cointreau. Continue to heat, while gently stirring, until the berries soften and form their own sauce. Remove from the heat.

Scoop the ice cream into 4 bowls or sundae glasses. Spoon the warm berries and sauce over the ice cream. Garnish with orange zest strips, if desired. Serve immediately.

CHEF'S TIP
The berry sauce can be made in advance and reheated when ready to serve.

KATIE BUTTON

Asheville, North Carolina

Chef/owner of Cúrate and Nightbell

CHEF SAYS

Items I always keep on hand for unexpected guests are . . .

Olives, cheese, charcuterie, pâté, crackers, and almonds.

When hosting a quick get-together, never overlook . . .

Dessert! It doesn't have to be anything fancy. Some chocolates will do just fine. But you need to end with something sweet!

My secret tip for successful last-minute entertaining is . . .

Stay calm, cool, and collected. And get your friends to help you cook!

One fun fact few people know about me is that . . .

I spent a year in Paris studying for my master's degree in biomedical engineering. While there, I taught myself how to make puff pastry on the floor of my apartment by marking off a square with duct tape and declaring that area an extension of my kitchen counter since it was so small. I walked around that square of floor the entire time I was in that tiny studio apartment!

MENU

Grilled Fish Collars

Sautéed Greens with Salted Yogurt, Curry Oil, Kalamata Olives & Dried Apricots

Eton Mess with Gin-Soaked Blackberries

CHEF'S PAIRING

Pitcher of white sparkling sangria

CHEF'S PLAYLIST

Lunático by Gotan Project

MAJOR KUDOS

Finalist for the James Beard "Rising Star Chef" award; winner of the Robb Report's "Next Culinary Masters" competition; winner of *Food & Wine*'s "Best New Chef" award; named "One of the 12 Places to Go for a Perfect Night Out in the U.S." by *GQ*

HER STORY

Katie's story is truly one for the books. In a nutshell, it goes something like this:

Girl goes to Cornell for a degree in biomedical engineering. Also gets a master's from École Centrale in Paris. Then gets accepted into a really, really prestigious PhD program. Experiences early-life crisis two weeks before classes begin. Drops out of program. Starts waitressing. Falls in love. Goes to Spain with boyfriend and interns at the ultra-famous, three-Michelin-starred El Bulli (once described as "the most imaginative generator of haute cuisine on the planet"). Incredibly, wows everyone—including herself. Returns to the States and interns with Jean-Georges Vongerichten and José Andrés. Marries boyfriend. Moves to Asheville. Opens tapas restaurant pronounced coo-rah-tay. Wows everyone . . . again. Opens second restaurant, this time focusing on local Appalachian ingredients. Wows once more. And lives happily ever after. Whew!

"I chose this meal," says Katie, "because I really wanted something easy, quick, but spectacular. I think lots of times when we're in a hurry to prep a meal for guests coming over, dessert often gets shrugged aside and forgotten. But it's my favorite course, and I think ending on a high note is incredibly important!"

Grilled Fish Collars

SERVES 4

"I chose to cook with fish collar," explains Katie, "because it's an inexpensive but extremely tender portion of the fish. It's also a relatively unknown-but-delicious and amazing ingredient. Get it from your fishmonger or Asian market. Or if your supermarket butchers their own fish, chances are they'll have collars around, and they'll sell them to you at a fraction of the cost." FYI, fish collars are exactly what the name suggests: a cut from along the fish clavicle, right behind the gills. Only two per fish.

FOR THE HARISSA MUSHROOM GLAZE

½ oz (14 g) dried mushroom blend

½ cup (120 ml) orange juice

2 tbsp (42 g) honey

2 tsp (10 ml) fish sauce

2 tbsp (30 g) chili paste (harissa or sambal oelek)

FOR THE FISH

3 lb (1.4 kg) fish collars of choice (salmon, yellowtail, or any other fish)

Olive oil

Salt

Freshly ground black pepper

Maldon or other flaky sea salt, for finishing

Small handful fresh cilantro leaves, for garnish

1 lime, cut into wedges, for serving

To prepare the harissa mushroom glaze, place the dried mushrooms in a small saucepot with 1½ cups (355 ml) water. Bring to a boil, then take off the heat, cover with a lid, and steep for 10 minutes.

Drain and discard the mushrooms, reserving liquid in a medium-size bowl. Add the orange juice, honey, fish sauce, and chili paste to the bowl. Whisk to blend, then set aside.

Preheat the grill to medium-high heat.

To prepare the fish, rub the fish collars with olive oil and season liberally with salt and pepper. Place on the grill, skin side down, and grill for 3 to 4 minutes, or until the skin is slightly crispy and releases from the grates without sticking. Turn over. Continue to cook for 2 to 3 minutes, or until the fish releases from the grill without sticking. Take off the heat and set aside.

Pour the mushroom glaze into a large sauté pan over medium heat. Once the glaze has reduced by half, about 3 to 4 minutes, add the fish collars. Finish reducing the glaze with the collars in the pan until the glaze is similar in consistency to honey, about 2 minutes. Take off the heat.

Finish with the tiniest amount of Maldon salt and garnish with the cilantro leaves. Serve with the lime wedges on the side.

CHEF'S TIP

Because this meal uses a few different cooking sources, you aren't fighting over space in the oven or on the stove top. I recommend preparing the meal in this order:

1. Get your meringue in the oven.

2. Start heating your grill.

3. Soak the blackberries.

4. Make the glaze for the fish.

5. Make the curry oil and salted yogurt for the sautéed greens.

6. Make the yogurt whipped cream.

7. Mise en place everything else so that it's out and ready for both savory dishes.

8. When your guests walk in the door, greet them and relax for a few minutes.

9. Pop the fish on the grill for a few minutes. Then glaze.

10. Finish making the sautéed greens.

11. Assemble the berry desserts just before time to serve them.

Sautéed Greens with Salted Yogurt, Curry Oil, Kalamata Olives & Dried Apricots

SERVES 4

"I use spinach or any baby-size green," says Katie, "like a baby kale or baby supergreens blend, which you can easily find in any supermarket. It usually also has baby bok choy, collards, or other veggies mixed in. This is a super-fast side, but it's also super flavorful."

⅓ cup (45 g) dried apricots

¼ cup (62 g) plain Greek yogurt

Salt, to taste

¼ cup (60 ml) extra virgin olive oil

½ tsp curry powder

2 tbsp (30 ml) canola oil

⅓ cup (60 g) pitted Kalamata olives, cut in half lengthwise

2 cloves garlic, minced

1 lb (450 g) hearty greens (baby chard, baby kale, or baby spinach blend)

1 tsp cider vinegar

⅓ cup (50 g) dry-roasted salted peanuts, chopped

Cut the apricots into small bite-size pieces. Place in a heatproof bowl and cover with 1 cup (235 ml) of hot water. Microwave on high for 1 minute, or until hot. Cover with plastic wrap and rehydrate until plump, about 5 minutes, then drain and set aside.

Whisk the yogurt and 1¼ tablespoons (17 ml) of water together in a small bowl, then season with salt until the yogurt tastes slightly tangy and salty, like cottage cheese. Place in the refrigerator.

Make a curry oil by heating the extra virgin olive oil in a small saucepan until just warm, then adding the curry powder and whisking to combine. Remove from the heat and set aside.

To prepare the sautéed greens, heat the canola oil in a large sauté pan over medium-high heat. Add the olives and the rehydrated apricots and sauté for 1 minute, then add the garlic and cook just until fragrant, about 30 seconds. Add the hearty greens and lightly sauté. Once the greens have started to wilt, about 1 to 2 minutes, remove from the heat. Immediately add the cider vinegar and toss. Check for seasoning.

Spoon the salted yogurt over a large serving platter, then drizzle on the curry oil from side to side in a zig zag motion. Arrange the sautéed greens down the middle and garnish with the chopped peanuts to serve.

Eton Mess with Gin-Soaked Blackberries

SERVES 4

"This is a truly amazing homemade dessert," admits Katie. "It's so impressive. The coconut meringue mixed in with the yogurt and gin-soaked berries is just delicious!"

FOR THE GIN-SOAKED BLACKBERRIES

2 cups (288 g) ripe fresh blackberries

¼ cup (50 g) sugar

Zest of 1 lemon

1 tbsp (15 ml) fresh lemon juice

¾ cup (180 ml) dry gin

2 fresh tarragon sprigs, leaves only

4 fresh basil leaves, thinly sliced

FOR THE TOASTED COCONUT BAKED MERINGUES

1 large egg white, at room temperature

¼ tsp sea salt

¼ cup (50 g) granulated sugar

⅛ tsp pure vanilla extract

½ cup (40 g) unsweetened flaked coconut, toasted (page 457) and cooled

FOR THE YOGURT WHIPPED CREAM

1 cup (240 ml) heavy cream, chilled

½ cup (56 g) powdered sugar, sifted

½ cup (125 g) Greek yogurt, chilled

½ tsp fresh lemon juice

Heavy pinch of salt

FOR THE OPTIONAL GARNISH

Fresh tarragon leaves

Thinly sliced basil leaves

Lemon zest

Preheat the oven to 325°F (165°C).

To make the gin-soaked blackberries, cut the blackberries in half lengthwise. Place them in a medium-size bowl. Sprinkle with the sugar and toss to coat. Add the lemon zest, lemon juice, and enough gin to almost cover the berries. Stir, folding lightly as to not crush the berries. Add the tarragon leaves and basil leaves. Fold together lightly. Let sit until ready to serve, gently tossing the mixture occasionally.

Prepare a sheet pan by spraying it with nonstick cooking spray, then line it with parchment paper.

To make the meringue, place the egg white and salt in a very clean stand mixer bowl. Using the whip attachment, start beating on low, gradually increasing the speed to high. When soft peaks form, reduce the speed to medium. Slowly add the sugar, a little at a time. Once all has been added, increase the speed to medium-high and whisk until the whites are stiff and glossy. Reduce the speed to medium-low and mix in the vanilla until incorporated. Remove the bowl from the mixer and fold in the toasted and cooled coconut by hand, taking care not to deflate the meringue.

Spread the meringue into a thin layer in the prepared sheet pan and bake for 20 minutes. Remove from the oven and let cool to room temperature.

To make the yogurt whipped cream, place the heavy cream, powdered sugar, yogurt, lemon juice, and salt in the cleaned-out bowl of the stand mixer. First whisk lightly by hand just to combine, then, using the whip attachment of the stand mixer, whisk on low speed, gradually increasing to medium-high as the mixture thickens. Bring the whipped cream to stiff peaks, then remove the bowl to the refrigerator and chill the yogurt whipped cream until ready to serve.

To serve, drain the gin-soaked blackberries (save the drained liquid to make blackberry gin and tonics!). Setting half the berries aside, divide the remaining berries among 4 individual 6- to 8-ounce (120- to 180-g) ramekins or serving bowls.

Next, break off about a third of the baked meringue and crumble it over the portions of berries. Cover each portion with yogurt whipped cream, using half of the cream. Break off another third of the meringue, crumble, and sprinkle over the cream. Then divide the remaining berries among the dishes. Add remaining baked meringue, crumbled, and top with the remaining yogurt whipped cream. If desired, garnish each dish with the tarragon, basil, and lemon zest. Serve immediately.

SHAUN HERGATT

New York, New York

Executive chef of 432 Park Avenue

CHEF SAYS

Items I always keep on hand for unexpected guests are . . .

A great bottle of wine, cheese, charcuterie, great bread, and a chocolate cake.

When hosting a quick get-together, never overlook . . .

Alcohol. Serve enough drinks so that everyone's happy. Start with a nice cocktail, followed by some good wine. Keep it coming and remember to enjoy yourself.

My secret tip for successful last-minute entertaining is . . .

Devise a plan to manage your time and tasks so you're not overwhelmed or unprepared for your guests. Remember that entertaining in your home is an opportunity to treat them to a special and personal experience.

One fun fact few people know about me is that . . .

I work out religiously. I have a very specific routine, and I train every day.

MENU

Creamy Cucumber Soup with Crab Meat & Dill

Fillet of Beef with Hon Shimeji Mushrooms, Wilted Tatsoi & Truffle Vinaigrette

CHEF'S PAIRING

Champagne with the soup

Pinot Noir with the beef

CHEF'S PLAYLIST

Beacon

MAJOR KUDOS

Two Michelin stars; James Beard nomination for "Best New Chef"; restaurant named a "Best New Restaurant" by both *Esquire* and *New York Magazine*; named "Best New Chef" by *New York Magazine*; across-the-board 29 of 30 ranking in Zagat; *Condé Nast Traveler*'s "Gold List"; gold medal from International Salon Culinaire

HIS STORY

As a young boy growing up in Australia, he aspired to be an art teacher. But as this Aussie lad got older, the culinary influences of his chef father and beloved Scandinavian grandmother were too strong to ignore. So, at seventeen, he started an intense four-year apprenticeship program with a fine dining restaurant in Cairns—and has been riding high ever since.

Shaun is now recognized worldwide as a technically accomplished chef with multiple Michelin stars. But he's just as well known for creating memorable dining experiences for his grateful customers. Which is probably why he was asked to run the exclusively private restaurant that occupies an entire floor in the tallest residential tower in the Western Hemisphere.

"I chose this meal because I wanted to create something simple but also fresh and tasty," says Shaun. "Both recipes are really easy to make at home, but they both taste incredible, which is exactly what makes them special. I want people to leave my home having forged lifetime memories. As for me, food is all about joy and experiences."

Creamy Cucumber Soup with Crab Meat & Dill

SERVES 4

"This soup is so simple, it only needs fresh ingredients and a blender," says Shaun. "Respecting and understanding ingredients is something that's central to my heritage, upbringing, and day-to-day life. My food philosophy revolves around the many micro-seasons that occur throughout the year, lasting for just a few weeks or an entire month." FYI, cukes are a warm-season veggie.

1½ lb (680 g) cucumbers, peeled, seeded, and rough chopped

½ cup (120 g) crème fraîche, plus additional for serving

1 bunch fresh mint, leaves only

1 bunch fresh cilantro, leaves only

½ tsp salt

½ tsp sugar

4 oz (112 g) cooked crab leg meat, broken up, for garnish

Olive oil, for drizzling

Fresh dill sprigs, for garnish

Combine the cucumbers, crème fraîche, mint, cilantro, salt, and sugar in a blender. Process to a fine purée, then pass through a fine sieve.

Pour the soup evenly into 4 soup bowls. Garnish each bowl with 1 ounce (28 g) of the crab meat. Top with a dollop of the crème fraîche and drizzle with the oil. Garnish with the dill.

Fillet of Beef with Hon Shimeji Mushrooms, Wilted Tatsoi & Truffle Vinaigrette

SERVES 4

What does it take to elevate a beautiful-yet-simple fillet of beef into a luxuriously elegant entrée? Think exotic, delicate, Asian mushrooms cooked to a rich, nutty flavor. Think succulent, tender, small, green, leafy Asian rosettes transformed to a subtle, warm earthiness. And think heady, aromatic drizzles of heaven-on-earth, more commonly referred to as truffle vinaigrette. Thanks to Shaun, that's precisely what this dish features!

FOR THE TRUFFLE VINAIGRETTE

¼ cup (60 ml) truffle juice (can be found at specialty food stores or online)

3 tbsp (45 ml) olive oil, divided

1 tbsp (15 ml) fresh lemon juice

2 tsp (10 ml) soy sauce

FOR THE SPICE MIX

1½ tbsp (6 g) freshly ground black peppercorns

1½ tbsp (7 g) ground ginger

1½ tbsp (7 g) ground star anise

1½ tbsp (7 g) ground coriander

FOR THE FILLET OF BEEF

2 lb (907 lb) fillet of beef, cut into 4 medallions

4 oz (112 g) hon shimeji (brown beech) mushrooms (can substitute any other mushrooms)

4 oz (112 g) tatsoi (can substitute any other greens, like baby bok choy, English spinach, or Tuscan kale)

Salt, to taste

Freshly ground black pepper, to taste

Prepare the truffle vinaigrette by thoroughly whisking together the truffle juice, 2 tablespoons (30 ml) of the olive oil, lemon juice, and soy sauce in a bowl. Set aside.

Prepare the spice mix by whisking the peppercorns, ginger, star anise, and coriander in a bowl. Sprinkle on both sides of the beef fillets to season.

Set a sauté pan over medium-high heat. Add the remaining 1 tablespoon (15 ml) olive oil. Pan sear the fillets, on both sides, until medium rare, reaching an internal temperature of 135°F (57°C), 3 to 4 minutes a side. Remove to a platter, tent with aluminum foil, and set aside to rest.

Reduce the heat to medium. Add the mushrooms and tatsoi to the sauté pan. Season lightly with salt and pepper. Sauté until wilted and cooked through, about 2 minutes.

Distribute the mushroom mixture evenly on 4 dinner plates. Place a beef fillet in the center of each plate and drizzle with the truffle vinaigrette. Serve immediately.

GAVIN KAYSEN

Minneapolis, Minnesota

Cheflowner of Spoon and Stable (Minneapolis) and Bellecour (Wayzata, Minnesata); founding mentor of the nonprofit ment'or BKB Foundation; head coach of the Bocuse d'Or USA team

CHEF SAYS

Items I always keep on hand for unexpected guests are . . .

Saba, fleur de sel, great "EVOO," European butter, and vanilla beans.

When hosting a quick get-together, never overlook . . .

Cooking some onions, garlic, and rosemary in a pan with butter before your guests show up. The house will smell divine.

My secret tip for successful last-minute entertaining is . . .

Make it so you can entertain. Do not be a slave in the kitchen while your guests are there.

One fun fact few people know about me is that . . .

I collect spoons from all over the world.

MENU
Chilled Sweet Corn Soup with Vanilla Oil

CHEF'S PAIRING
Riesling

CHEF'S PLAYLIST
Michael Jackson

MAJOR KUDOS

One Michelin star; *Food & Wine's* "Best New Chefs" award; James Beard "Rising Star" award; finalist for James Beard "Best New Restaurant" award; record-breaking gold and silver medals at Bocuse d'Or; guest judge on Bravo's *Top Chef*

HIS STORY

Gavin has had such incredible opportunities. A gig with the legendary Marco Pierre White in London. A stint with the revered Daniel Boulud in New York City. And a run at Bocuse d'Or in Lyon, France—one of the world's most prestigious cooking competitions.

So, what does this über chef choose to make for his own last-minute guests at home? Soup.

Not just any soup, mind you. A silky, velvety, luxuriously sumptuous essence-of-corn soup with a depth of surprising undertones.

"I love corn soup, especially in the summer," says Gavin. "It cools me down and brings back great memories I have of my father and me shucking corn in our backyard. Plus, it's quick."

As for his garnish, don't look for any parsley sprigs here. Gavin goes for something just a bit more exotic.

"Vanilla oil really ties it all together. At first it might not make sense, but try it!"

There's no way we wouldn't.

Chilled Sweet Corn Soup with Vanilla Oil

SERVES 4 TO 6

This recipe is all about the corn—and its natural sweetness. Don't even think about those cellophane-wrapped packages in your grocery store in the dead of winter. During its peak of freshness (July to September), look for heirloom varieties. From a local farmer. Or better yet, your own garden. And if you prefer to serve this magnificent soup as an hors d'oeuvre instead of a main course, try using espresso cups or shot glasses. Yes, very impressive.

¼ cup (60 ml) olive oil

1 vanilla bean, split

10 ears fresh sweet corn, shucked, kernels cut off (about 4 cups [575 g]) and cobs reserved

Grapeseed oil, for coating

4 oz (115 g, 1 stick) butter

1 cup (100 g) diced leeks (white part only)

½ cup (50 g) diced yellow onion

2 cloves garlic, minced

Water, vegetable stock, or chicken stock to cover

½ cup (120 ml) heavy cream

Salt, to taste

Juice of 1 lime

1 tsp hot sauce

Fennel fronds for garnish, optional

Preheat the oven to 425°F (218°C).

To make the vanilla oil, place the olive oil and split vanilla bean in a glass jar with a cover. Shake well and let sit. The longer this sits, the better it will get.

On a sheet pan, coat 6 of the reserved corn cobs with a small amount of the grapeseed oil. Bake until dark brown and burned, about 20 to 30 minutes. This will help create a savory/bitter flavor that will help offset the sweetness of the corn. Remove from the oven and set aside.

In a stockpot, melt the butter over medium heat. Add the leeks, onion, and garlic. Sweat until translucent, about 6 minutes.

Add the corn kernels (reserving 1 tablespoon [15 g] and setting aside for garnish), the burned cobs, and the remaining 4 raw cobs to the pot. Add enough water or stock to cover. Bring to a simmer and cook, uncovered, for about 35 minutes.

Remove the pot from the heat. Carefully remove the cobs with tongs and discard. Add the heavy cream to the liquid in the pot and let sit for 15 minutes.

Blend the soup until smooth. For an even smoother texture, strain through a fine-mesh sieve into a bowl after blending. If you prefer some texture, pour it into the bowl without straining.

If you plan to eat the soup hot, season it now, with the salt, lime juice, and hot sauce (see Chef's Tip). If not, set it, unseasoned, in its bowl, in a larger bowl of ice to let it cool quickly. Once cooled, season with the salt, lime juice, and hot sauce.

Divide the soup among 4 individual bowls. Drizzle the vanilla oil on top and garnish with the reserved corn kernels and optional fennel fronds.

CHEF'S TIP

When the soup is cold, it will generally take more salt and seasoning just because it is cold, so if you season it earlier, you'll just have to taste for seasoning again!

KRISTEN KISH

Boston, Massachusetts

Chef

CHEF SAYS

Items I always keep on hand for unexpected guests are . . .

Salt, pepper, oil, sherry vinegar, and maybe some leftover condiments that weren't used last time.

When hosting a quick get-together, never overlook . . .

Cloth napkins. Food, vibe, and drinks all can be very casual, but a cloth napkin is a small detail that I've learned to appreciate.

My secret tip for successful last-minute entertaining is . . .

Keep it simple. Entertaining can be overwhelming, and if cooking isn't your forte, then it can get real overwhelming. Don't be afraid to buy some premade goods to boost a meal. It's okay. And stay organized. That's huge! It keeps your mind less frazzled and, in turn, your food more focused. A meal in an hour can be daunting. At the end of the day, serve great food and enjoy your company.

One fun fact few people know about me is that . . .

Hmmm . . . well, I played the baritone in high school. Is that interesting enough?

MENU

Rib Eye Steak

Spring Pea Toast

CHEF'S PAIRING

Either Barolo wine or cans (not bottles) of Miller High Life beer

CHEF'S PLAYLIST

Chill music (jazz, Van Morrison)

MAJOR KUDOS

Winner of Bravo's *Top Chef*, season ten, plus *Last Chance Kitchen*; co-host of Travel Channel's *36 Hours* series; feature story in *Food & Wine*

HER STORY

Part culinary superstar, part down-to-earth role model, Kristen's the total package when it comes to being an inspiration both in and out of the kitchen.

Born in Seoul, Korea, Kristen was adopted by an American couple from Michigan when she was only four months old. Growing up, her favorite TV show was *Great Chefs*. So it came as no surprise that, after a year of studying international business in college, she up and left for Chicago, pursuing her true passion at Le Cordon Bleu instead.

Armed with a culinary degree, she then headed to Boston, where she worked at several über-high-profile restaurants (including Menton, where she served as their chef de cuisine). As luck would have it, she got to compete on *Top Chef*—and then, with nothing having to do with luck, she won . . . becoming only the second woman to ace this competition!

"For a quick meal for several people," explains Kristen, "cooking large format is easy and delicious. Nothing is particularly revolutionary about this meal—and in fact, that's the best part of it! It's so simple, yet stands out in flavor and execution. It truly hits the spot of satisfaction for me as a friend having friends over."

Rib Eye Steak

SERVES 4

"Roasting off a large piece of rib eye is tasty and takes very little babysitting," says Kristen. "Start with a great piece of beef, and all it needs is some great seasoning and a few aromatics. You can cut it into individual portions and plate each one. But I really prefer family style when among friends in my own home."

1 (2-lb [900-g]) rib eye steak, brought to room temperature 30 minutes before cooking

Salt, to taste

Freshly ground black pepper, to taste

2 tbsp (30 ml) grapeseed oil, plus additional if needed

2 shallots, quartered

8 fresh thyme sprigs

3 fresh sage sprigs

1 head garlic, unpeeled, split horizontally

3 tbsp (43 g) butter

Season the rib eye with salt and pepper.

Pour the grapeseed oil in a large cast-iron or heavy bottom pan. Add more if needed to disperse into a thin layer, then heat over medium-high heat. Place the steak in the pan and sear for 3 to 4 minutes on one side, or until the bottom has developed a golden-brown crust. Important: Do not touch or move around until ready to flip!

When the steak is ready, flip it. Scatter the shallots, thyme, and sage around the steak, and add the garlic, cut sides down. Cook for 3 to 4 minutes, or until you have nearly reached the desired doneness. Just before reaching the recommended internal temperature (118°F [48°C] for medium rare), add the butter and allow it to foam. Baste the steak with it 15 to 20 times.

Remove the steak from the pan, with the aromatics, to a platter and allow to rest for about 25 minutes before serving. The final internal temperature should be 123°F to 126°F (51°C to 52°C) for medium rare.

Spring Pea Toast

SERVES 4

"The idea for this side dish was a mash-up of shrimp toast and avocado toast," explains Kristen. "Both are delicious, so why not take some direction from each and create something new? I borrowed the hollowing-out and shallow-frying method from the shrimp toast, and the phenomenon of mashed avocado from the avocado toast. If the two had a baby, this would be it! It's effin' delicious."

3 tbsp (48 g) salt, plus additional for seasoning

1 cup (151 g) English peas

8 (1-inch [2.5-cm]) thick slices of ficelle bread, preferably rolled in seeds (can substitute French baguette)

Zest of 1 lemon

2½ tbsp (37 ml) olive oil

8 oz (230 g, 2 sticks) butter, divided

2 cloves garlic, smashed, divided

4 fresh thyme sprigs, divided

Red chili flakes (crushed red pepper), to taste

Freshly ground black pepper, to taste

Lemon wedge, for squeezing

2 red radishes, julienned

Pea tendrils, for garnish, optional

Preheat the oven to 350°F (177°C).

To blanch the peas, bring 3 quarts (2.8 L) of water to a boil over high heat. Meanwhile, prepare a bowl of ice water and set it near the stove. Add the 3 tablespoons (48 g) of salt to the boiling water, then the peas, and cook for 20 seconds, then drain and plunge the peas immediately into the ice bath. Let cool completely, about 3 to 4 minutes, then drain and pat dry with paper towels.

Arrange the bread slices in a single layer on a sheet tray. Place in the oven and bake until lightly dry and slightly crisped on the outside but still squishy in the center, about 5 to 8 minutes.

Remove from the oven. Once cool enough to handle, pinch out a small well in the center of each slice of bread, creating a mini bread bowl. Set aside.

In a bowl, mash the blanched peas, lemon zest, and oil with a fork until it looks like finely lumpy mashed potatoes. Season with salt. Pack 2 tablespoons (30 g) of the peas into the well on each slice of bread, creating a mound on top.

In a large skillet over medium-high heat, melt half the butter. Once it begins to bubble slightly (be sure not to burn), add 1 of the smashed garlic cloves and 2 of the thyme sprigs, then 4 of the bread slices. You are now shallow-frying the toast in an aromatic butter.

Once the bread is a nice golden brown, about 2 to 4 minutes, remove from the pan and place on a paper towel to absorb any excess fat. Dump out the used butter, wipe the pan clean, and repeat the process for the remaining 4 toasts, using the remaining butter, garlic, and thyme sprigs.

Arrange on a platter and season with extra salt if necessary. Sprinkle with the red chili flakes, pepper, and a squeeze of lemon juice. Garnish each toast with the radishes and pea tendrils, if using.

MICHAEL WHITE

New York, New York

Chef/co-owner of Altamarea Group, which includes Marea, Ai Fiori, Costata, and Vaucluse (New York); Osteria Morini (New York; Bernardsville, New Jersey; and Washington, D.C.); Nicoletta Pizzeria (New York and Bernardsville); The Barn at Bedford and Campagna (Westchester, New York); Due Mari (New Brunswick, New Jersey); Ristorante Morini (New York and Istanbul); Al Molo (Hong Kong); and Chop Shop (London)

CHEF SAYS

Items I always keep on hand for unexpected guests are . . .

Great olives, sliced prosciutto, and eggs, flour, and Parmigiano for last-minute handmade pasta.

When hosting a quick get-together, never overlook . . .

The lighting, music, wine, temperature, and dietary restrictions. Know who your guests are and seat them appropriately! Make sure there are objects to invoke conversation (i.e., interesting people, new ingredients, etc.).

My secret tip for successful last-minute entertaining is . . .

Choose a menu that allows you to enjoy your company (i.e., make-ahead food). Or plan on having lots of guests in the kitchen to congregate and keep you company.

One fun fact few people know about me is that . . .

I was a football player, had an injury, and then decided to pursue cooking. I'm from Beloit, Wisconson. I married an Italian woman and speak Italian fluently. I love orange soda.

MENU

Garganelli with Prosciutto, Cream & Arugula

Fluke Crudo with Lemon Thyme & Extra Virgin Olive Oil

Affogato

CHEF'S PAIRING

Fraciacorta

CHEF'S PLAYLIST

Action Bronson or Carmen Consoli

MAJOR KUDOS

Multiple Michelin stars; James Beard award for "Best New Restaurant"; four-time nominee for James Beard "Best Chef: New York City" award; "Best New Chef" award from *Esquire*; multiple 3-star reviews from the *New York Times*; multiple "Best Restaurant" accolades

HIS STORY

Although Michael, of Norwegian descent, grew up in Beloit, Wisconsin, his taste in food has drastically changed since the days of his youth. In fact, it's anything but midwestern.

You see, Michael LOVES (all caps intentional) authentic Italian cuisine. He even once famously stated, "I eat, sleep, live, and die Italian food!"

We don't doubt it.

In large part, this gastronomic "obsession" of his can be attributed to the seven years Michael spent in Italy under the tutelage of chef Gianluigi Morini. It was there that he immersed himself in all things Italian—from its culinary history and art of pasta making, to its language and art of love. (Yes, he met his wife, Giovanna, there.)

Which makes his dinner choice for this book no surprise whatsoever.

"This meal is light, delicious, and universally appealing," says Michael. "It's also so easy to throw together."

Pasta. Then fish. Then gelato. What could be more Italian? *Mangia!*

Garganelli with Prosciutto, Cream & Arugula

SERVES 4 AS A MAIN COURSE

When you're in a hurry to make a pasta dish for last-minute company, this elegant version makes it look like you slaved all day over it. Yet nothing could be further from the truth. Michael prefers to use garganelli pasta, which he considers to be "the finest of the short fresh pastas because of their textural complexity." Look for them in an Italian market or specialty shop.

Kosher salt

1 cup (151 g) fresh or frozen peas

2 tbsp (28 g) truffle butter (can substitute regular butter), divided

5 oz (140 g) thinly sliced prosciutto, cut into ½-inch (12-mm) wide strips

1½ cups (360 ml) heavy cream

1 lb (450 g) fresh or dried garganelli (can substitute gemelli or penne)

¾ cup (135 g) finely grated Parmigiano-Reggiano cheese, divided

Freshly ground black pepper

1½ cups (45 g) loosely packed arugula, washed, spun dry, and torn or cut into strips

Fill a medium-size pot about two-thirds full of water and salt it liberally. Bring to a boil over high heat. Add the peas and cook just until they start to turn bright green, about 30 seconds. Immediately drain them in a colander and rinse under gently running cold water to stop the cooking and preserve their green color. Set aside.

Fill a large pot about two-thirds full of water and salt it liberally. Bring to a boil over high heat.

Meanwhile, set a large heavy sauté pan over medium-high heat. Add 1 tablespoon (14 g) of the butter and let it melt, tipping and tilting the pan to coat. Add the prosciutto and cook, stirring with a wooden spoon, just to warm it and infuse the butter with its flavor, about 1 minute.

Stir in the cream and bring it to a simmer, then lower the heat and continue simmering gently until it reduces and thickens enough to coat the back of a spoon, about 5 minutes.

When the water comes to a boil, add the pasta and cook until al dente, about 2 minutes for fresh or 7 minutes for dried.

Meanwhile, stir the peas and the remaining 1 tablespoon (14 g) of butter into the sauce, letting the butter melt.

Drain the pasta and add it to the sauté pan. Toss to coat the pasta with the sauce, then stir in ½ cup (90 g) of the cheese until it melts and thickens the sauce.

Divide the pasta among 4 individual plates. Finish with a few grinds of black pepper, a sprinkling of the remaining cheese, and the arugula. Serve promptly.

Fluke Crudo with Lemon Thyme & Extra Virgin Olive Oil

SERVES 4

When buying fresh fluke (one of the common names of the summer flounder), it's essential to purchase it from a reliable purveyor and use it that same day. Make sure it's of the best, freshest quality. And tell your fishmonger you're planning to serve it raw. "For the most elegant cuts," explains Michael, "use a sharp knife and slide it forward and back like the blade of a slicing machine, rather than a more severe up-and-down chopping motion."

1 lb (450 g) sushi-grade fluke fillet (can substitute sushi-grade striped bass, snapper, trout, or yellowtail)

Extra virgin olive oil, for brushing

½ lemon

Fine sea salt, to taste

About 1 tbsp (3 g) fresh lemon thyme leaves (can substitute regular thyme), for garnish

Chill 4 small plates.

Using a sharp knife, slice the fluke diagonally against the grain into 16 or 20 slices, each ¼-inch (6-mm) thick. Arrange one quarter of the slices side by side on each of the chilled plates.

Brush the slices with the oil, then squeeze a few drops of the lemon juice over the slices. Season with sea salt and garnish each slice with a few thyme leaves.

Affogato

SERVES 4

Affogato (Italian for "drowned") is a coffee-based dessert many Italians enjoy after dinner. Hot espresso is actually poured over cold gelato, which makes for an incredible offset of temperatures and textures in your mouth. *Mamma mia*, now this is a dessert worth trying!

1 pint (480 g) vanilla gelato (can substitute excellent-quality vanilla ice cream)

¼ cup (60 ml) amaro, preferably Ramazzotti, divided

4 shots hot, freshly pulled espresso, divided

Freshly whipped cream, for garnish

Put a scoop of gelato in each of 4 serving dishes, coffee cups, or dessert glasses. Top each scoop with 1 tablespoon (15 ml) of the amaro, then 1 shot of the espresso. Finish each serving with a dollop of the whipped cream and serve immediately.

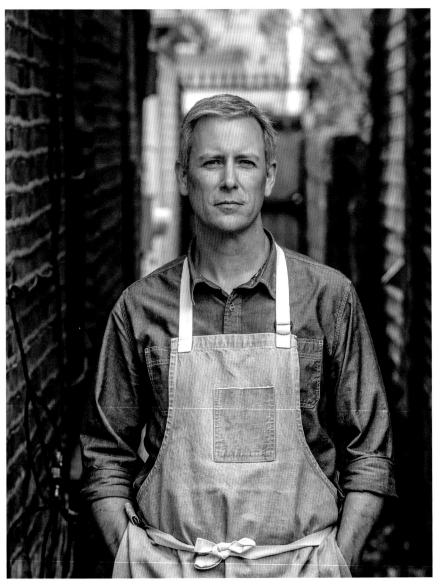

ANDREW ZIMMERMAN

Chicago, Illinois

Executive chef of Sepia; member of American Chef Corps

CHEF SAYS

Items I always keep on hand for unexpected guests are . . .

Bourbon, good red wine, great cheese, citrus, and chairs.

When hosting a quick get-together, never overlook . . .

Water, ice, and napkins.

My secret tip for successful last-minute entertaining is . . .

Don't try to overreach. Your guests should be there to hang out with you, not watch you win a Top Chef Quickfire Challenge.

One fun fact few people know about me is that . . .

Few people know about me.

MENU

Head-on Shrimp, Chili Salsa, Marcona Almonds & Crispy Ciabatta

Prime Rib Eye, Maitake Mushrooms, Fingerling Potatoes, Knob Onions & Ssamjang Butter

Buttermilk Panna Cotta with Berries & Gingersnap Crumble

CHEF'S PAIRING

A simple whisky smash and cold IPA beer

CHEF'S PLAYLIST

My Bloody Valentine, Slint, and Mogwai

MAJOR KUDOS

One Michelin star; AAA four-star rating; finalist and multiple nominations for James Beard award for "Best Chef: Great Lakes"; "Rising Star" award from StarChefs.com; winner of the Jean Banchet "Restaurant of the Year" award and nominee for their "Chef of the Year" award; winner of the Battle Cream Cheese on Food Network's *Iron Chef America*; "Humanitarian of the Year" award from *Plate*

HIS STORY

Andrew Zimmerman grew up in New York City in the '80s, and his dream—probably like most kids his age back then—was to become a rock star. But that takes money. So Andrew started washing dishes in a kitchen. Suddenly he got bitten by the cooking bug. Hard. And that brought his would-be music career to a screeching halt.

After learning the ropes of the industry through hands-on experience for three years, he enrolled in the prestigious French Culinary Institute—and graduated first in his class. He then moved to Chicago, worked at several top spots around the city, and now heads one of the finest restaurants in the Windy City.

"This meal is both simple and delicious," says Andrew. "Hopefully, it also impresses my guests," he adds with a sly smile. "There's very limited prep work, and most of it can be done on a good charcoal grill, which is always nice to stand around, enjoying a cocktail, while dinner is cooking. The focus is on great ingredients treated simply. Let the product do the work, not you."

Wise words from a wise chef.

Head-on Shrimp, Chili Salsa, Marcona Almonds & Crispy Ciabatta

SERVES 4

This über-elegant appetizer is sure to impress even your most discriminating guests. But in the spirit of full disclosure, Andrew really does prefer to make this recipe using his own shrimp stock from scratch. However, in order to save time, he acquiesced to using store-bought chicken stock. This time only.

16 large (U10 or U7) head-on shrimp

2–3 ancho chiles

2 cloves garlic, peeled

2–3 piquillo peppers, diced small

Salt, to taste

1½ tbsp (22 ml) sherry vinegar (can substitute red wine vinegar), or more to taste

1 cup (240 ml) extra virgin olive oil, or as needed, divided

3 slices good-quality ciabatta bread, cut ¾-inch (19-mm) thick, crusts removed

Freshly ground black pepper, to taste

3 tbsp (45 ml) low-sodium chicken stock

¼ cup (43 g) Marcona almonds, rinsed of excess salt, drained, dried, and coarsely chopped

¼ cup (12 g) thinly sliced scallions, rinsed in cold water, drained, and dried on paper towels

2–3 tbsp (9 g) coarsely chopped fresh flat-leaf parsley

4–8 slices ciabatta or good sourdough bread, grilled, for serving

Peel and devein the shrimp but leave the heads and tail shells intact. Keep the shrimp cold either in the refrigerator or on ice.

Stem and seed the ancho chiles. Lightly toast them in a dry pan over medium-high heat, pressing down on them gently for about 30 seconds a side. Put them in a bowl and cover with very hot water to rehydrate, about 10 minutes. Once they are rehydrated, drain and chop them roughly into pieces no bigger than ¼ inch (6 mm).

Using a microplane, grate the garlic into a large mortar. Add the chiles, piquillo peppers, and a pinch of salt. Grind everything together with a pestle into a chunky mess. Add the sherry vinegar and about 3 tablespoons (45 ml) of the olive oil. You should have a good mix of heat, sweet, and tart. Set the chili salsa aside.

In a large sauté pan, heat about ½ cup (120 ml) of the olive oil over medium-high heat. Add the crustless ciabatta slices and fry, flipping them to make sure everything gets evenly colored, until the bread is the color of cornflakes or a little darker, about 5 minutes. Drain the fried bread and chop roughly into small irregular-sized croutons not much bigger than, say, chocolate chips.

To pull it all together, pat dry the shrimp and season with salt and pepper. Heat the remaining 2 tablespoons (30 ml) or so of the olive oil in a large sauté pan over medium-high heat. Arrange the shrimp in the pan. Cook for 1 minute or so on the first side, and then flip. While still keeping the shrimp in the pan, stir in the chicken stock and let it come to a bubble, then spoon in about half the chili salsa. Swirl the shrimp and sauce around for another 1 to 2 minutes, or until the shrimp are almost, but not quite, done (they should still be a little translucent). Remove from the heat immediately. They will finish cooking in the heat of the sauce while you do the finishing touches. Overcooked shrimp are a bummer.

Transfer the shrimp to a platter or, if you're feeling fancy, to individual plates. Taste the remaining chili salsa and adjust the seasoning with more salt and/or vinegar if you feel it needs it. Then spoon it over the shrimp. Scatter the almonds, scallions, parsley, and ciabatta bread crumbs over everything. Serve with the grilled bread to mop up the extra sauce.

Prime Rib Eye, Maitake Mushrooms, Fingerling Potatoes, Knob Onions & Ssamjang Butter

SERVES 4

An elegant appetizer deserves an equally elegant entrée. And this one is it. Using a great cut of meat, prepared simply and carefully, is the first step. Adding some unusual veggies takes it up another notch. And then topping off with ssamjang butter is the crowning glory, so to speak.

1 (2-lb [907-g]) prime rib eye steak

Salt, to taste

Freshly ground black pepper, to taste

4 tbsp (58 g) butter, at room temperature

4 tbsp (60 g) ssamjang (can substitute white or red miso paste)

2 tbsp (30 ml) rendered duck fat (can substitute bacon fat or vegetable oil)

2 clusters maitake mushrooms, each cluster cut into 4 roughly equal slabs (can substitute oyster mushrooms or any other mushroom you like)

8–12 fingerling potatoes (depending on size), cut in half lengthwise

8 knob onions, trimmed to just a bit of green on top and cut in half vertically (can substitute cipollini onions)

3–4 fresh thyme sprigs

2 cloves garlic, lightly crushed

3 tbsp (45 ml) vegetable oil

2–3 tbsp (6–9 g) chopped fresh flat-leaf parsley

Season the steak generously with the salt and pepper about 30 minutes before you plan to cook it. If you have time (and the grill!), fire up a hardwood charcoal grill and let the coals get good and ready. If you don't have the time (or the grill), plan to cook the steak on the stove. Both methods have their charm.

Preheat the oven to 375°F (191°C). In a bowl with a wooden spoon, work the butter and ssamjang together to create a paste. Set aside.

In a large cast-iron or ovenproof stainless-steel sauté pan, heat the duck fat over medium-high heat. Arrange the mushrooms, potatoes, and onions in the pan, cut sides down. Season with a bit of salt and pepper, then add the thyme and garlic. Cook for about 3 to 4 minutes to start getting a bit of color on the vegetables. Place the pan in the oven and roast the vegetables for about 6 to 8 minutes. If there is good browning on the cut sides of the mushrooms, flip them and finish cooking the vegetables for about 15 more minutes. Remove from the oven and discard the thyme sprigs and garlic. Keep warm.

To cook the steak on the grill: Make sure the coals are very hot and the grate is clean and freshly oiled. Place the steak on the grill and cook for about 2 minutes without moving it. Turn it 45 degrees and cook 2 more minutes. Then flip it to the other side and repeat the process. Keep moving the steak around until the meat registers an internal temperature of 105°F (41°C). Remove from the heat and place on a rack to rest for about 10 minutes. Return the steak to the grill and cook, flipping often, until the internal temperature hits 120°F (49°C). Return to the rack and let rest. The internal heat will carry over to about 125°F to 128°F (52°C to 53°C) for medium rare. Delicious.

To cook the steak on the stovetop in a cast-iron pan: Preheat a large cast-iron skillet over medium-high heat for about 8 minutes. Add the oil and then the steak. Leave it alone to develop a good initial sear, about 2 minutes, then flip and cook another 2 minutes. Keep flipping the steak until the meat registers an internal temperature of 105°F (41°C). Remove from the heat and place it on a rack to rest for about 10 minutes. Return the steak to the pan and continue to cook, flipping often, until the internal temperature hits 120°F (49°C). Return to the rack and let rest. The internal heat will carry over to about 125°F to 128°F (52°C to 53°C) for medium rare. Again, delicious.

To serve, slice the steak across the grain into slices about ½-inch (12-mm) thick; you should get about 3 nice slices per person that way. Arrange the slices on each of 4 plates and slather each portion with some ssamjang butter. Toss the mushrooms and other vegetables with the parsley, then divide among the plates. It won't be fancy, so don't freak out.

Buttermilk Panna Cotta with Berries & Gingersnap Crumble

SERVES 4

A dessert this impressive may look like it took you all day to make, but it can easily be done in under an hour. However, that's our little secret. Shhh. . . .

1½ tsp (3 g) powdered unflavored gelatin

1¼ cups (300 ml) heavy cream

7 tbsp (90 g) sugar

Seeds scraped from 1 vanilla bean

Tiny pinch of salt

1¾ cups (420 ml) buttermilk

2 cups (288 g) assorted fresh berries

1 tsp Grand Marnier

1 tsp sugar

¼ cup (25 g) crushed gingersnap cookies

Fresh mint leaves for garnish, optional

Place the gelatin and 1 tablespoon (15 ml) of water in a medium-size bowl. Let the gelatin bloom for about 3 minutes.

Place the cream, sugar, vanilla bean seeds, and salt in a saucepan. Bring almost to a boil, then remove from the heat and let the cream steep for about 10 minutes. Pour into the bowl with the bloomed gelatin, add the buttermilk, and stir.

Strain the cream mixture, then divide among 4 bowls or ramekins. Chill in the refrigerator for about 45 to 50 minutes or until set.

Meanwhile, mix together the berries, Grand Marnier, and sugar. Allow to macerate until ready to serve.

To serve, top each panna cotta with some of the berries, the berry liquid, and the crushed gingersnaps. Garnish with mint from your garden if you wish.

JODY ADAMS

Boston, Massachusetts

Chef/co-owner of TRADE, Saloniki, and Porto; board member of Partners in Health; co-author of the cooking blog, The Garum Factory

CHEF SAYS

Items I always keep on hand for unexpected guests are . . .

Cashews, sparkling wine, really good olive oil, bottarga (salted, cured roe, typically of gray mullet or tuna), and spaghetti. And good dark chocolate, too.

When hosting a quick get-together, never overlook . . .

Setting a beautiful table with candles.

My secret tip for successful last-minute entertaining is . . .

Make what you know and keep it simple.

One fun fact few people know about me is that . . .

I love to dance.

MENU

Seared Loin Lamb Chops with Aleppo

Roasted Eggplant with Harissa

Cracked Wheat

Garlic Yogurt

Herb Salad

Ricotta with Cinnamon, Honey & Orange

CHEF'S PAIRING

A classic Chianti

With the dessert, a small glass of Malvasia

CHEF'S PLAYLIST

African music, in particular the artist Dobet Gnahoré

MAJOR KUDOS

James Beard award for "Best Chef: Northeast"; "Best New Chef" award from *Food & Wine*; four stars from the *Boston Globe*; "Humanitarian of the Year" award from Share Our Strength; inductee into the Massachusetts Hospitality Hall of Fame; contestant on season two of Bravo's *Top Chef Masters*; five-time rider in the Pan Mass Challenge

HER STORY

As an anthropology major, Jody always appreciated cultural themes. As a renowned chef who ran the award-winning restaurant Rialto for over twenty years, she does the same.

Having traveled the world over and sampled hospitality from Guatemala to Morocco and Portugal to Holland, when cooking at home, Jody likes to infuse her dishes with international flavors using locally sourced ingredients.

This meal, inspired by the eastern Mediterranean, is no exception.

For instance, notice her use of such exotic ingredients as Aleppo pepper and harissa. We're all in for a real treat.

"I have served this menu many times, and it's always a hit," says Jody. "To me, lamb means 'special,' and it stands up to the big, bold flavors I love. It's a menu you can make any time of year."

And if you happen to find yourself hesitating for even a nanosecond because of the number of dishes, rest assured they're all super quick and extra easy to prepare.

"Only two of the elements are actually cooked," explains Jody. "The rest are thrown together."

What could be simpler?

Seared Loin Lamb Chops with Aleppo

SERVES 4

These elegant lamb chops could not be any easier to prepare if you tried. However, what really takes them over the top is the Aleppo pepper. Used predominantly in Middle Eastern cuisine, it is fairly mild, with fruity, raisin-like undertones. But then its heat starts building slowly, ending with a substantial kick. Take our advice—leave your regular black pepper behind.

8 (5-oz [140-g]) loin lamb chops

Kosher salt

Aleppo pepper (can substitute a mixture of black pepper and sweet paprika)

2 tbsp (30 ml) vegetable oil

1 lemon, cut into wedges

Set a large sauté pan or stove-top grill pan over medium-high heat.

Season the lamb with salt and Aleppo pepper. Brush with the oil. Cook the chops to medium rare, about 5 to 7 minutes per side.

Serve 2 chops per person, with the lemon wedges.

Roasted Eggplant with Harissa

SERVES 4

Because eggplant is such a mild-tasting vegetable, it really allows the kick of the harissa to take it to the next level. This fiery-hot chili pepper paste from Tunisia can be found in cans and jars in Middle Eastern markets.

1 eggplant, about 1 lb (450 g)

Kosher salt

Freshly ground black pepper

2 tbsp (30 ml) extra virgin olive oil

1–2 tbsp (16–32 g) harissa, depending on the heat of the harissa and your taste

1 cup (245 g) tomato sauce

Preheat the oven to 500°F (260°C).

Cut the eggplant crosswise into ¾-inch (19-mm) slices. Season with salt and pepper to taste and brush with the oil. Set the slices on a baking sheet in a single layer and bake until golden brown and tender, about 10 to 12 minutes.

Meanwhile, mix the harissa with the tomato sauce in a bowl.

Move the eggplant slices into the center of the baking sheet so they touch, or place them in a baking dish. Spoon the tomato sauce over the eggplant and bake until bubbling, about 2 minutes.

Cracked Wheat

This is such an easy dish, and such a delicious addition to any meal! This recipe's main star is bulgur, made from the groats of durum wheat. Recognized as a whole grain by the USDA, it boasts a tender, chewy texture and offers a high nutritional value. What's not to love about it?

1 cup (140 g) bulgur

½ tsp ground cumin

½ tsp ground fennel seed

1 tsp ground coriander

½ tsp kosher salt

1½ cups (360 ml) boiling water

2 tbsp (30 ml) extra virgin olive oil

Toss the bulgur in a bowl with the spices and salt. Pour the boiling water over the bulgur, then cover with plastic wrap and let stand until the water has been absorbed, about 30 minutes.

Add the oil and fluff with a fork.

*See photo on page 193.

Garlic Yogurt

SERVES 4

"Garlic yogurt has a magical flavor and is wildly simple," says Jody. "It's just four simple ingredients, and it's something I have in my fridge all the time. I eat it on just about everything." Isn't it time you gave it a try?

1 cup (245 g) full-fat Greek yogurt

1 large clove garlic, peeled

Salt

Freshly ground pepper

Put the yogurt into a bowl. Grate the garlic with a microplane into the yogurt. Season with salt and pepper to taste and stir, then cover and refrigerate until needed.

*See photo on page 190.

Herb Salad

SERVES 4

"This salad can be made with any combination of herbs and greens that work together and that you have on hand," explains Jody. In other words, mix and match to your heart's content. Now, that's simple enough!

1 tbsp (3 g) minced fresh chives

¼ cup (10 g) fresh flat-leaf parsley leaves

¼ cup (10 g) fresh mint leaves

2 tbsp (5 g) fresh celery leaves

2 tbsp (5 g) fresh oregano leaves

1 cup (35 g) fresh watercress leaves

Extra virgin olive oil, for drizzling

1 lemon

Sea salt, to taste

Freshly ground black pepper, to taste

Mix the first six ingredients together. Drizzle with the oil and a squeeze of lemon juice, then season with salt and pepper and toss.

*See photo on page 193.

Ricotta with Cinnamon, Honey & Orange

SERVES 4

It might surprise you to discover a dessert this simple and quick is also so amazingly delicious. It's a treat Jody still remembers from her trip to Sardinia. However, there's one secret ingredient that is key: good ricotta. We mean, *really* good ricotta. Ideally, sheep's milk ricotta. It'll make all the difference in the world.

1 lb (450 g) high-quality, dry, hand-packed ricotta, divided

1 stick cinnamon

4 tbsp (85 g) honey, or to taste, divided

Zested strips from half a scrubbed orange

Crisp, thin cookies or tuiles, for serving

Put ½ cup (114 g) of the ricotta into each of 4 bowls. Run the cinnamon stick over a fine microplane to create a generous dusting over the ricotta. Drizzle with a heaping tablespoon (21 g) of honey (or more, if you prefer) and top with a few strips of orange zest. Serve with the crisp cookies.

CHEF'S TIP

I recommend the following agenda to help prepare this meal as efficiently as possible:

1. Preheat oven to 500°F (260°C).

2. Preheat grill.

3. Bring water to a boil.

4. Cut eggplant and put in oven.

5. Mix bulgur and spices with water.

6. Mix tomato sauce with harissa.

7. Grill lamb.

8. Finish eggplant with tomato sauce.

9. Make garlic yogurt.

10. Make herb salad.

11. Cut lemon.

12. Make dessert.

ZOI ANTONITSAS

Seattle, Washington

Consulting Chef at Omega Ouzeri

CHEF SAYS

Items I always keep on hand for unexpected guests are . . .

Champagne, dried pasta, anchovies/tinned sardines, yogurt, and ground lamb (usually in the freezer).

When hosting a quick get-together, never overlook . . .

Having plenty of wine and snacks. The rest is gravy.

My secret tip for successful last-minute entertaining is . . .

Try not to stress. The best parties are when the hosts and the guests are having a great time. Don't spend too much time fussing in the kitchen. Keep it simple so you can be part of the party.

One fun fact few people know about me is that . . .

Growing up, my grandparents were very good friends with Mr. and Mrs. Wilson, who happened to be the parents of Ann and Nancy Wilson of the '80s–present legendary rock band Heart! I have all their albums on vinyl, signed with love from the sisters. I still absolutely love them and consider them one of the best bands of my lifetime. And . . . they still rock it!

MENU

Chicken Legs with Greek Honey & Aleppo Chili

Skordalia

Spiced Hot Chocolate

CHEF'S PAIRING

Sparkling wine of any good quality, preferably Champagne, white and rosé

CHEF'S PLAYLIST

Hip-hop (Digable Planets, Guru, The Pharcyde, and Little Dragon)

MAJOR KUDOS

Named a *Food & Wine* "Best New Chef"; named one of the "Best New Restaurants" and "The Hot 10" by *Bon Appétit*; named one of the "Top 25 Best New Restaurants in America" by *GQ*; was a contestant on Bravo's *Top Chef*

HER STORY

She started out in the business slowly. It began with her fascination as a kid with the PBS series *Great Chefs*. (She would race home after school to catch an episode.) Her first job at sixteen was as a prep cook. And she would continue to work at various kitchens as a teen. But quite truthfully, her real ambition back then was to become an artist. So she enrolled in art school.

At some point, Zoi changed her mind and dropped out. She backpacked across Europe, then landed in San Francisco, where she trained under Chef Loretta Keller. She eventually worked her way back to her hometown of Seattle, marking the beginning of a new chapter in her life: that of an award-winning chef.

"I chose this meal because I adore these particular ingredients and bold, delicious flavors," says Zoi. "It's easy to make, and it'll impress your friends because of its beautiful simplicity. Plus, I love to grill, even on a cold day in Seattle. I think cooking outside with fire is by far the most delicious way to cook. So get out there, light a fire, and get grilling!"

Chicken Legs with Greek Honey & Aleppo Chili

SERVES 4

The sweet-and-tangy mixture Zoi uses to marinate her chicken includes one secret ingredient: Aleppo pepper (a Turkish crushed chili). It has perfectly balanced heat and amazing flavor, best described as rich, sweet, and almost smoky. And since it's chunkier than paprika, the flavor has more "pop." Zoi gives us dual instructions below, depending on whether you'd rather grill or roast. Either way, the result is phenomenal.

⅓ cup (112 g) honey, preferably Attiki's Greek Forest

⅓ cup (80 ml) red wine vinegar, preferably Greek

2 tbsp (32 g) kosher salt

6 cloves garlic, microplaned or finely minced

½ cup (120 ml) extra virgin olive oil, preferably Greek Kalamata

3 tbsp (18 g) Aleppo pepper (can substitute a mixture of black pepper and sweet paprika)

1 tbsp (3 g) finely chopped fresh rosemary

1 tbsp (2 g) finely chopped fresh thyme

4 whole chicken legs (legs separated from thighs)

1 tbsp (16 g) finishing salt, preferably Jacobsen or Maldon flake sea salt

In a large bowl, combine the honey and red wine vinegar. Whisk well to dissolve the honey. Add the salt, garlic, olive oil, Aleppo pepper, rosemary, and thyme and mix well. Remove 2 tablespoons (30 ml) of the marinade to a small bowl and refrigerate.

Add the chicken to the remaining marinade and toss well to coat. Cover and refrigerate for about 30 minutes.

If grilling, preheat the grill on medium heat. If roasting, preheat the oven to 400°F (204°C).

When ready to cook, remove the chicken from the marinade and place on a wire rack over a baking tray to allow any excess marinade to drip off.

If grilling, place the chicken, skin side up, on the grill but not directly over the flame and cook for 15 minutes. Turn skin side down and grill, still not over the flame, for 10 more minutes, or until the juices run clear. Because of the honey in the marinade, the skin will burn if placed over a direct flame, so be careful.

If roasting, place the chicken skin side up on a foil-lined sheet pan for 40 minutes, or until the juices run clear.

To serve, place the chicken on a platter, drizzle with the reserved 2 tablespoons (30 ml) of marinade, and season with the finishing salt.

Skordalia

Skordalia, one of the most traditional Greek dishes, is often described as garlic mashed potatoes. It's simple to make, requires just a few everyday ingredients, and is crazy delicious. (Bonus: It's vegan, too!)

4 russet potatoes, peeled and cut into small cubes

2 tbsp (32 g) salt

6 cloves garlic, microplaned or very finely minced

Juice of 2 lemons

¾ cup (180 ml) extra virgin olive oil, preferably Greek Kalamata

⅓ cup (80 ml) Champagne (can substitute white wine vinegar)

1 tbsp (16 g) kosher salt

Place the potatoes in a pot and cover with cold water and salt. Cook on medium-high heat, making sure that the potatoes never boil but that they cook in a gentle simmer until tender when pierced with a knife, about 20 minutes.

Once the potatoes are cooked, drain immediately. Quickly put them through a ricer or smash them in a bowl while they are still piping hot. If the potatoes cool, they will become clumpy and gummy.

Add the garlic, lemon juice, olive oil, Champagne, and salt. For a silkier consistency, pass through a fine-mesh strainer. Serve slightly warm or at room temperature.

*See photo on page 198.

Spiced Hot Chocolate

What a wonderful way to end this fabulous meal! But rest assured that this is no ordinary hot chocolate. The addition of Urfa biber really makes all the difference. This luscious chili flake from Turkey has an earthy, smoky edge that hints at chocolate and tobacco and offers a mild heat. Just imagine what it adds to an otherwise-straight chocolate dessert beverage. Be prepared to be amazed! Please note: The cocoa mix will yield much more than is called for to make the hot chocolate. Store the rest in an airtight container for many more hot chocolates to come!

FOR THE COCOA MIX

1 cup plus 2 tbsp (226 g) sugar

1 cup (80 g) cocoa powder

½ tsp ground cinnamon

½ tsp ground cayenne pepper

¼ tsp Urfa biber (can substitute chili powder)

¼ tsp ground allspice

Pinch of ground cloves

FOR THE HOT CHOCOLATE

3 cups (720 ml) half-and-half

½ cup (120 ml) heavy whipping cream, whipped, for garnish

Sea salt flakes, for sprinkling

To prepare the cocoa mix, whisk together the sugar, cocoa powder, cinnamon, cayenne, Urfa biber, allspice, and cloves in a medium-size bowl. Set aside.

To prepare the hot chocolate, combine ¼ cup (60 g) of the cocoa mix with the half-and-half in a heavy-bottomed saucepot. Cook on low heat, stirring frequently, for 20 minutes, or until thick. Pour evenly into 4 mugs. Serve each with a generous dollop of the unsweetened whipped cream and a pinch of sea salt flakes on top.

NYESHA J. ARRINGTON

Los Angeles, California

Chef/partner of LEONA

MENU

Strawberry Brown Butter Streusel Cake

CHEF'S PAIRING

Blood orange mimosa

CHEF'S PLAYLIST

Reggae (specifically "I Love My Life" by Demarco)

MAJOR KUDOS

"Chef of the Year" award from Los Angeles Eater; named a "Rising Star" by Angeleno; winner of Food Network's *Chef Hunter*; winner of Esquire Network's *Knife Fight*; contestant on Bravo's *Top Chef: Texas*; guest judge on Esquire Network's *Knife Fight*; recognized by Zagat as one of "30 Under 30: LA's Hottest Up-and-Comers"

HER STORY

What six-year-old do you know who loves to play restaurant? I mean, for real. With friends who are invited over to actually cook—with adult supervision, of course.

That's exactly what happened with Nyesha. And she's been happily "playing" restaurant ever since!

As a graduate of the culinary program at the Art Institute of California–Los Angeles, Nyesha paid her dues all over the country, from Hawaii, Santa Monica, and Las Vegas to Orlando and the Virgin Islands. (She even spent time on tour with Stevie Wonder as his personal chef!) All the while, she was honing the skills her Korean grandmother taught her.

"I chose this particular recipe because my father used to make it for me when I was a kid," says Nyesha. "It brings me fond memories. Plus, I love to use items I can get from the farmers' market, and strawberries are so delicious during the summer season! Gaviota strawberries are my favorite."

Nyesha adds, "This recipe is also perfect for last-minute entertaining because the simplicity of the preparation doesn't sacrifice the depth of the flavor."

We can't wait to try it!

Strawberry Brown Butter Streusel Cake

SERVES 9

What a wonderful, luscious dessert to serve your guests for an impromptu visit or quaint afternoon tea! The secret is the brown butter, which lends a rich, complex, and nutty flavor, making it exponentially even more amazing. And it's not overly sweet either. With juicy, sun-kissed, just-picked strawberries thrown into the mix, it's just perfect—and beautiful, too.

FOR THE CAKE

4 oz (115 g, 1 stick) unsalted butter, plus additional for greasing

4½ cups (563 g) all-purpose flour

2¼ cups (450 g) sugar

6 tbsp (90 g) baking powder

Pinch of salt

2¼ cups (540 ml) whole milk

3 large eggs

¼ tsp pure vanilla extract

6 cups (865 g) fresh strawberries, preferably the Gaviota variety, diced, plus additional for garnish, optional

FOR THE STREUSEL TOPPING

1½ cups (330 g) brown sugar, firmly packed

1 cup (125 g) all-purpose flour

3 pinches of salt

4 oz (115 g, 1 stick) plus 1 tbsp (16 g) unsalted butter, cut into ½-inch (12-mm) slices, at room temperature

Freshly whipped cream, for garnish, optional

Preheat the oven to 350°F (177°C). Lightly grease a 9 x 9–inch (23 x 23–cm) baking pan.

To brown the butter, place the butter for the cake in a pan with a light-colored bottom. Melt over medium heat, swirling occasionally. As the butter melts, it will begin to foam, and the color will progress from lemony yellow to golden tan to, finally, toasty brown. Once you smell that nutty aroma, remove from the heat and transfer to a heatproof bowl to cool. Straining is optional.

To make the cake, sift together the flour, sugar, baking powder, and salt into one bowl. In the bowl of a stand mixer, using the paddle attachment, beat together the milk, eggs, and vanilla, then beat in the cooled brown butter.

Add the flour mixture gradually to the egg-butter mixture, beating after each addition on low speed. Slowly, as the paddle continues to fold the mixture, add the diced strawberries. When thoroughly incorporated, spoon the batter into the prepared baking pan.

Place the pan in the oven and set the timer for 35 minutes.

Meanwhile, to make the streusel topping, combine the brown sugar, flour, salt, and butter slices in the bowl of a food processor and pulse until crumbly, or combine the ingredients in a bowl and mix to crumbliness using a pastry blender or two knives.

When 35 minutes is up, remove the pan from the oven and spread the streusel topping evenly over the cake. Bake for an additional 15 minutes, or until a toothpick inserted in the center comes out clean and the topping is light golden brown.

Remove from the oven and allow to cool on a wire rack before serving. If desired, garnish with whipped cream and strawberries.

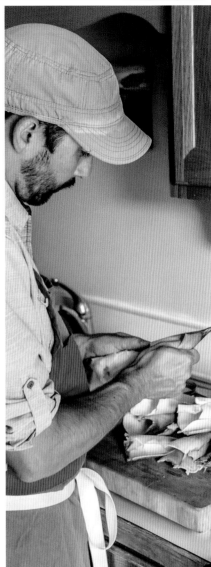

CLARK BARLOWE

Charlotte, North Carolina

Chef/owner of Heirloom; adjunct professor at the Art Institutes in Charlotte; founding member of the Mecklenburg Community Food Health Coalition

CHEF SAYS

Items I always keep on hand for unexpected guests are . . .

Pickles (any and all kinds), good bread, cheese, fish sauce (adds a quick umami hit with almost no work), and cured pork products (quick and always a crowd pleaser).

When hosting a quick get-together, never overlook . . .

Having a variety of dishes, as well as dishes that appeal to a large demographic and a variety of allergies and dietary restrictions. These are always a surprise, but if you plan the food accordingly, it makes dealing with them when they arise much easier.

My secret tip for successful last-minute entertaining is . . .

Have things prepared that you are confident with and like to talk about. This makes the multitasking that often happens with dinner parties much more comfortable.

One fun fact few people know about me is that . . .

I'm an avid beekeeper. We have ten hives on the roof of the restaurant that I was working on for years prior to our opening. I love the relationship I've formed with the bees and think this is an aspect of our pantry that elevates our food unconsciously.

MENU

Seasonal Salad with Honey Vinaigrette

Spaghetti Squash Carbonara

Pan-Roasted Duck Breast

Pickled Bamboo

CHEF'S PAIRING

Jones von Drehle Petite Manseng for a white offering

Jones von Drehle Malbec or Petite Verdot for a red offering

CHEF'S PLAYLIST

Mipso, Avett Brothers

MAJOR KUDOS

Contestant on Food Network's *Chopped* and *Beat Bobby Flay*; named one of the "100 Best Restaurants in the Country for Foodies" by Opentable

HIS STORY

There's no two ways about it. Clark is the poster child for North Carolina! In fact, this proud chef oozes all things North Carolina, including every element in this meal—from ingredients to beverage to even music.

It's no surprise, then, that Clark actually grew up in North Carolina, just down the road from a farm his family's worked on for seven generations! He studied at Johnson and Wales University in Charlotte. He worked at Mama Ricotta's down the street. And then he did the unthinkable. He left the state.

However . . . he left to join, not one, but two of the most famous restaurants in the world: The French Laundry in California's Napa Valley and El Bulli in Roses, Spain.

Finally, armed with an impressive pedigree, Clark returned home and fulfilled his lifelong dream of opening a local farm-to-fork restaurant before he was thirty.

"When I'm entertaining at home," says Clark, "I like to keep it simple and let the flavors of what I'm working with shine through. I also love for my food to tell a story, and this meal is no exception. It combines some interesting techniques and ingredients with skills that are easily executable and still impressive. In my opinion, it's the perfect short-notice dinner party preparation."

Seasonal Salad with Honey Vinaigrette

SERVES 6 TO 8

"When I think of salad, I think of several components rather than a recipe," explains Clark. "This makes it easy to adjust no matter what you have in the pantry. For instance, this simple vinaigrette can be adjusted to add different flavors (replace the honey with another flavor you prefer), and it works with a variety of fresh salads. I always have a salad on my table when guests come over. It starts the meal off on the right foot and awakens everyone's palate."

FOR THE HONEY VINAIGRETTE

1½ cups (225 g) minced shallots

¾ cup (180 ml) sherry vinegar (can substitute red wine vinegar)

3 tbsp (63 g) local honey

1½ tsp (4 g) chopped fresh thyme

1 tbsp (16 g) honey mustard, preferably Lusty Monk brand

½ cup (120 ml) neutral oil (canola, grapeseed, etc.)

¼ cup (60 ml) olive oil

Salt, to taste

Freshly ground black pepper, to taste

FOR THE GREENS

Varies by season, but could include lettuce, mustard greens, kale, Asian greens, or even baby root vegetable tops

FOR THE CRUNCH ELEMENT

Could include nuts, croutons, roasted vegetables, etc.

FOR THE FATTY ELEMENT

Could include cheese, hard-boiled egg, olives, etc.

FOR THE GARNISHES

Something to round out the salad and provide a contrasting or complementary flavor. Could include radishes, tomatoes, carrots, cucumbers, squash, or onions, depending on availability and personal preference.

To make the honey vinaigrette, place the minced shallots in a medium-size bowl. Add the sherry vinegar and honey to cover. Stir together. Allow to macerate for at least 15 minutes. Add the thyme and mustard. Whisk vigorously to combine. While still whisking, slowly drizzle in both the neutral oil and the olive oil. Season with salt and pepper. This will keep for up to 1 week in the refrigerator, although it's best enjoyed the day of preparation.

To assemble the salad, choose one or more ingredients from each of the greens, crunch element, and fatty element suggestions. Drizzle with the vinaigrette. Top with one or more ingredients from the garnishes suggestions. Toss at the table.

CHEF'S TIP
If you like your vinaigrette more acidic, simply add more vinegar. For less acidic, add more neutral oil. Either way, always adjust while tasting. And if the vinaigrette begins to separate at any time, simply whisk in a small amount of mustard to re-form the emulsification.

Spaghetti Squash Carbonara

SERVES 6 TO 8

"I think everyone sees spaghetti squash at the market and is intimidated by it," admits Clark. "Truthfully, with the recent explosion of allergies and dietary restrictions, spaghetti squash is a great dish to prepare for your guests because you get the look and mouthfeel of pasta without the gluten."

2 spaghetti squashes

2 cups (480 ml) vegetable stock

6 cloves garlic, peeled

1 cup (225 g) diced bacon

2 cups (480 ml) heavy cream

1 cup (151 g) English peas

2 egg yolks

Salt, to taste

Freshly ground black pepper, to taste

Cut the top and bottom off both squashes so they stand upright. Split each lengthwise and remove the seeds. (You can toast the seeds—see page 457—for a later snack or discard.)

Place all 4 squash halves cut side down in a microwaveable container. Add the stock and garlic and cover with plastic wrap, folding the wrap back on one edge of the container to allow steam to vent. Microwave on high for about 15 to 25 minutes until the squashes are tender, stopping to check for doneness after 15 minutes. Remove the container with the squashes from the microwave. Discard the stock and garlic and allow the squashes to cool.

Holding each squash half lengthwise, use a fork to remove the flesh. It should come out in strands similar in appearance to pasta. Set the strands aside in a bowl, discarding the skins.

Set a large sauté pan over medium heat and add the bacon. Cook until crispy and the fat is rendered out, about 6 to 7 minutes. Reduce the heat to medium-low and add the cooked spaghetti squash, followed quickly by the cream. Without stirring, allow the cream to reduce slightly, about 1 minute. Add the peas and remove from the heat. Add the egg yolks slowly, stirring constantly, so the egg yolks cook and the sauce is emulsified. Season with salt and lots of pepper and serve hot.

Pan-Roasted Duck Breast

SERVES 6 TO 8

"I love duck," admits Clark. "It's so versatile and the flavor is so complex, it's by far my favorite protein." He goes on to add, "Preparing a duck breast is very simple. Just think low and slow and you're halfway there. Start this breast as soon as you know your guests are on their way, and you'll be carving right before they arrive—or for the showman, once they've arrived!" And for those of you who are super ambitious and have extra time on your hands, try Clark's Duck Jus. It's outrageously decadent!

3 whole duck breasts

Salt, to taste

Freshly ground black pepper, to taste

1 tsp rendered duck fat (can substitute butter)

Your favorite steak sauce, for serving (can substitute Duck Jus, recipe follows)

Score the fat side of the duck breasts in a crisscross pattern with shallow slices. Season with salt and pepper. Place in a room-temperature sauté pan, fat side down. Add the duck fat. Cook on medium-low heat, allowing the fat to slowly render out of the breasts. The best way to think about cooking a duck breast is that you are cooking a steak with a slab of bacon on top. You want the bacon to be crispy and not burned, and you also want the breast to be cooked medium at the thickest part.

Allow the breast to cook fat side down, checking often to spoon off the excess fat. Once the skin is golden brown and crispy, about 15 minutes, roll the breasts over and cook quickly on the flesh side, about 1 to 1½ minutes.

Remove the breasts and allow to rest at least 2 to 3 minutes on a plate lined with paper towels, skin side up so it stays crispy. Cut into thin slices. Serve about a half breast per guest with steak sauce.

Bonus Recipe: Duck Jus
MAKES ABOUT 2 CUPS (1 PINT)

1 tbsp plus 1 tsp (20 g) butter

3 shallots, sliced

10 cloves garlic, sliced

8⅓ cups (2 L) red burgundy wine

2 fresh thyme sprigs

1 tbsp (15 g) black peppercorns

4¼ qt (4 L) duck stock (can substitute chicken stock)

Salt, to taste

Melt the butter in a large pot. Add the sliced shallots and garlic. Sweat for about 5 minutes. Add the wine, thyme, and peppercorns. Reduce to about 1 cup (240 ml). Add the stock and reduce to about 2 cups (480 ml). Strain the jus through a fine-mesh strainer. Season with salt.

Pickled Bamboo

MAKES 2 QT (1.9 L)

"I would help harvest bamboo as a kid every summer," recalls Clark. "It was something I looked forward to all year. What kid wouldn't? You get to swing a knife around and cut down these invasive plants, all just to make pickles. This pickling solution and method can actually be used for a variety of veggies—from tomatoes, to okra, to green beans. So, go ahead, pickle and eat right then, or save in the refrigerator for a treat year 'round." Chef's note: Bamboo shoots can be found in most Asian markets. You can also substitute green beans with the exact same preparation. They would then be called "Southern Dilly Beans."

2½ lb (1.1 kg, 5 to 6) fresh, tender bamboo shoots (can substitute 1½ lb [680 g] green beans)

1 tbsp (15 g) red chili flakes (crushed red pepper)

4 cloves garlic, peeled

1 bunch fresh dill

2 cups (480 ml) white wine vinegar

1¾ cups (420 ml) water

4 tbsp (64 g) kosher salt

Carefully strip the outer husk of each bamboo shoot, similar to peeling an ear of corn. Working quickly, slice into rings (you should have about 8 cups [25 kg]). Bamboo begins to harden when it's exposed to air, so it's easier to immediately slice each section as it's peeled. While slicing, if you notice a dull sound, discard the bamboo since it will be too tough for pickling.

Prepare a large bowl of ice water and set aside.

After all the bamboo is sliced, place in a large stockpot, cover with water, and bring to a gentle boil. Continue to cook for 10 minutes, or until tender and the bamboo breaks easily. Drain and immediately place the bamboo in the ice water bath.

Place the chilled bamboo rings, red chili flakes, garlic, and dill into any large plastic or glass container with a lid. Set aside.

To make the pickling solution, place the vinegar, water, and salt into a large pot over high heat. Continue stirring until the salt dissolves. Bring to a boil, then pour into the container of bamboo. Secure the lid and refrigerate. It will keep for months in the refrigerator.

JOEY BEATO

Chicago, Illinois

Executive chef/partner of Community Tavern and Cochinita Taco Co.

CHEF SAYS

Items I always keep on hand for unexpected guests are . . .

Beer, dry pasta, some sort of sauce in the freezer, cheese, and Wheat Thins. Plus rice and canned goods that can quickly get turned into something good.

When hosting a quick get-together, never overlook . . .

Having the cocktails ready when people show up.

My secret tip for successful last-minute entertaining is . . .

Stay calm. Last-minute planning can get stressful. Keep calm, make a list, and abide by the list.

One fun fact few people know about me is that . . .

I was a gymnast in high school.

MENU

Scallion Pancakes with a Fried Egg & Zucchini-Carrot Slaw

Roast Pork Tenderloin with Chinese Mustard Sauce & Broccoli Rabe

Danny's Fried Rice

CHEF'S PAIRING

An Alsatian Pinot Gris

CHEF'S PLAYLIST

Hail Mega Boys by J. Roddy Walston and the Business

MAJOR KUDOS

Zagat's "30 Under 30" honoree; *Chicago Magazine*'s "Best New Restaurants" and "Chefs You Should Know" awards

HIS STORY

Joey likes to eat breakfast—for dinner. At least that's how it was when he was growing up in Park Ridge, Illinois.

During high school, he taught himself to cook, specializing in omelets. He decided cooking really was his thing, so he got his first job at a pizzeria (although he quit when the owner threw a pizza at him). He then enrolled at Le Cordon Bleu in Chicago.

Several high-level stints later—including one as sous chef at Momofuku Má Pêche in New York—he found himself opening his own place with a partner. And it's right in his new Windy City neighborhood: Portage Park.

"This meal is quick, interesting, and easy to produce," says Joey. "I especially like cooking Asian food for guests because it's an easy way to wow them with some things they're not used to. Plus, I have almost all the ingredients I need stocked at home. Any leftovers are great for the next day."

You mean, if there are any leftovers!

Scallion Pancakes with a Fried Egg & Zucchini-Carrot Slaw

SERVES 4

Sure, we all enjoy breakfast pancakes slathered in maple syrup. But savory pancakes? Ahhh, now that's an interesting concept! Joey makes his batter with flour, eggs, and milk—as expected. But then he also adds in coconut milk, fish sauce, sambal (a chili garlic paste found in most grocery stores), and vodka, of all things. The result, trust us, is an appetizer no one is soon to forget!

8 large eggs, divided

¼ cup (60 ml) vodka

¼ cup (60 ml) sambal

2½ cups (200 ml) whole milk

½ cup (120 ml) coconut milk

¼ cup (60 ml) fish sauce

4 cups (500 g) all-purpose flour

¼ cup (50 g) sugar

2 tbsp plus 2 tsp (40 g) baking powder

2 bunches scallions, thinly sliced

2 cups (290 g) julienned zucchini

2 cups (290 g) julienned carrots

Olive oil, for tossing

Fresh lime juice, for tossing

Kosher salt, to taste

1 tbsp (14 g) butter

In a small bowl, whisk together 4 of the eggs, the vodka, sambal, milk, coconut milk, and fish sauce to combine. In another, larger bowl, mix together the flour, sugar, and baking powder. Add the wet ingredients to the flour mixture, and stir slowly until just combined. Then fold in the scallions. Do not overmix; some lumps are okay. Let rest for a few minutes.

In the meantime, toss the zucchini and carrots in a bowl with a little olive oil and a bit of lime juice just enough to coat. Season with salt. Set aside.

Preheat a large nonstick sauté pan or griddle on medium heat. Ladle on batter for 2 pancakes, using about ¼ cup (60 ml) of batter for each pancake. Cook until golden brown on one side. Flip, reduce the heat to low, and cook for about 2 more minutes, or until the pancakes are golden brown on both sides. Remove from the pan and keep warm. Repeat.

Wipe the pan clean, then preheat again on medium heat. Add the butter and lightly fry the remaining 4 eggs until they are done, once over easy.

To serve, place 1 pancake on each of 4 plates. Add an egg on top and place the zucchini-carrot slaw on the side. Serve warm.

Roast Pork Tenderloin with Chinese Mustard Sauce & Broccoli Rabe

SERVES 4

This company-worthy entrée will be the talk of the town once your guests get a taste of it. Tender, succulent pork tenderloin is accompanied by fork-tender broccoli rabe enveloped in a tangy mustard sauce. The contrast is divine. The taste, equally so.

1 cup plus 2 tbsp (270 ml) canola oil, divided

2 limes, zested and juiced

½ cup (20 g) chopped fresh cilantro

1 tbsp (7 g) minced fresh ginger

2 cloves garlic, minced

2 lb (907 g) pork tenderloin

1 lb (450 g) broccoli rabe (broccoli raab, broccoli rape, or rapini)

1 cup (240 g) crème fraîche

¾ cup (187 g) Chinese mustard

¼ cup (62 g) Dijon mustard

2 tbsp (42 g) honey

2 tsp (5 g) mustard powder

Salt, to taste

2 cups (480 ml) chicken stock

4 oz (115 g, 1 stick) cold butter, cut into small pieces

Preheat the oven to 350°F (177°C).

In a large bowl, combine the 1 cup (240 ml) of oil, lime juice and lime zest, cilantro, ginger, and garlic. Add the pork tenderloin to submerge and marinate while you prepare the rest.

Have ready a bowl of ice water. Bring salted water to boil in a saucepan and add the broccoli rabe. Blanch for 20 seconds, then drain and shock in the ice bath. Drain again and set aside.

In a small bowl, mix together the crème fraîche, Chinese mustard, Dijon mustard, honey, mustard powder, and salt to taste. Set aside.

Set a large cast-iron pan or ovenproof skillet over medium heat. When hot, add the remaining 2 tablespoons (30 ml) of oil. Sear the drained pork on one side for 3½ minutes. Flip and sear the other side for 1 more minute. Place in the oven and bake for 12 minutes if you want your pork a little on the medium side (it's okay!) or for 19 minutes if you prefer it cooked all the way through.

Meanwhile, place the chicken stock in a large pot and bring to a boil on high heat. Add the butter and whisk until combined, then whisk in the mustard mixture.

Divide the broccoli rabe evenly among 4 plates. Drizzle with the mustard sauce. Slice your tenderloin thin and set it on top of the broccoli rabe, dividing evenly. Serve immediately.

Danny's Fried Rice

SERVES 4

This delicious side dish is named after one of Joey's cooks (last name withheld to protect the innocent). "Danny makes this fried rice for our staff meals," explains Joey, "and it's absolutely amazing." If Joey's wowed by it, you can be sure your guests will be, too.

1 cup (185 g) uncooked jasmine rice

1 tbsp (14 g) butter

2 large eggs, lightly beaten

1 tbsp (15 ml) canola oil

1 shallot, thinly sliced

1 tbsp (7 g) minced fresh ginger

4 cloves garlic, minced

8 oz (224 g) mushrooms (any), thinly sliced

½ cup (25 g) julienned carrots

2 tbsp (30 ml) good-quality soy sauce

2 tsp (10 ml) good-quality toasted sesame oil

1 tbsp (15 ml) sambal

2 tsp (10 ml) fish sauce

½ cup (20 g) chopped fresh cilantro, for garnish

Prepare the jasmine rice according to instructions on the box. Set aside.

Set a large sauté pan over medium heat. Add the butter. Pour the eggs in and cook slowly, while stirring continuously with a spatula until set. Remove the eggs from the pan and shred into a bowl. Set aside.

Wipe the pan clean. Add the oil and heat on medium-high heat. Add the shallot, ginger, and garlic and sauté for 1 minute. Add the mushrooms, carrots, and rice and cook for another 2 minutes (keep stirring!). Add the soy sauce, sesame oil, sambal, and fish sauce, then remove from the heat and stir to combine. Fold in the cooked eggs and place in a large bowl. Garnish with the cilantro to serve.

EMMA BENGTSSON

New York, New York

Executive chef of Aquavit (New York and London)

CHEF SAYS

Items I always keep on hand for unexpected guests are . . .

Wine, coffee, chocolate, cheese, and marmalade. Those will tide you over in almost any situation.

When hosting a quick get-together, never overlook . . .

Pouring yourself a glass of wine before anyone arrives. No one will be able to enjoy the beautiful meal if the host isn't relaxed and having fun, too.

My secret tip for successful last-minute entertaining is . . .

Don't stress too much and overcomplicate things. Remember that they are there because they want to see you. Flavor is more important than fancy ingredients.

One fun fact few people know about me is that . . .

I'm a world traveler. I love to visit different countries and experience them from a local's perspective. I try to live and eat as I would if I lived there. I always set myself to a minimum budget just to get the most out of it. So far I've visited over thirty-five countries and hope to reach forty within the next few years. It's getting harder and harder, especially since I've already done most of Europe.

MENU

Seared Cod, Potatoes, Cucumbers & Dill Mayonnaise

CHEF'S PAIRING

Sancerre white wine

CHEF'S PLAYLIST

Melissa Horn, Rebecka Törnqvist, and Lisa Ekdahl

MAJOR KUDOS

Two Michelin stars; three stars from the *New York Times*; "Best Chef" award from the *Village Voice*; finalist for the Eater "Chef of the Year" award; nomination for *Food & Wine*'s "Best New Pastry Chef" award

HER STORY

She's considered New York City's most prized and decorated female chef. (Supporting reason: She's the only woman in the city with two Michelin stars—and one of only three in the country!)

Emma didn't always strive for such fame. In fact, as a little girl growing up in a quaint fishing town on Sweden's west coast, all she wanted to do was cook with her grandmother. So it was natural that when it came time to choose a career, she opted to attend the prestigious Stockholm Hotel and Restaurant School.

After working at many of Sweden's most acclaimed and established restaurants, she was offered a pastry chef position at Aquavit in New York. She jumped at the chance. And when the position of executive chef opened up, she was the natural choice. In fact, the best choice.

"This dish, in addition to being a fast recipe for the home cook, has a lot of personal significance for me," says Emma. "Being Swedish, these flavors, which are very common in Nordic cuisine, remind me of home. I love it."

Seared Cod, Potatoes, Cucumbers & Dill Mayonnaise

SERVES 4

"The ingredients in this dish are easy to find in most grocery stores," says Emma, "plus almost everything can be prepared ahead, so you can spend more time with your guests." As to making your own mayonnaise as called for in this recipe, Emma explains, "People always ask me about it. They have this idea that it's super hard and that you have to be a chef to do it correctly. It's actually pretty simple." And super delicious.

2 tbsp (32 g) salt, plus additional to taste

2 small Persian cucumbers

12 potatoes, preferably baby, or as small as possible

3 large eggs, hard-boiled (page 456) and cooled

1 big bunch fresh dill, saving some for garnish

2 cups plus 2 tbsp (510 ml) canola oil, divided

2 large egg yolks

1 tsp Japanese mustard (can substitute any other hot mustard)

1 tsp white wine vinegar

1 tsp fresh lemon juice

4 (6-oz [168-g]) cod pieces

4 oz (115 g, 1 stick) butter

1 lemon, halved, for drizzling

CHEF'S TIP

If you'd like to achieve the foam effect as in the photo, after the cod is transferred to the serving platter, carefully mix the remaining browned butter in the skillet with a stick blender before adding the potatoes and egg whites.

Preheat the oven to 325°F (165°C).

Mix together the salt and 1 cup (240 ml) cold water. Peel the cucumbers. Cut into smaller irregular pieces. Place them in a container and pour the salt water over it and let it sit at room temperature for at least 30 minutes—or better, if you have the time, store the cucumbers, covered, in the refrigerator overnight.

Bring a pot of salted water to a boil. Add the potatoes and cook until tender, about 15 minutes. Drain and cut the potatoes in half if small, or into more pieces if larger. Set aside in a bowl.

Peel the hard-boiled eggs. Carefully separate the egg whites from the yolks, then tear the whites into smaller pieces. Add the whites to the same bowl as the boiled potatoes and set aside. Save the cooked egg yolks for another use.

Place the dill in a food processor. Add the 2 cups (480 ml) oil and mix at full speed until smooth. Press through a strainer, discarding the contents of the strainer and saving the green oil. Clean out the processor bowl and add the 2 raw egg yolks, the mustard, and vinegar. Start processing on medium speed and, in a slow pour to prevent the mixture from breaking, add the dill oil. If the mixture looks like it's about to break, you can add one or two drops of cold water and then continue adding the oil. Season with the lemon juice and salt, process briefly to mix, and set aside.

Place a cast-iron or other ovenproof skillet over medium-high heat. Add the remaining 2 tablespoons (30 ml) oil. When hot, add the cod, flat side down, and cook until golden brown on the seared side, about 5 minutes. Remove the pan from the heat and season the cod with salt. Add the butter, in pieces, to the hot pan and, using a spoon, scoop up the butter as it melts and pour it over the cod, basting for 2 to 3 minutes. Place the skillet in the oven until the inner temperature of the cod reaches 100°F (40°C), about 10 minutes. Remove from the oven and carefully transfer the cod to a serving platter and set aside.

Add the halved potatoes and egg whites to the remaining browned butter in the skillet and give them a quick heat and stir until just warm. Season with salt, then place on a platter around the cod. Use some of the dill mayonnaise to decorate the platter, reserving the remainder as an accompaniment for the cod platter. Squeeze some lemon juice over the fish and garnish with fresh dill. Drain the salt brine from the cucumbers. Transfer the cucumbers to a serving bowl and serve with the cod platter.

JONATHAN BENNETT

Cleveland, Ohio

Chef/partner of Moxie, the Restaurant and 811 Kitchen, Bar, Lounge (Cleveland), and Red, the Steakhouse (Cleveland and Beachwood, Ohio; South Beach, Florida; Indianapolis; and Pittsburgh)

CHEF SAYS

Items I always keep on hand for unexpected guests are . . .

Cheese (like Jeff's Gouda and Adams Reserve Cheddar), lots of hot sauces, ice cream (at least 3 flavors), homemade chocolate syrup (for hot chocolate, mochas, or ice cream sauce), and hot tea.

When hosting a quick get-together, never overlook . . .

Something to nibble on when guests walk through the door. Slice some cheese, and pull out a little honey and some crackers. Have them help you with that if you're tied up at the moment.

My secret tip for successful last-minute entertaining is . . .

Keep it simple. The most important thing is to enjoy your friends. You can't do that if you're fussing around with making a complicated dinner that keeps your head down over a cutting board.

One fun fact few people know about me is that . . .

The wet bar in my basement is actually a full-blown espresso bar, with a commercial machine, grinder, and under-counter fridge. I bring my wife a latte every morning. I even pour a pretty little heart on top!

MENU

Grilled Leg of Lamb Steaks

Shaved Artichoke & Tomato Salad

Chewy Brownies with Hot Fudge Sauce

CHEF'S PAIRING

La Croix (pamplemousse for me, pure for my wife)

CHEF'S PLAYLIST

Classic rock, probably Springsteen or Kansas

MAJOR KUDOS

James Beard award nominee for "Rising Star Chef"; named one of the "Best Places to Eat in America" by *Gourmet*; named one of the "Five Best Steakhouses in the U.S." by *Esquire*; named one of the "Ten Best Steakhouses in the U.S." by *Playboy*; given "Best Chef" award by *Northern Ohio Live*

HIS STORY

He grew up on a 400-acre farm in Ellerbe, North Carolina (population: 1,000). More specifically, a pig farm. With 2,500 pigs. Which clearly explains his affinity for pork. But that's another story.

When Jonathan was seven, his mother took him to a Japanese steakhouse for the very first time. He was so awestruck that the next day he set up a makeshift hibachi and prepared stir-fry for his parents and brother. That was the precise moment he knew he wanted to someday become a chef.

So, after high school Jonathan headed straight to the Culinary Institute of America. After several notable stints, he landed in Cleveland, his wife's hometown, and hasn't looked back since.

"I love to grill at home," says Jonathan. "It's no mess and really flavorful. Plus, it doesn't heat up the kitchen. As for this meal, the timing works out great. First the brownies go in the oven. While they're baking, the lamb gets its love. Then the salad. And just as the hot fudge sauce is coming off the stove, you're ready to serve the lamb. While you're eating, the brownies and sauce are cooling down and ready to eat when you are!"

Grilled Leg of Lamb Steaks

SERVES 6

"I really love leg of lamb steaks," says Jonathan. "They've got such great flavor to begin with. And being a thinner piece of meat, they cook quickly. The rub really has an impact on every bite!"

6 bone-in leg of lamb steaks

2 tbsp (30 ml) extra virgin olive oil

1 tbsp (16 g) kosher salt

1 tbsp (6 g) fennel seeds

6 cloves garlic, crushed

2 tsp (4 g) freshly ground black pepper

1 tsp guajillo chile flakes, coarsely ground (can substitute ¼ tsp crushed red pepper)

Preheat your grill as hot as it will get.

Rub down each lamb steak with oil. Continue rubbing both sides with the salt, fennel seeds, garlic, pepper, and ground guajillo chile flakes.

Place the steaks on the hottest part of the grill, flipping as needed until they reach an internal temperature of 130°F (50°C), about 7 to 10 minutes. Let rest for 15 minutes before serving.

Shaved Artichoke & Tomato Salad

SERVES 6

"For my wife and me," says Jonathan, "it doesn't really matter what the weather is like outside. We both think a nice salad with some protein on top is the perfect meal." This favorite of theirs uses raw artichokes—yes, raw!—to lend great texture and flavor.

3 raw globe artichokes, cleaned

2 lb (907 g) heirloom tomatoes, cut into bite-size wedges

Zest and juice of 1 lemon

3 tbsp (45 ml) extra virgin olive oil

Salt, to taste

Freshly ground black pepper, to taste

8 oz (224 g) arugula

2 tbsp (3 g) thinly sliced fresh mint leaves

4 oz (112 g) goat cheese, fresh or soft ripened, crumbled or sliced into bite-size pieces

Remove all the dark, tough outer artichoke leaves and discard, until only the pale yellow and green leaves remain. Trim the dark green off of the stem and bottom of the artichoke. Cut each artichoke in half lengthwise, remove the little purple leaves, and scoop out the fuzzy choke. Using a paring knife, serrated knife, or mandolin, carefully shave or very thinly slice everything that remains, starting with the flat side of each artichoke.

Place the artichokes in a bowl and add the tomatoes. Toss gently with the lemon juice and zest, oil, salt, and pepper. Let stand for 5 minutes.

Add the arugula, mint, and goat cheese and season with a touch more salt. Toss and serve.

Chewy Brownies with Hot Fudge Sauce

MAKES 12 (3 X 3-INCH [8 X 8-CM]) BROWNIES; ABOUT 3 CUPS (720 ML) SAUCE

"I'm a firm believer that most of the stuff we buy at grocery stores could—and should—be made at home from scratch instead," says Jonathan. "It's healthier and leagues tastier. Specifically, brownies and hot fudge sauce (recipe below) are super easy to make and so much better!" Add a scoop of French vanilla ice cream à la mode for an even tastier treat (if that's possible).

FOR THE CHEWY BROWNIES

2 cups (400 g) sugar

8 oz (230 g, 2 sticks) unsalted butter, melted

½ cup (120 ml) vegetable oil

1 tsp salt

4 large eggs, at room temperature

2 tsp pure vanilla extract

1 cup (125 g) all-purpose flour

¾ cup (60 g) cocoa powder

½ tsp baking powder

FOR THE HOT FUDGE SAUCE

¾ cup (180 ml) heavy cream

4 tbsp (58 g) unsalted butter

½ cup (100 g) granulated sugar

½ cup (110 g) brown sugar, firmly packed

¾ cup (60 g) cocoa powder

½ tsp kosher salt

1 tsp pure vanilla extract

Powdered sugar, for dusting

Preheat the oven to 350°F (177°C). Grease a 13 x 9–inch (33 x 23–cm) pan, or spray with nonstick cooking spray.

To make the chewy brownies, mix the sugar, melted butter, oil, and salt together with an electric hand mixer or in a stand mixer. Scrape the bowl, then slowly beat in the eggs and vanilla. Remove the bowl from the mixer and fold in the flour, cocoa powder, and baking powder by hand.

Pour the batter into the prepared pan and bake for 30 minutes, or until a tester inserted in the middle comes out clean. Remove from the oven and let cool, in the pan, on a wire rack.

Meanwhile, to make the hot fudge sauce, bring the cream and butter to a boil in a saucepan. Add the granulated sugar and brown sugar and stir to combine, then return to a boil. Stir in the cocoa powder and salt. Once the mixture returns to a final boil, remove from the heat and whisk smooth. Whisk in the vanilla.

Cut the cooled brownies into 3-inch (8-cm) squares. Place a brownie on each of 6 plates, dust with powdered sugar, and spoon the hot fudge sauce over to serve. Leftover brownies may be frozen.

DANTE BOCCUZZI

Cleveland, Ohio

Chef/owner of Dante, Ginko, Next Door, Coda, and Dante's Inferno (Cleveland); D.C. Pasta Co. (Strongsville, Ohio); DBA and Northeast Speakeasy (Akron)

CHEF SAYS

Items I always keep on hand for unexpected guests are . . .

Arborio rice, Parmigiano-Reggiano cheese, De Cecco pasta, Dante pasta sauces, and pancetta/prosciutto.

When hosting a quick get-together, never overlook . . .

Knowing your guests. Make sure your dish complements their dining habits. It should be new and exciting but not over their heads.

My secret tip for successful last-minute entertaining is . . .

To try making a complete dish that contains the protein, starch, and vegetable all in one to avoid making sides or sauces. The only additional item I would make is a dessert, salad, or cheese.

One fun fact few people know about me is that . . .

I enjoy woodworking and building furniture.

MENU

Risotto alla Carbonara

Arugula Salad with Goat Cheese Fritters, Green Apples & Pomegranate

CHEF'S PAIRING

2012 Rocche Costamagna Barbera d'Alba

CHEF'S PLAYLIST

Into the Wild by Eddie Vedder

MAJOR KUDOS

One Michelin star; multiple James Beard award nominations; named one of "America's Top 5 Culinary Talents" by *Robb Report*; placed first as the Pacific regional winner of a Cervena Plates competition; named a "Rising Star" by StarChefs; winner of the Maker's Mark Chef Challenge sponsored by the Rock and Roll Hall of Fame + Museum; "Best Culinary Scene Stealer" award by *Cleveland Scene*; *Food & Wine*'s "Best New Wine List" award

HIS STORY

Born and raised in Parma, Ohio, Dante left as a relatively naïve and sheltered eighteen-year-old kid and returned years later as a culinary superstar.

Along the way, he attended the Culinary Institute of America . . . traveled all across the country . . . jet-setted around the world . . . and eventually settled right back home again to start his own family and help lead Cleveland's exploding food scene.

Some of Dante's more exciting ventures included privately cheffing for Robert DeNiro; heading both the famed Aureole restaurant in New York City and the elite Silks restaurant in San Francisco's Mandarin Oriental Hotel; "staging" in London, Sardinia, Mougins, Hong Kong, and Taiwan; and serving as executive chef of the chic Armani/Nobu restaurant housed on the first floor of Giorgio Armani's flagship boutique in Milan.

"I chose this particular main dish because it's a twist on two Italian classics," explains Dante. "Risotto is a great last-minute dish. It only takes about thirty minutes to cook, and the flavor combinations are endless, all depending on what's in your pantry."

Sounds simply marvelous.

Risotto alla Carbonara

SERVES 4

What do you get when you marry risotto with carbonara sauce? A decadently rich, silky, and creamy rice dish that's beyond your wildest expectations. "But what's really unique in this version," explains Dante, "is that a poached egg is used as the garnish. You just break the egg and cream the yolk right into the risotto!"

1 small white onion, diced

4 tbsp (58 g) butter, divided

1¼ cups (230 g) uncooked Arborio rice

2 cups (480 ml) white wine

1½ qt (1.4 L) hot chicken stock, divided

Salt, to taste

Freshly ground black pepper, to taste, plus additional for garnish

2 tbsp (30 ml) extra virgin olive oil

1 shallot, minced

½ cup (115 g) diced pancetta

1 cup (240 ml) heavy cream

1 tbsp (15 ml) vinegar

4 small eggs

1 cup (180 g) grated Parmigiano-Reggiano cheese, plus additional for garnish

Fresh parsely chiffonade, for garnish, optional

Truffle oil, for drizzling, optional

Sweat the onion in 2 tablespoons (28 g) of the butter in a skillet over low heat for about 5 minutes. Add the rice and sweat together for 3 minutes. Add the wine, simmer, and reduce until dry, about 7 to 8 minutes. Add enough stock to just cover the rice, about 1 cup (240 ml). Season with salt and pepper. Stir and simmer until the rice is dry, about 2 minutes. Repeat until the stock is used up and the rice is cooked, about 30 to 40 minutes. Set aside.

In a sauté pan, heat the oil over medium heat. Add the shallot and pancetta and slowly cook until browned, about 7 to 8 minutes. Add the heavy cream and reduce, about 4 to 5 minutes. Set aside.

Place 3 quarts (2.8 L) of water in a large pot and bring to a boil. Add the vinegar. Reduce the heat to under a simmer. Crack the eggs into the water, one at a time. Let the eggs cook/poach until they are firm on the outside and runny on the inside, about 2 to 3 minutes.

Stir the Parmigiano-Reggiano cheese and the remaining 2 tablespoons (28 g) of butter into the rice to finish it.

Spoon the risotto evenly onto 4 plates. Lay 1 poached egg in the center of each portion of rice, then spoon the pancetta cream lightly over the egg. Garnish with the Parmigiano-Reggiano cheese, pepper, and parsley chiffonade, if using. If desired, drizzle with the truffle oil.

Arugula Salad with Goat Cheese Fritters, Green Apples & Pomegranate

SERVES 4

While the poet Gertrude Stein once said, "A rose is a rose is a rose," as soon as you see—and taste—this salad by Dante, you'll conversely say, "A salad is *not* a salad is *not* a salad!" That's because this refreshing and aesthetic dish combines such a beautiful and unusual array of colors, textures, and flavors. Your salad will never be the same again. Note: Pomegranate molasses can be found in any Middle Eastern grocery store.

1 cup (125 g) all-purpose flour

2 large eggs

½ cup (60 g) fine bread crumbs

1 small log of goat cheese, chilled and cut into ¼-inch (6-mm) slices

¾ cup (180 ml) olive oil

¼ cup (84 ml) pomegranate molasses

3 tbsp (45 ml) red wine vinegar

4 green apples, divided

2 tbsp (28 g) butter

2 cups (480 ml) vegetable oil, for frying

Salt, to taste

Freshly ground black pepper, to taste

4 cups (120 g) arugula leaves

Juice of 1 lemon

Pomegranate arils, for garnish

Place the flour in a shallow bowl. Lightly beat the eggs in another shallow bowl. Place the bread crumbs in a third shallow bowl. Dredge each slice of the goat cheese first in the flour, then the eggs, and finally the bread crumbs. Make sure that within each step, the cheese is completely coated. Set the cheese slices aside on a wire rack.

In a separate bowl, combine the olive oil, pomegranate molasses, and vinegar. Whisk together, then set aside.

Peel 2 of the apples and cut into wedges. In a small saucepan, warm the butter over medium-high heat. Add the apples and cook for about 2 minutes. Add ¼ cup (60 ml) water and cook until the apples are tender, about 4 minutes. Remove from the heat and purée until smooth.

In a medium-size pot, heat the vegetable oil to 425°F (218°C). Fry the goat cheese slices until golden brown, about 1 minute. Remove from the oil and drain on paper towels. Season with salt and pepper.

Core the remaining 2 apples, leaving on the peel, then cut into julienne slices, preferably with a mandoline. In a bowl, combine the julienned apples with the arugula and lemon juice. Season with salt and pepper and toss.

To serve, spoon a pool of the apple purée in the center of each plate and top with some of the arugula mixture. Evenly lay the fritters on top. Drizzle pomegranate vinaigrette around, then garnish with pomegranate arils.

STUART BRIOZA & NICOLE KRASINSKI

San Francisco, California

Chef/proprietors of State Bird Provisions and The Progress

CHEFS SAY

Items we always keep on hand for unexpected guests are . . .
Marcona almonds, Gouda, crudité veggies (i.e., carrots, fennel), dates, and bourbon.

When hosting a quick get-together, never overlook . . .

Starting with a few easy snacks and a glass of Champagne. It can buy you more time for getting the rest of the dinner done.

Our secret tip for successful last-minute entertaining is . . .
One-pot cooking!

One fun fact few people know about us is that . . .

After the holidays, we like to throw our Christmas tree out the window of our second-story apartment.

MENU

Chicken & Ginger Rice Soup

Persian Cucumbers with Kinako Dressing

Poppy Seed Shortcakes with Orange Blossom Cloud Cream & Blackberries

CHEFS' PAIRING

Chrysanthemum tea

CHEFS' PLAYLIST

Cambodian surf rock

MAJOR KUDOS

One Michelin star; James Beard "Best New Chefs: West" and "Best New Restaurant" awards; nomination for James Beard "Best New Restaurant" award; "Best New Restaurant" award from *Bon Appétit*; named one of the "10 Best New Chefs" and "Restaurants of the Year" by *Food & Wine*; named one of the "Best New Restaurants in America" by *Esquire*

THEIR STORY

In the world of creative arts, there was Frida and Diego. Fred and Ginger. And now, Stuart and Nicole.

Having grown up only ten miles from each other in the South Bay suburbs of San Francisco, Stuart and Nicole never actually met until they were art students together at the same college. He then left for the Culinary Institute of America, and she got a job as a pastry chef at a bakery in Chicago, where they hooked up again after he graduated. After a couple of stints together at really great places, they landed right back in San Francisco, eventually opening a place of their own.

And what a place it is! Award after award even prompted them to open a second place. And the awards just keep coming.

"This is the dinner we make most often at home," says Nicole. "It's so satisfying and doesn't require any special hard-to-find ingredients. Plus, anything left over makes a great breakfast!"

Chicken & Ginger Rice Soup

SERVES 6

"This is a chicken soup with no chicken stock," explains Stuart. "But since you cook the chicken on the bone and then remove and cook the rice in that same water, you would think it was fortified with stock." Healthy, hearty, delicious. The perfect trifecta.

FOR THE SOUP

1½ lb (680 g) chicken legs

½ tsp sea salt

3 tbsp (45 ml) fish sauce, preferably Red Boat brand

1 tbsp (15 ml) vegetable oil

1½ cloves garlic, thinly sliced

¾ cup (138 g) uncooked rice, preferably long-grain jasmine, rinsed and drained

1½ tbsp (10 g) minced fresh ginger

FOR GARNISH

3 scallions, sliced

6 fresh cilantro stems, thinly sliced

3 tbsp (30 g) dry-roasted peanuts, crushed

Freshly ground black pepper

To make the soup, season the chicken legs with salt.

Bring 2 quarts (1.9 L) water and the fish sauce to a boil in a large stockpot. Add the chicken and lower the heat to a very delicate simmer.

Meanwhile, heat the oil in a sauté pan over medium heat. Add the garlic, rice, and ginger. Cook, stirring constantly, until the rice grains are opaque, about 3 to 4 minutes.

Add the rice mixture to the chicken in the stockpot. Continue cooking until the chicken is done, about 25 minutes. Remove the chicken and let cool on a plate until it's easy to pick and shred the meat. Continue to cook the rice until slightly overcooked and thicker.

Ladle the soup into warm bowls. Garnish with the shredded chicken, scallions, cilantro, peanuts, and pepper.

Persian Cucumbers with Kinako Dressing

SERVES 6

This unexpectedly refreshing side has the Persian cucumber at center stage. A little sweeter and much smaller (only 4 to 6 inches [10 to 15 cm] long) than your common green-skinned cuke, it's seedless and available year-round in most grocery stores. Fun fact: Despite its nomenclature, it's known to have originated in India and is now a staple of Mediterranean cuisine! And the kinako powder can be found online or in Asian markets.

FOR THE DRESSING

1½ cups (190 g) kinako powder (roasted soybean flour)

1 tbsp (16 g) kosher salt

1½ tsp ground ginger

¾ cup plus 3 tbsp (225 ml) grapeseed oil

¾ cup plus 3 tbsp (225 ml) toasted sesame oil

⅓ cup plus 1 tsp (85 ml) unseasoned rice vinegar

FOR THE CUCUMBERS

6 crunchy Persian cucumbers, cut into irregular 1 × ½ × ½-inch (2.5 cm × 12 mm × 12-mm) pieces (can substitute 2 English cucumbers)

1½ tbsp (24 g) kosher salt

1 tbsp (7 g) grated fresh ginger

1 tbsp (9 g) black sesame seeds, toasted (page 457)

½ tsp Maldon or other flaky sea salt

1 tbsp (5 g) kinako powder, for sprinkling

To make the dressing, whisk together the kinako powder, salt, and ginger in a medium bowl. Slowly pour in the grapeseed oil, sesame oil, and rice vinegar, whisking constantly until the dressing is well combined. Set aside.

About half an hour before serving, prepare the cucumbers. Combine the cucumbers, kosher salt, and ginger in a bowl and let sit for 30 minutes.

Meanwhile, combine the toasted sesame seeds and sea salt in a mortar and pound until the mixture resembles coarsely ground black pepper. Set aside.

At serving time, drain the cucumbers in a fine-mesh strainer to extract any excess liquid. Pour about ¼ cup (60 ml) of the dressing on a large serving platter and arrange the cucumbers over the dressing. First sprinkle the cucumbers with the kinako powder, then sprinkle with the sesame mixture. Serve immediately.

Poppy Seed Shortcakes with Orange Blossom Cloud Cream & Blackberries

SERVES 6

Wow, where to even begin? Nicole's sweet creation is simply above and beyond. Forget your ordinary shortcakes (which are still pretty awesome, don't get us wrong). Instead, these cakes feature tangy yogurt, aromatic orange zest, and crunchy poppy seeds instead. Then whip up billowy cream featuring goat cheese, mascarpone, and orange blossom water. Finally, pick the freshest sun-kissed blackberries you can find. And voilà! Heaven on earth.

FOR THE SHORTCAKES

2 cups (250 g) all-purpose flour

¼ cup (50 g) sugar

1 tbsp (15 g) baking powder

½ tsp salt

2 tsp (6 g) poppy seeds

4 oz (115 g, 1 stick) unsalted butter, cut in small dice

1 large egg

½ cup (125 g) unflavored whole-milk yogurt

2 tsp (6 g) orange zest

¼ cup (60 ml) heavy cream

1 tbsp (8 g) poppy seeds

1 tbsp (16 g) Maldon or other flaky sea salt

FOR THE ORANGE BLOSSOM CREAM

½ cup (75 g) goat cheese

½ cup (100 g) sugar

¼ tsp kosher salt

½ cup (114 g) mascarpone

¾ cup (180 ml) heavy cream

1½ tsp (7 ml) orange blossom water

2 cups (288 g) fresh blackberries

Preheat the oven to 400°F (204°C). Line a baking pan with a sheet of parchment paper.

To make the shortcakes, whisk together the flour, sugar, baking powder, salt, and poppy seeds in a large bowl until combined. Chill in the refrigerator for 15 minutes.

Remove the bowl from refrigerator and add the butter. Using a pastry blender or two knives, cut the butter into the flour mixture until you have a good combination of small and large pieces of butter.

In a separate small bowl, whisk the egg, yogurt, and orange zest. Add to the butter-flour mixture and stir until the ingredients are just combined. Turn the dough onto a lightly floured surface and roll into a square about ½-inch (12-mm) thick. Cut into 6 equal pieces, then place the pieces on an ungreased baking sheet and chill in the refrigerator for 15 minutes.

Brush each shortcake with the heavy cream, then sprinkle with the poppy seeds and salt. Bake for 10 to 12 minutes, or until the bottoms of the shortcakes are golden brown. Remove from the oven and let cool.

To make the orange blossom cream, place the goat cheese, sugar, and salt in the bowl of a standing mixer. Using the paddle attachment, beat on medium speed until creamy and a little fluffy. Add the mascarpone and beat until well incorporated. Reduce the speed to low and stream in the heavy cream and orange blossom water, beating just until combined. Turn into a jar with a lid and refrigerate, covered, until ready to serve.

To serve, split each shortcake crosswise in half and place on a plate. Garnish with a large dollop of the cream and top with some of the blackberries.

ZACK BRUELL

Cleveland, Ohio

Chef/owner of Parallax, L'Albatros, Chinato, Cowell & Hubbard, DYNOMITE, Alley Cat Oyster Bar, Exploration, and Zack Bruell Events; consulting chef/restaurateur of Table 45 at The InterContinental Cleveland and The Burnham at the Cleveland Hilton

CHEF SAYS

Items I always keep on hand for unexpected guests are . . .

Wine, olives, sea salt, kala namak salt, and jalapeño chiles. Also, sour cream, a type of lettuce, yogurt, cheese, and salsa.

When hosting a quick get-together, never overlook . . .

A clean bathroom with toilet paper.

My secret tip for successful last-minute entertaining is . . .

Stay calm.

One fun fact few people know about me is that . . .

I hit golf balls on a daily basis.

MENU

Seared Salmon

Braised Fennel

Baked Potato That Will Blow Your Mind

Shredded Romaine Salad

Greek Yogurt with Berries & Honey

CHEF'S PAIRING

A great Sauvignon Blanc or Grüner Veltliner

CHEF'S PLAYLIST

Frank Sinatra and Teddy Pendergrass

MAJOR KUDOS

Multiple James Beard semifinalist nominations for "Best Chef: Great Lakes," three-time winner of *Esquire*'s "Best New Restaurants in America" award; three Santé Awards of Innovation; listed as one of *Cleveland Magazine*'s "Best New Restaurants"; and named one of the "Top 100 Restaurants in America" by OpenTable

HIS STORY

He's gone where no man has gone before—at least not in Cleveland. Because Zack's the only restaurateur in this city to have nine (count 'em, *nine!*) establishments within the city limits. Oh, yeah, plus he's got a line of gourmet coffees, balsamic vinegars, olive oil, and sauces, too.

For the record, Zack is no stranger to hard work and taking detours as needed. He started out at an Ivy League university. Got drafted. Served. Finished his business degree in Colorado. Impulsively changed career paths and headed to The Restaurant School in Philadelphia. Went back west to work with his old classmate—and famed chef—Michael McCarty, who had just opened his own pioneering California nouvelle eatery in Santa Monica called Michael's.

Zack eventually made his way back home to Cleveland. And the rest of his remarkable story ends with him opening one successful restaurant after another.

"I chose this meal because it's easy and can relate to everyone's palate," says Zack. "It's light and seems complicated, but it can be done pretty quickly."

Seared Salmon

Zack's secret to this amazing dish involves seasoning the freshest salmon you can find with a pretty unique spice, Hatch chile powder. Hatch chile peppers are grown exclusively in the Mesilla Valley near Hatch, New Mexico. Many consider them to be one of the most flavorful peppers in the world. And while they're only available fresh one month out of the year (in late summer), you can get them in powdered form, both mild and spicy hot, anytime. Look for the powder in a Hispanic grocery store or specialty spice shop, or online.

4 (5–6-oz [140–168-g]) boneless salmon fillets

Ground cumin

Hatch chile powder (can substitute regular chili powder)

Salt, to taste

Freshly cracked black pepper, to taste

¼ cup (60 ml) extra virgin olive oil, plus additional for drizzling

2 tsp (9 g) butter

1 lemon, halved

Liberally season the salmon with the cumin, chili powder, salt, and pepper. Set aside.

In a heavy-bottomed sauté pan, heat the oil until almost smoking. Add the butter and then immediately add the salmon. Cook for about 2 to 3 minutes on each side, then remove from the heat to serving plates. Squeeze lemon juice on top, then add a light drizzle of oil.

Braised Fennel

A side dish this elegant and delicious would seem, at first glance, to require a lot of work. But nothing could be further from the truth. You just parboil and sauté. That's it! And if you've never given this bulbous vegetable a try, it's high time you did. It's crunchy and slightly sweet, with a mild but distinctive anise flavor. Peak season: October through April.

2 whole fennel bulbs, trimmed of stalks

½ cup (120 ml) extra virgin olive oil

2 tbsp (28 g) butter

Salt, to taste

Freshly ground black pepper, to taste

Bring a large saucepan of water to a boil. Place the fennel in the boiling water and cook until the bulbs begin to soften and are extra fork tender, about 45 minutes.

Meanwhile, prepare a bowl of ice water and set near the stove.

Drain the fennel and chill in the ice bath. Once chilled, drain and pat dry thoroughly with paper towels. Cut each bulb in half.

Heat the oil in a sauté pan over medium-high heat. Add the butter. Just before the butter begins to brown, add the fennel. Cook for about 2 minutes, then lower the heat slightly. Continue cooking until the fennel halves are browned on one side. Flip and continue to cook until browned on the other sides. Cooking time will depend on the size of the bulbs.

Remove from the heat and season with salt and pepper.

Baked Potato That Will Blow Your Mind

SERVES 4

With such a fun and quirky recipe name like this, who wouldn't want to give it a try? The beauty is in its simplicity of preparation and surprise use of oil instead of butter. Frankly, it's not your mother's baked potato. (Sorry, Mom.)

4 medium-size Idaho potatoes

Extra virgin olive oil

Sea salt

High-quality sour cream, for serving

Freshly cracked black pepper

Scallions, sliced or chopped, for garnish

Preheat the oven to 500°F (260°C).

Scrub the potatoes and dry well. Poke with a fork several times. Rub the potatoes with oil, lightly salt them, then place in a baking dish and bake for about 45 minutes, or until soft.

Remove from the oven and slice open the top of the potatoes. Squeeze the sides of the potatoes to loosen the flesh inside, then pour a liberal amount of oil into each (way more than you think, at least 2 to 4 tablespoons [30 to 60 ml]). Top with the sour cream. Add salt, pepper, and scallions to taste.

Shredded Romaine Salad

SERVES 4

This salad is not just any salad. With such fun ingredients as olives, cilantro, feta, and avocado, it's more like a Greek fiesta in your mouth! Enjoy.

2 romaine hearts, torn apart

1 ripe tomato, diced

¼ cup (45 g) imported olives, pitted and julienned

1 bunch fresh cilantro, leaves torn

½ cup (75 g) crumbled feta cheese

½ avocado, peeled, seeded, and diced

Sea salt, to taste

Freshly cracked black pepper, to taste

½ cup (120 ml) white balsamic vinegar, preferably Zack Bruell brand

½ cup (120 ml) extra virgin olive oil

Combine the romaine, tomato, olives, cilantro, feta, avocado, salt, and pepper in a large bowl. Drizzle with the balsamic vinegar and oil when ready to serve.

Greek Yogurt with Berries & Honey

SERVES 4

If you think a dessert needs to be fancy or labor intensive to be delicious, this recipe will totally prove you wrong. Just a few simple-but-high-quality ingredients are the secret. And be sure to use authentic Greek honey. It'll amaze you. (BTW, this makes a fabulous treat for breakfast or brunch, too!)

2 cups (490 g) high-quality Greek yogurt

1 cup (123 g) fresh raspberries

1 cup (140 g) fresh blueberries

1 cup (144 g) fresh blackberries

Greek honey, to taste

Divide the yogurt among 4 bowls. Place the berries on top, then drizzle lightly with the honey to serve.

CESARE CASELLA

New York, New York

Dean of Italian Studies at the International Culinary Center; owner of Republic of Beans

CHEF SAYS

Items I always keep on hand for unexpected guests are . . .

Salami, cheese, eggs, good-quality canned tomatoes, and pasta. Plus bread, too.

When hosting a quick get-together, never overlook . . .

The presentation of your dishes. It's key. And always set the table.

My secret tip for successful last-minute entertaining is . . .

Keep it simple and have fun.

One fun fact few people know about me is that . . .

I'm funny.

MENU

Insalata di Pontormo

Antipasto del Mercato

Spaghetti con Acciughe

CHEF'S PAIRING

Bubbles to start, then a red wine from Tolaini Vineyards

CHEF'S PLAYLIST

Classical music

MAJOR KUDOS

One Michelin star; Silver Spoon Award from *Food Arts*; named one of "New York City's 17 Greatest Chefs" by the *Village Voice*; Distinguished Service Award by the Italian Trade Commission; founder of the International Day of Italian Cuisine

HIS STORY

Everyone knows him by the small bouquet of fresh rosemary sprigs he always keeps tucked in his shirt pocket. You could say it's his signature style. But Cesare would rather say it's a reminder of his childhood in the Tuscan countryside, where rosemary grows wild and rampant.

Cesare's parents owned a trattoria just outside Lucca, Italy. He used to help out there—and found he loved it. So, at fourteen, he decided to enroll in culinary school. His parents were totally against it and tried to bribe him with a new car to go to law school instead. But Cesare's mind was made up.

When he returned home, he immediately began updating his parents' traditional recipes with new twists of his own. Slowly, the restaurant he'd opened drew more and more attention, until one day it received the greatest honor a restaurant could receive: a Michelin star. The son did well. Really well.

"These here are some of my favorite dishes whether or not I have any time constraints," admits Cesare. "I believe in simple, honest, authentic cooking using the best ingredients you have access to. The meal doesn't have to be extravagant. Italian cooking is all about simplicity . . . and hosting is all about warmth and love."

Insalata di Pontormo

SERVES 4

Cesare's signature salad of market greens with soft-scrambled eggs, *guanciale*, and pancetta is a dish he created while running his parents' kitchen in Lucca. "This dish was inspired by the Italian artist Pontormo," explains Cesare. "I was reading his biography where he talked about looking out his window and seeing the garden (greens), chicken coop (eggs), and hanging carne secca (bacon). From there I created my Pontormo salad!"

FOR THE PONTORMO DRESSING

1 tbsp (15 ml) red wine vinegar

1 tbsp (15 ml) balsamic vinegar

1 tbsp (15 ml) red wine

¾ tsp salt

½ tsp freshly ground black pepper

¼ cup (60 ml) extra virgin olive oil

FOR THE SALAD

4 oz (112 g) guanciale, pancetta, or prosciutto (can substitute bacon), cut into thin strips about ½-inch (12-mm) long

2 tbsp (5 g) minced mixed fresh herbs (use any combination of rosemary, thyme, basil, savory, chives, marjoram, and oregano) (can substitute 1 tsp dried herbs)

1 tbsp (15 ml) extra virgin olive oil

6 large eggs

Salt, to taste

Freshly ground black pepper, to taste

4 cups (120 g) washed, mixed salad greens, torn into bite-size pieces

1 cup (180 g) shaved Parmigiano-Reggiano cheese, for garnish

To make the Pontormo dressing, whisk all the ingredients in a small bowl. Set aside.

To make the salad, place the guanciale, herbs, and oil in a nonstick sauté pan. Cook over medium heat until the mixture begins to color and is aromatic, about 3 minutes. You don't want the meat too crispy.

Take the pan off the heat. Crack the eggs into it. Add salt and pepper. Return to the heat and cook, stirring occasionally with a heat-resistant rubber spatula so that the yolks and white are still recognizable but mixed slightly. Cook gently until the eggs are just set but still a little soft, about 2 minutes. Take off the heat.

Dress the salad greens with 3 tablespoons (45 ml) of the Pontormo dressing. Pour the egg/meat mixture over the greens and toss well. The greens will begin to wilt, so serve immediately, garnished with the cheese and finished with pepper.

Antipasto del Mercato

SERVES 4 TO 6

Cesare says you can make this luscious, oven-roasted market vegetable recipe using any vegetables you have available. "This dish is very flexible and so are the ingredients," he explains. "When I'm in Italy, I'll select whatever is growing right outside in my garden." You should, too.

1 small eggplant, cut lengthwise into ¼-inch (6-mm) thick slices

1 small bunch broccoli, cut into small florets

1 small zucchini, cut lengthwise into ¼-inch (6-mm) thick slices

10 red cherry tomatoes

10 yellow cherry tomatoes

½ medium-size head fennel, cored and cut lengthwise into ¼-inch (6-mm) thick slices

1 medium-size carrot, cut diagonally into ¼-inch (6-mm) slices

¼ lb (112 g) shiitake mushrooms, cleaned and sliced

4 scallions, trimmed

1 bunch asparagus (about 16 stalks), tough ends trimmed

10 radishes, halved

1 head radicchio, cut into 8 lengthwise pieces

½ red bell pepper, seeded and cut into thick slices

½ yellow bell pepper, seeded and cut into thick slices

¼ cup (60 ml) extra virgin olive oil

¼ cup (60 ml) white wine

2 tbsp (30 ml) water

1 tsp salt

½ tsp freshly ground black pepper

Preheat the broiler.

Place all the vegetables in a large roasting pan.

In a bowl, whisk together the oil, wine, water, salt, and pepper. Drizzle over the vegetables and toss to coat them well.

Place the pan under the broiler for about 10 to 15 minutes, stirring occasionally and watching so the vegetables don't burn but become slightly grilled and tender. Remove from the oven and turn into a bowl or a platter to serve.

Spaghetti con Acciughe

SERVES 4

"I chose this dish of spaghetti with anchovies (*acciughe*) because I really am an anchovy lover," admits Cesare. "In oil or under salt. I always have them in my house, even since the time I was a young boy. I think it was because it was my grandfather's favorite food. Another great way to eat anchovies is with toasted bread. Spread on some butter and then add the salty anchovies on top. *Buonissimo*!"

1½ cups (195 g) cauliflower florets

3 tbsp (45 ml) extra virgin olive oil, divided

1½ tbsp (24 g) salt, plus additional to taste

Freshly ground black pepper, to taste

8 oz (224 g) anchovies preserved in olive oil, divided

1 clove garlic, crushed

¼ tsp red chili flakes (crushed red pepper)

½ cup (120 g) peeled, chopped ripe tomatoes (can substitute canned Italian tomatoes)

2 tbsp (20 g) chopped walnuts, toasted (page 457)

8 oz (224 g) spaghetti

½ cup (90 g) grated Parmigiano-Reggiano cheese

2 tbsp (5 g) finely chopped fresh Italian parsley

2 tbsp (16 g) bread crumbs, toasted (page 457), for garnish

Preheat the oven to 350°F (177°C).

Place the cauliflower florets in a small baking dish with 1 tablespoon (15 ml) of the oil. Season with salt to taste and pepper. Bake for 20 minutes. Remove and let cool, then roughly chop.

In a large pot, bring 3 quarts (2.8 L) of water to a boil with the 1½ tablespoons (24 g) of salt.

Meanwhile, rinse the anchovies under running water. Set aside.

Place the remaining 2 tablespoons (30 ml) of oil and the garlic in a large sauté pan. Cook over medium heat until the garlic turns golden, about 5 minutes. Add the red chili flakes, 6 ounces (168 g) of the anchovies (reserving the rest for use later), salt, and pepper. The anchovies will dissolve as they cook.

Reduce the heat to low, add the tomatoes, and break them up with the side of a spoon. When the tomatoes are slightly reduced, about 5 to 10 minutes, add the cauliflower and continue cooking for 2 to 3 more minutes. Lower the heat and stir in the toasted walnuts. Remove from the heat and set aside.

Add the spaghetti to the pot of boiling salted water. When the pasta is very al dente, drain and add to the anchovy sauce. Cook over medium heat for 2 to 3 minutes, then remove from the heat and stir in the Parmigiano-Reggiano and parsley.

Divide the pasta among 4 bowls. Garnish with some of the toasted bread crumbs and the remaining whole anchovies before serving.

JIM CHRISTIANSEN

Minneapolis, Minnesota

Chef/co-owner of Heyday

CHEF SAYS

Items I always keep on hand for unexpected guests are . . .

Good-quality crackers, cheese, chicken in the freezer (wings and thighs), bread in the freezer, and good-quality condiments.

When hosting a quick get-together, never overlook . . .

The idea of hospitality. Be a generous host, and always ensure the guests are taken care of first.

My secret tip for successful last-minute entertaining is . . .

Keep it simple! Don't overthink anything, and to ensure your personal touch is included in the meal, let the recipe be only a guide. Don't like chives? Don't use them!

One fun fact few people know about me is that . . .

A salad may be my most favorite food of all time.

MENU

Charred Green Peppers with Chicken, Cotija Cheese & Lime

Wild Garden Salad

Coconut Granola with Frozen Red Berry Ice & Amaro Whipped Cream

CHEF'S PAIRING

Classic rum daiquiri

CHEF'S PLAYLIST

"Mare" by Julian Lynch

MAJOR KUDOS

Multiple James Beard award semifinalist; named a "Best New Chef" by *Food & Wine*; named "Best New Restaurant" by *Mpls. St. Paul Magazine*

HIS STORY

He's a local kid. Born and bred in the Twin Cities. But don't think for a minute he hasn't been around the block.

You see, after Jim finished working his first job at McDonald's, concluded his culinary training, and completed his stints at noted restaurants throughout Minneapolis, he left the area. Actually, he left the country. And it wasn't to just anywhere. It was to Copenhagen, at the best restaurant in the world (per *Restaurant* magazine): Noma.

After an awe-inspiring internship there, Jim returned home and eventually opened his own place. Everyone took notice, and today he's a culinary star (yet as humble as ever).

"I chose this meal because it's based on foods that I grow in my garden," says Jim. "In the summer I'll go outside and clip any edible greens, wild or cultivated, and combine them in a salad. More often than not it, it's more complex and delicious than any forced composed salad I can come up with. Each week brings a different green, herb, bitterness, etc., to the mix, which makes it really exciting. Plus, there's no need to go to the store! All of these recipes can be loosely adapted to work last minute."

And that's just perfect.

Charred Green Peppers with Chicken, Cotija Cheese & Lime

SERVES 4

What a unique and unexpected twist on the traditional stuffed peppers. Good-bye, mild bells. Hello, spicy poblanos! Add a filling that's chock-full of moist chicken and a robust, salty, Hispanic-style cheese, and you're in for quite a delightful surprise.

FOR THE STUFFED PEPPERS

8 mildly spicy peppers such as poblano, cut in half lengthwise and seeded

4 boneless, skinless chicken thighs, chopped into ½-inch (12-mm) dice

1 clove garlic, finely grated on a microplane

Juice of 2 limes

4 oz (112 g) cotija cheese, crumbled (can substitute mozzarella)

1 bunch fresh cilantro, roughly chopped

Sea salt, to taste

FOR GARNISH

Sliced red radish

Sliced jalapeño chiles

Fresh cilantro sprigs

Freshly squeezed lime juice, to taste

Sea salt, to taste

Preheat a charcoal grill on medium-high heat.

To prepare the peppers, place them, cut side up, on a baking sheet.

Combine the chicken, garlic, lime juice, cheese, cilantro, and salt in a bowl and stir well. Fill the pepper halves up to the top with the mixture, and make sure they are stuffed tight.

Place the baking sheet on the grill and cook until the peppers are completely black and charred on the underside, about 15 minutes. Transfer to the side of the grill with less direct heat and continue cooking until the fillings are bubbling and cooked through. Take off the grill and let rest for 10 minutes.

Right before serving, garnish with the radish, jalapeño, cilantro, lime juice, and salt.

Wild Garden Salad

SERVES 4 TO 6

Now, you may take one look at Jim's ingredients list and feel a bit intimidated. "Where on earth am I going to find all these exotic items?" you might wonder. But the truth is, you're certainly welcome to wildly improvise, which will make this recipe all that much more fun and interesting. Now go for it!

12 lacinato kale leaves, thick stem removed

12 romaine lettuce leaves

12 large wild garlic mustard leaves

12 large French sorrel leaves

8 wild leek greens

1 large handful fresh radish-top greens

1 bunch fresh dill, roughly picked to include large sprigs

1 handful fresh chives, finely minced

1 handful wild wood sorrel

1 pint cherry tomatoes, halved

1 cucumber, thinly sliced

4 radishes, thinly sliced

Roasted almond oil, to taste (can substitute olive oil)

Fresh lemon juice, to taste

Sea salt, to taste

2 large handfuls fresh raspberries, sliced in half

1 handful fresh green gooseberries, sliced in half (can substitute strawberries, other berries, or any fruit)

¼ cup (45 g) hazelnuts, toasted (page 457) and chopped

To make the salad, tear the kale, romaine, mustard leaves, sorrel leaves, leek greens, and radish tops into bite-size pieces. Place in a large bowl. Add the dill, chives, sorrel, tomatoes, cucumber, and radishes. Toss.

Drizzle the oil and lemon juice over the salad. Season with salt. Gently toss and taste until it suits you well.

Divide the salad among 4 to 6 plates. Garnish with the raspberries, gooseberries, and toasted hazelnuts.

Coconut Granola with Frozen Red Berry Ice & Amaro Whipped Cream

SERVES 4

For a quick, light, colorful, and anything-but-ordinary dessert, nothing beats this combination. Jim knows how to perfectly incorporate a great variety of flavors, textures, and even temperatures to create the most memorable end to any special meal.

FOR THE RED BERRY ICE

1 cup (140 g) fresh red currants (can substitute fresh pitted cherries)

1 cup (123 g) fresh red raspberries

¼ cup (84 g) honey

Juice of 1 lemon

FOR THE COCONUT GRANOLA

¼ cup (84 g) honey

2 tbsp (30 ml) almond oil (can substitute olive oil)

Pinch of sea salt

1 cup (80 g) unsweetened flaked coconut

½ cup (40 g) rolled oats

2 tbsp (18 g) golden flax seeds

FOR THE AMARO WHIPPED CREAM

1 cup (240 ml) heavy cream, chilled

2 tbsp (26 g) sugar

Fernet-Branca or other amaro, to taste (can substitute crème de menthe, dark rum, or Angostura aromatic bitters; for a nonalcoholic version, use 1 tbsp [3 g] finely chopped fresh spearmint)

Fresh strawberries, halved, for garnish, optional

To make the red berry ice, combine all the ingredients in a blender and blitz quickly to a purée. Press through a fine-mesh strainer into a glass baking dish, forming a shallow layer. Freeze, then reserve in the freezer until ready to assemble the dessert.

To make the coconut granola, preheat the oven to 325°F (165°C). Combine the honey, oil, and salt in a saucepan. Bring to a boil, then take off the heat. Combine the coconut, oats, and flax seeds in a bowl. Add the honey mixture and stir until combined. Spread on a baking sheet and bake until toasted to a light gold, about 15 to 20 minutes. Be sure to stir the mixture throughout the baking time to ensure even baking.

To make the amaro whipped cream, whisk the heavy cream and sugar until light and fluffy. Add enough amaro to your liking, depending on your taste.

To serve, divide the cream among 4 bowls. Top with the granola. Scrape the red berry ice with a fork until lightly and fluffy. Top the cream and granola with the desired amount of ice. If desired, garnish with strawberries. Serve immediately.

SONYA COTÉ

Austin, Texas

Chef/owner of Hillside Farmacy, Eden East, and Coté Catering; co-founder of The Homegrown Revival

MENU

Oysters on the Half Shell with Horseradish & Cucumber Mignonette

Grilled Lobster & Curry Grits with Red-Eye Gravy & Melted Leeks

Corn in the Husk with Smoked Chili Flakes, Butter & Rosemary

CHEF'S PAIRING

Campari and soda with a twist of orange

CHEF'S PLAYLIST

Donna Summer

MAJOR KUDOS

Voted one of the *Daily Meal*'s "Top 10 Badass Women Chefs in America"; named one of "The Best Spots in America to Taste the Revival" by *Bon Appétit*; named one of *Marie Claire*'s "Women on Top"; appearance on Food Network's *Chopped*; named one of *Austin Monthly*'s "Best New Restaurants"; winner of TasteMade's "Grill Iron" championship

HER STORY

As an artist, Sonya loves to paint food. (She was once an illustrator for Whole Foods, after all.) Conversely, as a chef Sonya draws on her artistic skills to make her gastronomic presentations remarkably beautiful.

"I like to create edible pieces of art," says Sonya. Which is why her meal here—based on the best ingredients summer has to offer—is so elaborate.

"This menu was created as southern cuisine meets New England," she explains. "I prepared this menu in Rhode Island during a summer trip and wanted to expose the community of Westerly to some southern flavors.

"I decided to use grilled lobster, which isn't done very often, as a play on the traditional southern dish of shrimp and grits. It takes only 15 minutes to cook. And the oysters are served raw, so there's no need to prep there."

Fast. Easy. Fresh. Delicious. Seriously, what's not to love?

Oysters on the Half Shell with Horseradish & Cucumber Mignonette

SERVES 4

No seafood feast would be complete without tasty, briny raw oysters. They're surprisingly easy, affordable, and fun, too! Just be sure to buy them from a trusted source. And if you're not planning to serve them right away, store unopened in the fridge, covered with a wet towel, curved side down. They can be kept quite happy and alive this way for several days.

FOR THE CUCUMBER MIGNONETTE

1 large cucumber, peeled, seeded, and diced

¼ tsp salt

1 tbsp (15 ml) champagne vinegar

1 tsp honey

1 tsp fresh lemon juice

2 tsp (7 g) super finely chopped shallot

Pinch of cayenne pepper

Freshly cracked black pepper (about 8 turns on a peppermill)

FOR THE OYSTERS

12 fresh oysters, preferably an East Coast variety

Crushed ice or wet rock salt

Fresh horseradish (can substitute prepared horseradish in a jar)

Trout roe caviar, for garnish, optional

Chopped fresh parsley, for garnish, optional

To make the cucumber mignonette, in a small bowl toss the diced cucumber with the salt. Place in a blender. Start to blend and slowly add the vinegar. Blend until smooth.

Pour through a fine-mesh strainer into a measuring cup. Place ¼ cup (60 ml) of the strained liquid in a small bowl. Add the honey, lemon juice, shallot, cayenne, and black pepper. Whisk and chill until ready to use.

To prepare the oysters, shuck the oysters by holding firmly in place on a flat surface using a mitt or heavy towel. Insert the tip of a sharp knife between the shell halves of each oyster and work from side to side as you pry them open. Cut the muscle away from the top flat shell. Bend the shell back and discard. Then run your knife under the oyster meat and detach it completely but keep in the shell. Be careful not to cut the meat itself. Continue to do the same with the rest of the oysters.

Create a bed of ice on each of 4 plates. Nestle 3 oysters into each ice bed to keep them steady.

If using fresh horseradish, zest lightly over the oysters. If using prepared horseradish, serve alongside the oysters. Spoon about 1 teaspoon of the cucumber mignonette over each oyster. Garnish with caviar and parsley, if using.

Grilled Lobster & Curry Grits with Red-Eye Gravy & Melted Leeks

SERVES 4

With lobster as the centerpiece of this undeniably impressive dish, the rest may seem like just eye candy. But don't be fooled. There are plenty of complementary textures and flavors going on here, too. From the spicy grits to the tenderly creamy leeks and coffee-laced red-eye gravy, it's no wonder this is one heckuva meal!

FOR THE CURRY GRITS

2 tbsp (30 ml) grapeseed oil (can substitute clarified butter, page 456)

1 small onion, finely diced

2 cups (320 g) organic yellow corn grits

2 qt (1.9 L) water

1 (13.5-oz [400-ml]) can coconut milk

2 tbsp (30 g) red curry paste

1 tbsp (5 g) Indian spice blend (or muchi curry powder)

Salt, to taste

Freshly ground black pepper, to taste

FOR THE RED-EYE GRAVY

2 tbsp (28 g) butter

2 tbsp (16 g) all-purpose flour

½ onion, finely chopped

2 cups (480 ml) chicken stock

2 tbsp (30 ml) freshly brewed, wicked strong-ass coffee

FOR THE MELTED LEEKS

1 tbsp (14 g) butter

1 tbsp (15 ml) vegetable oil, such as grapeseed or safflower

2 leeks, light green and white parts, cleaned and trimmed (page 456), finely chopped

Salt, to taste

Freshly ground black pepper, to taste

FOR THE LOBSTERS

4 whole live lobsters (1½ lb [680 g] each)

1 scallion, chopped, for garnish

Preheat the grill to very hot.

To make the curry grits, place the oil in a large pot over medium heat. Add the onion and sweat for about 7 minutes. Add the grits, stir, and toast for about 5 minutes.

Lower the heat to low, add the water, and keep cooking until done, about 20 minutes. Stir in the coconut milk, curry paste, spice blend, salt, and pepper. Remove from the heat and keep warm.

To make the red-eye gravy, melt the butter in a sauté pan over medium heat. Whisk in the flour. Add the onion, stir, and continue to simmer for about 10 minutes. Add the chicken stock and coffee. Simmer for an additional 10 minutes. Remove from the heat.

To make the melted leeks, place the butter in a sauté pan over medium heat and watch carefully until just melted. Add the oil until just warmed, then add the leeks. Reduce the heat to low and cook until transparent and very tender (like they will "melt" in your mouth). Season with salt and pepper.

To prepare the lobsters, first make a quick incision through the head shell of each lobster about 1 inch (2.5 cm) from the eyes, pushing down hard to instantly kill the lobster. Place the lobsters on the grill for about 15 minutes, turning once or twice.

Transfer to a platter. Sprinkle the chopped scallion around the lobsters for garnish. Serve family style.

Corn in the Husk with Smoked Chili Flakes, Butter & Rosemary

SERVES 4

There's nothing that screams summer louder than freshly picked sweet corn still in its husk. Throw in a smoky spice, some creamy butter, and an aromatic sprig of fresh rosemary, and you've got yourself a side dish to die for.

4 ears fresh corn

Salt, to taste

4 tbsp (58 g) whipped butter

1 tbsp (5 g) smoked chili flakes (can substitute crushed red pepper)

4 fresh rosemary sprigs (each about 3 inches [8 cm] long)

Preheat the grill to very hot.

Peel back the husk of the corn without pulling it all the way off. Remove the silk.

Soak the corn in a large bowl full of salt water for 30 minutes.

Remove from the water and allow to dry out on a sheet tray (or a picnic table in the sunshine), about 10 to 15 minutes.

Coat each corn cob with 1 tablespoon (14 g) of the whipped butter. Sprinkle each cob with ¼ tablespoon of the chili flakes. Place a rosemary sprig lengthwise on each cob. Wrap the husks back up and tie with kitchen twine.

Place on the grill for about 7 to 10 minutes, or until the kernels are tender. Arrange on a platter and serve warm.

GREG DENTON & GABRIELLE QUIÑÓNEZ DENTON

Portland, Oregon

Chef/owners of Ox Restaurant and SuperBite

CHEFS SAY

Items we always keep on hand for unexpected guests are . . .
Liquor and/or wine, good olive oil, cheese, dry pasta, and something briny, like olives, capers, or pickles.

When hosting a quick get-together, never overlook . . .
Cleaning as you go. Nothing is more daunting than trying to clean up when you are sleepy and full of food and booze.

Our secret tip for successful last-minute entertaining is . . .
As soon as you've decided what you're going to serve, move quickly and efficiently in order to get it all prepped out. Then slow down, tidy yourself up, and set out your beverage and glassware selection. No one will mind that you may still have a couple more things to do to get dinner on the table if everyone has a drink in their hand. Making people feel at home is crucial to good hospitality, and the key to this is letting go of any anxiety before your guests approach your front door.

One fun fact few people know about us is that . . .

When we first met, we used to sneak into hot spring pools in Napa Valley to unwind after a hard night's work.

MENU

Summer Squash Carpaccio with Spanish Chorizo, Manchego & Marcona Almonds

Black Pepper–Seared Tuna & Balsamic Soy Cream with Mustard Greens, Roasted Tomatoes & Corn

Ice Cream with Bittersweet Chocolate Magic Shell & Crumbled Honeycomb Candy

CHEFS' PAIRING

Ice cold white txakoli with the first course

Rosé txakoli with the entrée

Sherry or bourbon with the dessert

CHEFS' PLAYLIST
Cesária Évora

MAJOR KUDOS

James Beard award for "Best Chef: Northwest"; numerous James Beard award finalist nominations; named two of *Food & Wine*'s "Best New Chefs"; listing in *Bon Appétit*'s "Top 50 Best New Restaurants"; "Portland Restaurant of the Year" award from Eater; "Restaurant of the Year" award from the *Oregonian*; winner of Esquire Channel's *Knife Fight*

THEIR STORY

This dynamic duo have a lot in common. They both had a passion for food at a young age. They both graduated from culinary school with honors. And they both worked their way up at Michelin-starred Terra in Napa Valley.

Together Greg and Gabrielle make the perfect couple—both personally and professionally. Which is why the meal they chose to serve their own last-minute guests is so special.

"We'd feel proud to serve this menu at any time to anyone," says Gabrielle. "The food appears beautiful on the plate, and each dish is brightly flavored and balanced. It's also easy to make and so adaptable. In fact, it can be adjusted to suit any season."

In a word, perfect.

Summer Squash Carpaccio with Spanish Chorizo, Manchego & Marcona Almonds

SERVES 4

If you're lucky enough to make this dish during the peak of summer freshness, wonderful! If not, don't fret. "Just trade out the summer squash for some thinly sliced and quickly roasted winter squash, such as delicata or butternut," says Gabrielle, "or even some thinly sliced fresh pears instead. Because other than the produce, the rest of the ingredients are pantry staples." Easy enough!

1 medium-size zucchini

1 medium-size yellow squash

2 oz (56 g) cured Spanish chorizo (can substitute any dry salami or pepperoni)

3 tbsp (45 ml) extra virgin olive oil

Flaky sea salt, to taste

Small chunk of Manchego cheese (about 2 oz [56 g]) (can substitute Parmigiano-Reggiano or any other hard, aged cheese)

¼ cup (40 g) Marcona almonds (can substitute almond slices or slivers, toasted (page 457)

Slice the zucchini and yellow squash into thin rounds (about ⅛-inch [3-mm] thick). Divide among 4 medium-small plates, alternating and slightly overlapping the slices carpaccio-style.

Cut the Spanish chorizo into ¼-inch (6-mm) cubes. Scatter evenly over the squash. Drizzle the olive oil over the squash and chorizo. Lightly season the squash with salt.

Thinly shave the cheese with a vegetable peeler and garnish each dish. Lightly crush or crack the toasted almonds and scatter over each plate.

Serve at room temperature.

Black Pepper–Seared Tuna & Balsamic Soy Cream with Mustard Greens, Roasted Tomatoes & Corn

SERVES 4

Besides being utterly delicious, this dish is also extremely versatile. As for the balsamic soy cream, "It always surprises people when we tell them that not only is the sauce vegetarian, but it's made from only three ingredients!" says Gabrielle.

FOR THE BALSAMIC SOY CREAM

½ cup (120 ml) balsamic vinegar (basic, not fancy)

¼ cup (60 ml) soy sauce (preferably gluten-free)

1 cup (240 ml) heavy cream

FOR THE TOASTED GARLIC–LEMON OIL

½ cup (120 ml) extra virgin olive oil

2 tbsp (7 g) thinly sliced garlic

3 tbsp (45 ml) fresh lemon juice

½ tsp kosher salt

Pinch of freshly ground black pepper, to taste

2 small ears of corn, husk and silk removed

2 bunches mustard greens (about 1 lb [450 g]), stems removed

Kosher salt, to taste

6 tbsp (90 ml) extra virgin olive oil, divided

1 pint (300 g) heirloom grape tomatoes

2 tsp (2 g) fresh thyme leaves (or ½ tsp dried)

4 (5-oz [140-g]) sashimi-grade tuna loin steaks

2 tbsp (10 g) crushed or cracked black peppercorns

16 fresh tarragon leaves, for garnish

Preheat the oven to 400°F (204°C).

To make the balsamic soy cream, in a small, nonreactive saucepan over medium heat, bring the balsamic vinegar and soy sauce to a boil. Immediately lower to a simmer and cook until reduced by half. Add the cream and bring back up to a boil, then simmer lightly for 2 minutes. Remove from the heat and keep warm until ready to serve.

To make the toasted garlic–lemon oil, place the oil and garlic in a medium-size stainless-steel saucepan and place over medium heat. Stir the garlic, then cook until it starts to brown and smell toasty. Remove from the heat and immediately add the lemon juice. Stir, then season with salt and pepper. Keep warm.

Bring a large pot of salted water to a boil. Add the corn and cook until heated through, about 7 minutes. Remove the corn from the water, but keep the pot over the heat to blanch the mustard greens. Let the corn cool. Prepare a large bowl of ice water and place close to the stovetop. Add the mustard greens to the boiling water and cook for 1 minute, until just tender. Immediately drain the mustard greens and place in the bowl of ice water to cool rapidly and prevent from overcooking. Once chilled, remove the greens from the water to drain again, then squeeze out as much water as you can. Set aside. Once the corn is cool enough to handle, cut the kernels from the cob into a small bowl. Season with salt and stir in 1 tablespoon (15 ml) of the olive oil. Set aside.

Place the tomatoes in a bowl and gently toss with some salt, 1 tablespoon (15 ml) of the olive oil, and the thyme. Transfer to a sheet pan and roast in the preheated oven until lightly dehydrated and wrinkly, about 7 to 10 minutes. Remove from the oven.

Place the toasted garlic-lemon oil in a medium-size pan with the blanched mustard greens. Heat over medium heat until hot, stirring frequently. Remove from the heat.

In a large sauté pan, heat the remaining 4 tablespoons (60 ml) of olive oil over medium heat. Season the tuna steaks evenly on both sides with the salt and crushed peppercorns, pressing the peppercorns into the flesh with your palms to help them adhere. When the oil is hot and starting to shimmer, place the tuna steaks carefully in the pan. Sear for 30 to 45 seconds on one side. Turn over and sear for another 30 seconds on the second side. Remove from the pan and place on a cutting board.

To serve, pour about ⅓ cup (80 ml) of the balsamic soy cream onto each of 4 serving plates, then center a mound of the mustard greens over the cream. Cut each tuna steak into ½-inch (12-mm) slices and arrange on top of the mustard greens. Scatter some of the corn across the center of the tuna slices, then garnish with the roasted tomatoes and tarragon. Serve any remaining balsamic soy cream on the side.

Ice Cream with Bittersweet Chocolate Magic Shell & Crumbled Honeycomb Candy

SERVES 4

When you have such a spectacular meal, it would be a shame—a crime, really—to end it with anything less than an equally spectacular dessert. And this is the one! Not only is it quick and easy to prepare, but it also makes for quite an impressive, interactive experience. Now how many desserts can you say that about? Not many at all.

FOR THE BITTERSWEET CHOCOLATE MAGIC SHELL

8 oz (224 g) bittersweet chocolate

2 tbsp plus ½ tsp (33 ml) virgin coconut oil

Pinch of kosher salt

FOR THE HONEYCOMB CANDY

Vegetable oil, for greasing the pan

1½ tsp (7 g) baking soda

¾ cup (150 g) sugar

2 tbsp (42 g) honey

2 tbsp (30 ml) water

1 pint (480 g) vanilla ice cream (can substitute any other basic flavor such as strawberry or coffee)

To make the bittersweet chocolate magic shell, fill a medium saucepan with 1 to 2 inches (2.5 to 5 cm) of water and bring to a simmer. Place a heatproof bowl on top of the pot (water should not touch the bottom of the bowl). Add the chocolate and let melt, stirring frequently. Stir in the coconut oil and salt. Keep warm until ready to use.

To make the honeycomb candy, rub or spray a baking sheet or silicone baking mat with vegetable oil. Measure out the baking soda and place close to the stove.

In a medium-size heavy-bottomed, stainless-steel saucepan, combine the sugar, honey, and water. Heat over medium-high until the mixture registers 300°F (149°C) on a candy thermometer. Immediately remove from the heat and whisk in the baking soda, then quickly pour the mixture onto the prepared sheet pan; do not move the pan while you're doing this, or you will lose the air pockets that make this candy so light and crisp.

Let cool to room temperature until the toffee-like candy is crispy and crunchy on the outside yet slightly aerated on the inside. Break off shards of the candy, crumbling some and leaving others in larger pieces.

Scoop ice cream evenly into four bowls. Serve the warm chocolate mixture on the side so that your guests may drizzle as much as they like over the ice cream.

Pass around the honeycomb candy and encourage guests to crumble the shards over the top of their ice cream and chocolate sauce. Wait 1 minute before digging in so that the chocolate hardens into a shell.

TIFFANY DERRY

Dallas, Texas

Chef/owner of Roots Southern Table, Roots Chicken Shack, The Cupboard, and Tiffany Derry Concepts; national spokesperson for Novo Nordisk

CHEF SAYS

Items I always keep on hand for unexpected guests are . . .

Pasta, cooked rice, tomato sauce in the freezer, some greens, and two or three types of kimchi (it's my obsession).

When hosting a quick get-together, never overlook . . .

Flavor. Just because it's last minute doesn't give you excuses for a subpar meal. Keep it simple but flavorful!

My secret tip for successful last-minute entertaining is . . .

Remember the saying "stay ready so you don't have to get ready." Always keep a few staples in the house.

One fun fact few people know about me is that . . .

I am a good mix of introvert and extrovert. I am outgoing in certain situations, but when meeting people, I am nervous and shy. If you don't really know me, you would never know it, but I am. The thought of small talk terrifies me, but I push through anyway.

MENU

Spaghetti Aglio e Olio

Arugula Salad with Warm Bacon Balsamic Vinaigrette

CHEF'S PAIRING

Nicolas-Jay Pinot Noir 2014

CHEF'S PLAYLIST

My own Pandora station, which has the music I grew up on (Gerald Levert, Case, Beyoncé, Xscape, Creed, Michael Jackson, and more)

MAJOR KUDOS

Host of Spike TV's *Hungry Investors*; finalist on both Bravo's *Top Chef* and *Top Chef: All Stars*; guest judge on Food Network's *Chopped Junior* and *Bobby's Dinner Battle*; celebrity chef on NBC's *Foodfighters*; named one of the "Best Chefs in Dallas-Ft. Worth" by the *Dallas Morning News*

HER STORY

What started as an after-school job at the International House of Pancakes at age fifteen serendipitously turned out to be Tiffany's foray into a highly successful and fascinating culinary career. Yet even with multiple TV, restaurant, and spokeswoman credits to her name, she still finds time to entertain.

"People just popping by at my house is a weekly event for me!" says Tiffany. "Sometimes I get a heads-up, and sometimes I just get a text that they're in the neighborhood. My family lives close by."

So why this dish?

"I love pasta!" exclaims Tiffany. "Hands down this is one of my favorite dishes to make and eat. The longest part is waiting for the water to boil. Once that's done, the pasta dish is done. We all need quick meals, and this is my go-to. Plus, I've personally never seen anyone disappointed with a big, oversize bowl of pasta sitting in the middle of the table. It's about the simplicity of flavors and having a great time over a meal."

Now, c'mon everyone, *mangia*!

Spaghetti Aglio e Olio

SERVES 4

This spaghetti dish features *aglio* (Italian for garlic) and *olio* (Italian for oil). But it doesn't stop there. "I always ask my guests whether they like anchovies," says Tiffany. "The majority of the time they say no. So they're blown away when they find out it's in here. That's because the underlying flavors you get from anchovies are amazing. The umami! Also, even though this dish is very simple to make, it does require all your senses. Pay attention, because it goes by so quick, and each step is important. The garlic needs to go almost to the edge of brown, but you need to smell and make sure it doesn't go too far. The tomatoes need to burst open, and the anchovies need to cook into the oil. Ohhh, and listen to the sound the parsley makes when hitting the hot oil! Each step is important and lends to the flavor of the dish."

2 tbsp (32 g) salt

1 lb (450 g) spaghetti

2 tbsp (30 ml) olive oil

4 cloves garlic, roughly chopped

2–3 anchovies, minced

1 cup (149 g) cherry tomatoes

Red chili flakes (crushed red pepper), to taste

½ bunch fresh parsley, chopped

Kosher salt, to taste

Freshly ground black pepper, to taste

2 cups (60 g) arugula

1 cup (100 g) grated Pecorino Romano cheese, divided

Bring a large pot of water to a boil. Add the salt and pasta. Cook according to package directions. Be sure to reserve 1½ cups (360 ml) cooking water before draining the pasta.

Meanwhile, heat the oil in a 12-inch (30-cm) sauté pan or large, shallow saucepan over medium-high heat. Add the garlic and cook for 2 minutes, stirring frequently, until it just begins to turn golden on the edges. Add the anchovies and tomatoes. Cook for 1 minute, or until the anchovies dissolve into the oil and a few of the tomatoes start to pop.

Add the chili flakes and cook for 30 more seconds. Add the parsley; you will hear it fry in the oil. Add the drained pasta and toss. Ladle in about ½ cup (118 ml) pasta water and season lightly with salt and pepper. Remove from the heat.

Add the arugula and half the cheese and toss well. Allow the pasta to rest for 5 minutes so the sauce gets absorbed, then season with salt and pepper. Serve warm, garnished with the remaining cheese.

Arugula Salad with Warm Bacon Balsamic Vinaigrette

SERVES 4

There are salads. And then there's *this* salad, which makes all the others pale in comparison. That's because it combines so many different flavors and textures. Take, for instance, the aromatic, peppery flavor of arugula. Add the rich, buttery flavor and crunch of pecans. Then throw in the sweet-sour flavor of dried cherries with the complex, full-bodied, salty/savory flavor of creamy blue cheese—and get ready for a salad you won't soon forget!

FOR THE BACON BALSAMIC VINAIGRETTE

5 slices thick-cut bacon, cut into ½-inch (12-mm) pieces

2 tbsp (20 g) minced shallots

1 tbsp (9 g) minced garlic

⅓ cup (80 ml) balsamic vinegar

1 tbsp (16 g) Dijon mustard

1 tsp brown sugar, firmly packed

¾ cup (180 ml) olive oil

Salt, to taste

Freshly ground black pepper, to taste

FOR THE SALAD

4 cups (120 g) arugula, washed

½ cup (60 g) pecans, toasted (page 457), divided

½ cup (80 g) dried cherries, divided

⅓ cup (50 g) blue cheese, crumbled, divided

Kosher salt, to taste

Freshly ground black pepper, to taste

To make the bacon balsamic vinaigrette, first cook the bacon in a skillet over medium heat until crisp. Using a slotted spoon, transfer the bacon to paper towels. Set aside for use as a garnish in the salad.

Remove the skillet with the reserved bacon drippings from the heat. Add the shallots and garlic and stir. Add the balsamic vinegar, mustard, and brown sugar. Stir vigorously, then add the oil, salt, and pepper. Whisk until well combined. Keep warm until needed.

To make the salad, in a large salad bowl toss together the arugula, half the pecans, half the dried cherries, and half the blue cheese. Season with salt and pepper.

When ready to serve, drizzle the salad with the warm vinaigrette and toss. Taste and adjust the seasoning with salt and pepper if needed. Garnish with the remaining toasted pecans, dried cherries, and blue cheese, and reserved cooked bacon from the vinaigrette recipe.

Serve immediately.

TRACI DES JARDINS

San Francisco, California

Chef/owner of Jardinière, Mijita Cocina Mexicana, Public House, The Commissary, Arguello, and TRANSIT

CHEF SAYS

Items I always keep on hand for unexpected guests are . . .

Salsas and tortillas in the freezer, beans, Jack cheese (as nothing quite beats a killer quesadilla), cooking oil, and my homemade chips.

When hosting a quick get-together, never overlook . . .

Having an array of great beverages on hand, from a nice bar selection and good wine in the fridge, to good soft drinks like drinking vinegars and delicious kombuchas, sparkling water (or a soda stream), and ice. Also, a well-stocked pantry and freezer allow you to throw together a great meal without having to venture to the store. Think frozen pasta, Bolognese sauce, a nice chunk of Parmigiano-Reggiano, and maybe even an herb garden where you can clip a little basil and fresh parsley.

My secret tip for successful last-minute entertaining is . . .

Have great reliable staples on hand and don't be overly ambitious. Go with what you know works and are very comfortable with.

One fun fact few people know about me is that . . .

People always wonder why I have done a few Mexican restaurants with my oh-so-French last name and rather fair appearance. They don't realize I'm half Mexican and grew up eating Mexican food every day. It is absolutely my soul food, and I'm passionate about it.

MENU

Taco Bar with Carne Asada, Salsa & Pink Beans

CHEF'S PAIRING

Great Mexican beer, a margarita, or Tequila & Squirt (or grapefruit soda) with lime

CHEF'S PLAYLIST

A whole range of music, from Leon Bridges to Chris Stapleton to David Bowie

MAJOR KUDOS

James Beard awards for "Best Chef: Pacific" and "Rising Star Chef of the Year"; semifinalist for James Beard "Outstanding Chef" award; nomination for James Beard "Best New Restaurant" award; winner of Esquire Network's *Knife Fight*; winner of Food Network's *Iron Chef America*; finalist on Bravo's *Top Chef Masters 3*; "Chef of the Year" award by *San Francisco Magazine*; "Best New Chef" award by *Food & Wine*; "Best New Restaurant" award by *Esquire*

HER STORY

With a surname as French as Des Jardins (meaning "of the gardens"), it may come as a surprise to some that Traci's passion is Mexican cuisine. But then again, it's no surprise at all if you knew her maternal family is from Mexico.

Traci eventually worked her way up from hand-rolling tortilla dough with her grandmother to working alongside some of the most respected chefs at the most acclaimed restaurants around the world.

Yet her initial passion never wavered. Which brings us to this fabulous Mexican meal—one of Traci's favorites.

"I love tacos!" exclaims Traci enthusiastically. "I make all kinds, but the carne asada is one of the fastest and easiest. It's also a crowd pleaser. Everyone loves it!"

She adds, "When I make this dish at home, I already have the salsa, beans, and sometimes even the tortillas in the freezer. Salsas that are boiled then blended freeze incredibly well. I always keep an assortment on hand, since they're easy to use as a foundation for all kinds of meals: enchiladas, chile rellenos, huevos rancheros, and chilaquiles."

Let's get started!

Taco Bar with Carne Asada, Salsa & Pink Beans

SERVES 4

Nothing screams "party" like a fun, festive taco bar! Plus, it's interactive, too—making it the perfect entertainment experience. P.S. Since this book's concept restricts preparation time to one hour, Traci allowed for canned beans to be used. However, she's also sharing her popular recipe for Homemade Beans (see below). Just get started early in the day—or make ahead, freeze, and defrost. The secret is to use only beans that are extremely fresh or "new crop."

FOR THE CARNE ASADA

½–¾ lb (224–336 g) butcher steak, flat iron, hanger, flank, or tri-tip

Salt, to taste

Freshly ground black pepper, to taste

2 cloves garlic, crushed

Juice of 4 key limes or 2 regular limes

FOR THE SALSA

8 oz (224 g) tomatillos

8 oz (224 g) tomatoes

½ onion, thinly sliced

2 cloves garlic

1 tbsp (15 ml) canola oil

1–3 canned chipotle chiles en adobo (depending on how spicy you like it), seeded

½ cup (120 ml) water

½ tsp dried oregano

Salt, to taste

Freshly ground black pepper, to taste

FOR THE TACOS

1 can pink beans, drained and warmed (can substitute pinto beans or Homemade Beans, recipe follows)

½ white onion, finely diced

½ bunch fresh cilantro leaves, roughly chopped

1 serrano chile, finely minced

8 key limes, halved

¼ cup (45 g) grated Cotija cheese

12 good-quality all-corn tortillas, kept warm

To make the carne asada, preheat a gas grill, grill pan, or heavy sauté pan.

Season the steak well with salt and pepper, then rub with the garlic and place in a glass baking dish. Pour in the lime juice and marinate for 15 minutes.

Remove the steak from the dish. Cook on the grill or grill pan, or in the sauté pan, until it reaches an internal temperature of 135°F (57°C). Remove from the heat and let rest for 10 minutes before slicing. Slice very thin.

To make the salsa, preheat the oven broiler to high. Place the tomatillos and tomatoes in a glass baking dish. In a bowl, toss the onion and garlic with the oil, then pour over the tomatoes. Place under the broiler for about 15 minutes, or until they are thoroughly "wilted" and slightly blackened, stirring as necessary to prevent the top layer from burning. Remove from the broiler and set aside.

Heat the oven to 350°F (177°C). Place the tomatillo mixture in a saucepan. Add the chipotle chiles, water, and oregano. Bring to a boil, then reduce the heat and simmer for 10 minutes. Carefully transfer to a blender and process until it's the consistency you like. Season with salt and pepper.

Set out the beans, onion, cilantro, chile, limes, cheese, carne asada, salsa, and warmed tortillas, family style. Allow everyone to build their own tacos.

Bonus Recipe: Homemade Beans
MAKES 6 CUPS (1200 G)

2 cups (400 g) dried pink or pinto beans

1 white onion, finely diced

1 head garlic, split

1 bunch fresh cilantro, tied tightly with kitchen string

Salt, to taste

Place the beans in a pot and cover with 1 gallon (3.8 L) of water. Add the onion, garlic, and cilantro. Bring to a boil, then turn down the heat and simmer for about 2 hours. Add a generous amount of salt. Cook for 1 more hour, or until completely tender. Taste again and add salt if necessary. Drain, discarding the garlic and cilantro. The beans will keep for about 4 to 5 days in an airtight container. May also be frozen.

RON DUPRAT

Los Angeles, California

Consulting partner with International Hospitality; culinary liaison with Vie Cachée; consultant with Rastelli Direct

CHEF SAYS

Items I always keep on hand for unexpected guests are . . .

Valmas Cremas, Rhum Barbancourt, Prestige beer, Black Elk wine, and prosciutto.

When hosting a quick get-together, never overlook . . .

Time, guests' allergies, and culinary diversity.

My secret tip for successful last-minute entertaining is . . .

Keep it simple and sexy so it can be entertaining.

One fun fact few people know about me is that . . .

I donated my adult life to give back to the less fortunate.

MENU
Coq au Vin

CHEF'S PAIRING
Black Elk red wine and Valmas Cremas

CHEF'S PLAYLIST
Beyoncé

MAJOR KUDOS
Contestant on Bravo's *Top Chef*; starred in Spike TV's *Bar Rescue*; appointed culinary ambassador by Hillary Clinton; named one of "10 Black Chefs That Are Changing the Food World as We Know It" by *Huffington Post*; listed in the article "How 12 Black Chefs Cooked Their Way to the Top of the World" by the *Washington Post*'s TheRoot.com

HIS STORY

If Haitian Creole influences with French-Asian-Caribbean fusion cuisine doesn't sound exotic to you, I don't know what does. But that's exactly the type of food Ron loves to prepare for the president, Jay Z, Beyoncé, and Usher, plus you and me.

Even though Ron came from a very poor background, his humble beginnings were full of love. Born and raised in Haiti, he would spend many a comforting day in his grandmother's kitchen, watching her make mouth-watering dishes in a nod to their heritage.

But when he was sixteen, he and his family left for the United States, spending twenty-seven harrowing days at sea in a small boat in order to reach Florida.

After Ron landed his first job there as a dishwasher, he was hooked. He quickly rose through the ranks of that kitchen. He left to train at École de Cuisine La Varenne in Paris. Then he came back, rising with one executive position after another. Today all he wants to do is give back.

"I chose this meal because it's artistic, creative, and not your everyday meal," says Ron. "It's also easy to make. Not complicated at all!"

Coq au Vin

SERVES 4

Even though coq au vin is a classic French dish, Ron adds his own unique and distinctive twist using airline chicken breast. By definition, it's a boneless, skin-on chicken breast with the first wing joint (drumette) still attached. Also known as "Statler chicken breast" or "chicken suprême," it makes an impressive presentation and is commonly used in fine dining restaurants. Fun fact: This term "airline chicken breast" first became popular in the 1960s when commercial airlines would use a small breast portion but keep part of the wing to make it appear bigger than it actually was.

4 airline chicken breasts (about 6 oz [168 g] each), skin on (can substitute boneless, skin-on chicken breasts)

½ cup plus 3 tbsp (87 g) all-purpose flour, divided

Maldon or other flaky sea salt, to taste

Freshly ground black pepper, to taste

1 lb (450 g) slab bacon, preferably Nueske's, cut into ½-inch (12-mm) cubes

2 cups (320 g) small-diced Vidalia onion

2 cups (150 g) thinly sliced cremini mushrooms

¼ cup (40 g) chopped shallots

2 tbsp (18 g) chopped garlic

3 to 4 fresh thyme sprigs

2 bay leaves

3 cups (720 ml) young, full-bodied red wine, preferably Black Elk

2 cups (480 ml) brown chicken stock (can substitute regular chicken stock)

4 tbsp (58 g) French butter, at room temperature (can substitute regular butter), divided

1 tbsp (3 g) finely chopped fresh parsley

4 small Yukon Gold potatoes

Microgreens (can substitute finely chopped fresh parsley), for garnish

Season the chicken and the ½ cup (65 g) flour separately with salt and pepper. Dredge the chicken in the seasoned flour, coating each side completely. Reserve the remaining flour.

Set a large ovenproof skillet over medium-high heat, and when hot, add the bacon and cook until crispy and the fat is rendered out, about 6 to 8 minutes. Remove the bacon, drain on paper towels, and set aside.

Lay the chicken, skin side down, in the hot bacon fat. Brown for 3 to 4 minutes on each side, then remove from the pan and set aside.

Add the Vidalia onion to the pan and sauté for 2 to 3 minutes, or until tender. Add the mushrooms, shallots, and garlic, then season with salt and pepper. Sauté for 2 minutes. Add the thyme and bay leaves. Return the chicken to the pan, add the red wine and chicken stock, and bring to a simmer. Cover and cook until very tender, about 30 to 35 minutes, skimming off the fat. Remove the chicken from the pan and set aside. Remove the bay leaves.

Blend the remaining flour and 2 tablespoons (28 g) of the butter together into a smooth paste (in French, *beurre manié*). Whisk the paste into the hot liquid in the pan, then bring to a simmer and cook for 3 to 4 minutes. Return the chicken to the pan and continue to cook for 5 minutes. Stir in the parsley. Season with salt and pepper, if needed.

Bring water to a boil in a medium-size saucepan. Add the potatoes and parboil for 5 minutes, or until just fork tender. Drain the potatoes, then cut into quarters.

Melt the remaining 2 tablespoons (28 g) of butter in a sauté pan over medium-high heat. Add the quartered potatoes and cook, turning occasionally, until lightly golden brown.

Place the potatoes on one side of each of 4 plates. Lay the chicken next to the potatoes, then spoon the sauce over it. Garnish with the reserved crispy bacon and microgreens.

FORD FRY

Atlanta, Georgia

Chef/managing partner of JCT. Kitchen & Bar, no. 246, The Optimist, King + Duke, St. Cecilia, The El Felix, Superica, Marcel, Beetlecat, and Bar Margot (Atlanta), and State of Grace (Houston)

CHEF SAYS

Items I always keep on hand for unexpected guests are . . .

A range of different types of beers, still and sparkling water, wine, a good collection of vinyls, and a couple of big fat prime steaks.

When hosting a quick get-together, never overlook . . .

Music, for sure. Something interesting and not a commercial "dinner party" CD!

My secret tip for successful last-minute entertaining is . . .

Keep it super simple and don't try to do too much.

One fun fact few people know about me is that . . .

After "being on stage" (talking to people all day/night), I have to decompress to recharge. A true introvert.

MENU
Wood-Grilled Nam Prik Chicken Roti

CHEF'S PAIRING
Singha beer slushy

Thai coffee for dessert

CHEF'S PLAYLIST
"Zenyattà Mondatta" by The Police

MAJOR KUDOS

Multiple James Beard award nominations; "Empire Builder of the Year" award from Eater Atlanta; Crystal of Excellence Award for "Restaurateur of the Year" by the Georgia Restaurant Association; "Best New Restaurant of the Year" award from *Esquire*; named one of the "70 Best Restaurants in the World" by *Condé Nast Traveler*; named one of the "Best New Restaurants in America" by *Bon Appétit*

HIS STORY

They call him "part-human-part-restaurant-building-robot." (He owns eleven restaurants, for Pete's sake!)

As if that's not enough, he's also got his hand in a whole lot of other fun stuff, too. Like taking on a gig as Justin Bieber's personal chef. And coming up with a special burger for Shake Shack. And partnering with Uber on an exclusive lineup of curbside treats. And playing in an all-chef band (5 Bone Rack). And, seriously, who knows what else.

So, when it comes to at-home entertaining, you can bet Ford's got something really creative in mind.

"The first time I served this dish, the eyes-wide-open looks I got said, 'What is this? It's like crack!'" jokes Ford. "It was as if I had filled a tortilla with croissant dough! Your guests will truly be blown away by the flavors and how it was so easy to throw together. You just got to pretend that you came up with it off the cuff!"

Much easier for you to say, Ford, but we'll try.

Wood-Grilled Nam Prik Chicken Roti

SERVES 4

This recipe is incredibly easy to make, yet sophisticated and amazing at the same time. Just look for the *roti paratha* (a crispy and buttery Malaysian flatbread) in the frozen section of any Asian market. As for the Thai chili paste, Ford says, "I always keep a bottle of my favorite nam prik pao sauce in stock, which I love to use on wood-fired meats, in stir-fries, warming noodle soups, and more. There are a lot of authentic bottles you can find in specialty stores and online. But I do prefer making my own, which I store in the refrigerator." Since Ford's recipe takes at least a couple hours to make, we're offering it to you as a bonus recipe below!

1 cup (240 g) Thai chili paste, preferably Pantai or Maeri brand (can substitute Ford's Homemade Nam Prik Pao Sauce, recipe follows)

¼ cup (60 ml) peanut or canola oil

¼ cup (60 ml) lime juice

8 boneless, skin-on chicken thighs

8 frozen roti paratha, thawed

½ cup (120 ml) vegetable or peanut oil, for frying

FOR SERVING

¼–½ cup (60–120 g) crème fraîche

1 cucumber, peeled, seeded, and thinly sliced

1 bunch fresh Thai or regular basil, leaves only, roughly chopped

1 bunch fresh mint, leaves only, roughly chopped

1 bunch fresh cilantro, leaves only, roughly chopped

2 limes, halved

1 fresh Thai chile, thinly sliced, for garnish, optional

Combine the Thai chili paste, oil, and lime juice together in a glass jar with a lid and shake, covered, until well mixed. Pour half the mixture into a small bowl and set aside for later use. Add the chicken to the remaining chili paste mixture in a large bowl, toss, and marinate for 30 minutes in the refrigerator.

Meanwhile, preheat the grill (preferably wood or charcoal). When the chicken is done marinating, grill until just done, about 5 to 6 minutes per side or until each thigh reaches an internal temperature of 165°F (74°C), basting with the reserved chili paste mixture. Set aside.

Using a couple of skillets, panfry the roti over medium-high heat, using 1 tablespoon (15 ml) of oil per roti until golden brown on both sides. Remove the roti from the skillets as they are done and keep warm under a heavy kitchen towel while frying the remaining roti.

Slice the chicken and build the roti in this order: chicken, spoon of crème fraîche, cucumber, basil, mint, cilantro, and squeeze of lime. If desired, garnish with Thai chile slices.

Bonus Recipe: Ford's Homemade Nam Prik Pao Sauce

MAKES 1½ CUPS (360 ML)

10 Thai chiles, stemmed and roughly chopped

¼ cup (10 g) finely chopped fresh lemongrass (about 1 stalk, trimmed, outer leaves removed, pale green parts only)

2 tbsp (42 g) honey

1 cup (240 g) Thai chili paste, preferably Pantai or Maeri brand

¼ cup (60 ml) fresh lime juice

2 tbsp (30 ml) fish sauce

½ cup (20 g) loosely packed Thai basil leaves (can substitute regular basil)

Place the chiles and lemongrass in a food processor and process until finely minced. Combine the chile mixture with the honey in a small bowl. Allow to infuse for at least 1 hour or up to 4 hours in the refrigerator. Stir in the remaining ingredients, cover, and place in the refrigerator for at least 1 hour or overnight to infuse further. Remove and discard the basil before using. Will keep for up to 4 months in the refrigerator.

KENNY GILBERT

Jacksonville, Florida

Chef/owner of Gilbert's Underground Kitchen; president/CEO of Cook Like the Big Dogs LLC

CHEF SAYS

Items I always keep on hand for unexpected guests are . . .

Onions, crushed tomatoes, basil paste, garlic purée, and dried pasta.

When hosting a quick get-together, never overlook . . .

A clean home. Make sure bathrooms are stocked and fresh smelling, and that they have amenities available for guests (breath mints, flossers, etc.). Plus, always have a nice variety of beverages (both alcoholic and nonalcoholic), good coffee with appropriate accompaniments, and a signature drink for the evening. Great music is also a must!

My secret tip for successful last-minute entertaining is . . .

Be organized. Mise en place is critical. Having everything in its place is so key.

One fun fact few people know about me is that . . .

My mom taught me how to clean, cook, and sew from the age of three. She didn't have any girls, so she domesticated me and my brother early on. I also have a keen eye for interior design. I used to create concepts for the Ritz-Carlton Club Division.

MENU

Fried Western-Style Pork Ribs

Sour Cream New Potatoes

Hot Mustard Peppers & Onions

CHEF'S PAIRING

Knobb Creek bourbon with lemon juice, blackberries, black pepper simple syrup, and a few shakes of bitters over ice

CHEF'S PLAYLIST

Motown (Aretha Franklin, The Jackson 5, The O'Jays, Teddy Pendergrass, etc.)

MAJOR KUDOS

"Chef of the Year" and "Best Caribbean Restaurant" awards from *Folio: Magazine*; winner of Food Network's *Beat Bobby Flay* and *Cutthroat Kitchen*; contestant on Bravo's *Top Chef*

HIS STORY

Imagine a three-year-old being taught by his mom how to cook and by his dad how to grill. Is there any surprise he'd grow up to be a chef? Didn't think so.

Raised in Cleveland, Kenny was making Thanksgiving dinner by himself by the time he was eleven. By the time he was sixteen, he was cooking for his high school swim team on an electric burner in the locker room. And by the time he graduated from the Pennsylvania Culinary Institute, he landed his first job with the Ritz-Carlton Hotel Company in Florida.

In fact, by the time he turned twenty-three he had become the youngest African-American chef to ever run a AAA Five Diamond and Mobile Four Star Ritz-Carlton restaurant. Impressive, right?

"When I create food," says Kenny, "I do everything I can to create memorable and craveable flavors. That's why I chose this meal. Because I feel that once you try it, you'll always want more. Besides, it can easily be finished in one hour. You only need three burners: one to fry the pork, one to smother the peppers and onions, and one to boil the potatoes."

Fried Western-Style Pork Ribs

SERVES 4

"My father was from Chicago," explains Kenny. "He took me to Chinatown there when I was a kid, and there was a place that would serve a fried pork chop sandwich between two slices of Wonder bread, topped with smothered peppers and onions with a hot mustard sauce. I remember this was the most delicious combination I ever had. Even now after thirty-plus years, I still remember it." We bet you'll always remember this dish, too!

3 cups (375 g) all-purpose flour

1 cup (112 g) cornstarch

¼ cup (25 g) Chef Kenny's Fried Chicken Seasoning (can substitute Goya Adobo All Purpose Seasoning)

¼ cup (25 g) Chef Kenny's Raging Cajun Spice (can substitute Chef Paul Prudhomme's Blackened Redfish Magic Seasoning)

4 (4-oz [112-g]) western-style—not country—pork ribs (pork shoulder or Boston butt roast, cut into 2-inch [5-cm] thick strips)

2 cups (460 g) lard

2 cups (410 g) Crisco all-vegetable shortening

Salt, to taste

Freshly ground black pepper, to taste

Place the flour, cornstarch, and chicken seasoning in a bowl. Whisk together well.

Massage the Cajun spice into the ribs, then dredge the ribs in the flour mixture. Place on a baking sheet and allow to sit for 10 minutes. Dredge the ribs again in the flour mixture and set aside.

Place the lard and Crisco in a deep 12- to 14-inch (30- to 36-cm) cast-iron skillet over medium to medium-high heat. When hot, add the ribs and fry, rotating every 2 to 3 minutes, until fully cooked, about 9 to 10 minutes. The internal temperature should reach 155°F to 165°F (68°C to 74°C). If necessary, cook ribs two at a time.

Remove the ribs to a platter with tongs and season lightly with salt and pepper.

Sour Cream New Potatoes

SERVES 4

Rich. Rustic. Decadent. And pretty damn amazing. That's the best way to describe this deceptively easy recipe. And that's what you should come to expect every time . . . nothing less!

16 new potatoes, unpeeled

¼ cup (60 g) sour cream

3 tbsp (43 g) butter, at room temperature

¼ cup (12 g) sliced scallions

Salt, to taste

Freshly ground black pepper, to taste

Place the potatoes in a pot and cover with cold water. Bring to a boil, then reduce to a simmer. Continue to cook the potatoes until tender, about 15 to 20 minutes. Drain.

Crush the potatoes, skin and all, in a bowl with a masher or fork. Fold in the sour cream, butter, scallions, salt, and pepper. Serve warm.

*See photo on page 304.

Hot Mustard Peppers & Onions

SERVES 4

Just when you thought that caramelizing the onions and peppers was going to produce a sweet rendition of this mixture, Kenny goes and adds a 1:4 ratio of hot sauce to yellow mustard. Imagine the tang it produces now. Way to go, Kenny!

3 tbsp (43 g) butter

1 cup (100 g) julienned red onion

½ cup (45 g) julienned red bell pepper

½ cup (45 g) julienned poblano chile

1 tbsp (9 g) chopped garlic

1 tbsp (3 g) chopped fresh sage

1 tbsp (3 g) chopped fresh rosemary

1 tbsp (3 g) chopped fresh Italian parsley

1 cup (249 g) prepared yellow mustard

¼ cup (60 ml) Texas Pete Hot Sauce (can substitute Louisiana Hot Sauce)

1 tbsp (16 g) sugar

Salt, to taste

Freshly ground black pepper, to taste

Place the butter in a medium-size skillet over medium-high heat. Let cook for about 30 seconds, until lightly brown.

Add the onion, red pepper, and poblano chile. Continue to cook, stirring frequently, until caramelized, about 8 to 10 minutes. Add the garlic, sage, rosemary, and parsley. Turn the heat to low and sweat, about 3 to 4 minutes.

Add the mustard, hot sauce, and sugar. Simmer for 3 to 4 minutes, then remove from the heat and season with salt and pepper.

Transfer the pepper mixture to a bowl to serve.

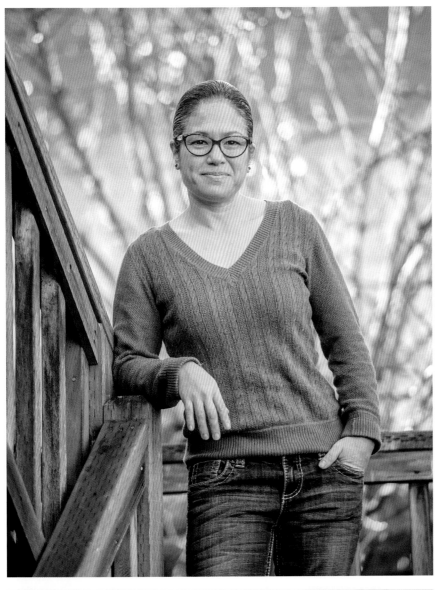

MARIA HINES

Seattle, Washington

Chef/owner of Tilth, Agrodolce, and Young American Ale House

CHEF SAYS

Items I always keep on hand for unexpected guests are . . .

Extra wine, bread, cheese, olives, and nuts.

When hosting a quick get-together, never overlook . . .

Having enough food. Nuts, olives, and cheese can go with any meal, so they make a nice buffer. It's great to have them on the table when people arrive, so if you're running behind in the kitchen, they'll have food to snack on. And make sure the wine is chilled and ready.

My secret tip for successful last-minute entertaining is . . .

One-pot dishes. For example, paella, cassoulet, chili, etc.

One fun fact few people know about me is that . . .

My diet is 85% vegetarian.

MENU

Fresh English Pea Soup

Salmon Cakes

Asparagus Salad

Blood Orange Gratin

CHEF'S PAIRING

A chilled rosé

CHEF'S PLAYLIST

Rodrigo y Gabriela

MAJOR KUDOS

James Beard award for "Best Chef: Northwest"; finalist for the James Beard "Outstanding Chef" award; named one of *Food & Wine*'s "Top 10 Best New Chefs in America"; named one of the "Top 10 Best New Restaurants in the Country" by the *New York Times*; contestant on Bravo's *Top Chef Masters*; winner of the Battle of Pacific Cod on Food Network's *Iron Chef America*

HER STORY

Her initial reason for becoming a chef was simple: She knew she'd always be able to find a job. But somewhere along the way, she found a much deeper meaning and genuine passion for the profession.

Raised in Bowling Green, Ohio, Maria got her first restaurant job at seventeen. She liked it so much ("I got paid for peeling carrots!") that she then went on to Mesa College in San Diego and got a culinary degree. After graduation, her jobs took her from a one-Michelin-star restaurant in France to a three-Michelin-star restaurant in New York.

But when it came time to settle down, she chose one of her favorite places on earth: Seattle. And after a few years making a name for herself there, she decided to open her own restaurant.

But not just any restaurant. Rather, a sustainable, eco-friendly restaurant and only the second one in the country to receive organic certification from Oregon Tilth, one of the toughest organizations to get certified through.

"I chose this meal," explains Maria, "because it's quick and elegant. A lot of it can even be prepared ahead of time." Now that, we like!

Fresh English Pea Soup

Shelling peas—also known as English or garden peas—are just that: peas that need to be removed from their pods before eating (unlike sugar or snap peas, which have edible pods). They're especially appreciated for their lovely vegetal sweetness. Buy them fresh or pluck them, if you can, from your garden in early spring. Otherwise, and only as a last resort, go ahead and use frozen peas (but thaw first).

1 tbsp (16 g) kosher salt, plus additional to taste

1 tbsp (13 g) sugar

2 lb (907 g) fresh English shelling peas, shelled

1½ qt (1.4 L) vegetable broth

Freshly ground black pepper, to taste

Unflavored yogurt or croutons, for garnish, optional

Place 1½ quarts (1.4 L) water, the salt, and sugar in a medium-size saucepan. Bring to a boil over high heat. Add the peas and blanch for about 2 minutes. Drain.

Add the peas and broth, in batches, to a blender or food processor and purée. Pour into a pot and warm through over medium heat. Season with salt and pepper. If desired, garnish with a dollop of yogurt or with croutons. Serve immediately.

*See photo on page 310.

Salmon Cakes

This all-star, easy-to-follow recipe makes full use of fresh, not canned, salmon for an authentic culinary experience. So much better than store bought!

¼ cup (25 g) diced yellow onion

1 tsp minced garlic

1 tbsp plus 2 tsp (25 ml) olive oil, divided

2 slices bacon, diced

1 lb (450 g) salmon (can be trim pieces), cut into small dice

2 tbsp (5 g) mixed fresh herbs (fresh dill, parsley, chives, tarragon), minced

Salt, to taste

Freshly ground black pepper, to taste

Store-bought pesto, for garnish, optional

In a sauté pan, sauté the onion and garlic in 1 tablespoon (15 ml) of the olive oil over medium heat until soft, about 2 to 3 minutes. Set aside to let cool.

In another pan, cook the bacon over low heat for several minutes to render out the fat. Take off the heat, then remove the bacon to a paper towel–lined plate with a slotted spoon and blot away the excess grease.

In a medium-size bowl, combine the onion-garlic mixture, salmon, bacon pieces, herbs, salt, and pepper. Form into 4 thick cakes. Heat the remaining 2 teaspoons (10 ml) of olive oil in a pan over medium heat. Add the salmon cakes and cook about 2 to 3 minutes per side, or to desired doneness. Do this 2 patties at a time, if necessary. If desired, garnish with pesto. Serve warm.

Asparagus Salad

Not only is this salad a cinch to make, but Maria makes it into such a beautiful presentation. Your guests will be totally wowed!

2 large eggs, hard-boiled (page 456), cooled and peeled

1 tbsp (16 g) crème fraîche

1 tsp strong Dijon mustard

Salt, to taste

Freshly ground black pepper, to taste

1 fresh tarragon sprig

1 fresh dill sprig

1 fresh flat-leaf parsley sprig

2 tbsp (5 g) chopped fresh chives

FOR THE VINAIGRETTE

3 tbsp (45 ml) truffle oil (can substitute extra virgin olive oil)

1 tbsp (15 ml) champagne vinegar (can substitute white wine vinegar)

Salt, to taste

Freshly ground black pepper, to taste

24 medium-thick asparagus spears, stems peeled

Slice the eggs in half and gently remove the yolks from the whites. Grate the yolks into a small bowl, then mix in the crème fraîche, mustard, salt, and pepper. Spoon the yolk mixture back into the whites and set aside.

Strip the leaves off the stems of the fresh herbs, then combine all the herbs and set aside.

To make the vinaigrette, combine the oil, vinegar, salt, and pepper in a second small bowl and mix well.

Bring a pot of water to a boil. Add the asparagus and blanch for about 8 minutes. Drain, then place the blanched asparagus in a large bowl and drizzle with the vinaigrette. Sprinkle with the herb mixture and gently toss.

Divide the asparagus among 4 plates. Place an egg half on top of each serving and serve immediately.

Blood Orange Gratin

SERVES 4

This elegant dish requires a simple method called, in French, *brûlée*. "You need to sprinkle the sugar very evenly on the orange slices," explains Maria, "and evenly torch the sugar until it melts and gets a nice caramel color. Then it should be cooled until it looks glassy. This provides a nice candy-crunch texture on top of the oranges."

4 blood oranges (can substitute regular navel oranges), peeled of both rind and white pith

4–6 tbsp (27–40 g) chopped hazelnuts, toasted (page 457), divided

4 tsp (18 g) sugar

1 tbsp (15 ml) canola or vegetable oil

2 tsp (10 g) coarse sea salt

Aged balsamic vinegar (or see page 456), for drizzling

Slice each orange crosswise into 12 slices.

Overlap the slices of one orange per person on each of 4 dessert plates into a straight row, alternating each slice with sprinkles of some toasted hazelnuts. Sprinkle a teaspoon of sugar over each row to coat.

Using a kitchen blowtorch, melt the sugar to create a crust, holding it 2 to 3 inches (5 to 8 cm) above the sugar surface, moving it back and forth to ensure even browning. Let the sugar cool before touching it (see Chef's Tip).

Toss the remaining hazelnuts with the oil and salt. Sprinkle onto the orange stacks to garnish. Add a light drizzle of balsamic vinegar, which should have a thick, syrupy consistency, and serve.

CHEF'S TIP

If you don't have a kitchen blowtorch, you can use your broiler. However, if you do use the broiler, be sure to place the orange slices on an ovenproof dish first, broil *very* briefly—just a few seconds—and then carefully transfer the glazed orange slices to the serving plates.

CHRIS HODGSON

Cleveland, Ohio

Chef/co-owner of Hodges; president of Driftwood Catering; consulting chef for Driftwood Restaurant Group

CHEF SAYS

Items I always keep on hand for unexpected guests are . . .

Saffron, Hodges Spice Blend (paprika, cinnamon, chili powder, garlic powder, onion powder, black pepper, salt), Hodges Hot Sauce (honey, red wine vinegar, hot sauce, garlic, shallots), salsa verde, and different chutneys.

When hosting a quick get-together, never overlook . . .

The table setting. While it may be last minute, a nicely set table, wine, water pitcher, correct setting, napkins, etc., go a long way. It shows your guests you put some effort into the meal and it was important to you.

My secret tip for successful last-minute entertaining is . . .

Do a favorite with a twist. People love familiar foods—just add something a little out of the box.

One fun fact few people know about me is that . . .

I started cooking and working in restaurants in order to afford a guitar for my now wife back when I was only fifteen.

MENU
Eggs in a Nest

CHEF'S PAIRING
For the kids, freshly squeezed orange juice

For the adults, a nice Greyhound cocktail

CHEF'S PLAYLIST
Funk music

MAJOR KUDOS

Won "The People's Best New Chef: Great Lakes Region" award from *Food & Wine*; was runner-up on Food Network's *Great Food Truck Race*, a finalist on their *Food Network Star* show, and featured on their *Unique Eats* show

HIS STORY

Chris graduated from Le Cordon Bleu culinary school, went to live in New York City, and then, after being inspired by what he saw in the Big Apple, came back home to Cleveland with a brilliant-beyond-brilliant idea.

He wanted to start this city's very first food truck. Which he did—and playfully called it Dim and Den Sum.

After quickly gaining a loyal, cult-like following and lots of praise, he started a second food truck, this time calling it Hodge Podge. It, too, was a huge success, garnering national attention on the Food Network.

As an encore, Chris went on to open an eponymous bricks-and-mortar restaurant (without wheels this time). And he's been keeping busy ever since.

"I remember my mom making this dish for me on special occasions," says Chris. "I found it to be so much fun. My favorite part was dipping the perfectly toasted round cut-out into the yolk as it first cracked and spilled over. Too few people make this anymore, but it's one of my best childhood memories." And that's what it's all about.

Eggs in a Nest

SERVES 2

This whimsical dish is a perfect choice when someone special drops by for breakfast or brunch. It combines a nice variety of flavors, textures, and aromas all at once to create something pretty delicious. You make it in parts, then put it together to craft one impressive meal that will have your guest wanting more (and more)!

6 tbsp (86 g) butter, divided

1 onion, thinly sliced

2 fresh sausage patties

2 slices challah bread, each cut 1-inch (2.5-cm) thick

Clarified butter (page 456), for brushing (can substitute regular butter, melted)

2 large eggs

1 potato, peeled, cut into ½-inch (12-mm) cubes, and set aside in cold water

¼ cup (60 ml) chicken stock

1 tsp minced garlic

Kosher salt, to taste

Freshly ground black pepper, to taste

1 tbsp (3 g) chopped fresh chives

In a nonstick sauté pan, melt 4 tablespoons (57 g) of the butter over medium heat. Add the onion and let cook down in the pan until lightly browned and caramelized, about 4 to 5 minutes, stirring occasionally. Remove from the heat and set aside.

Wipe out the sauté pan and set over medium heat. Flatten the sausage patties and add to the pan. Cook in the patties' own rendered fat until browned and cooked through, about 3 minutes per side. Set aside and keep warm.

Remove the center of each challah slice with a round 3-inch (8-cm) cookie cutter or an Old-Fashioned rocks glass. Toast the round centers in a toaster until light brown on both sides. Brush one side with the clarified butter. Set aside.

Brush the hollowed-out challah slices with clarified butter on both sides. Place in a nonstick sauté pan over medium heat. Carefully crack 1 egg into the center of each slice. When the egg whites are firm but yolks are still uncooked, and the bread is lightly toasted, about 2 to 3 minutes, carefully turn each bread slice over in the pan, using a wide spatula. Brown on the other side for about 1 minute, but do not overcook the egg. The yolks should remain soft. Remove from the heat and set aside to keep warm.

Drain and pat the potato cubes dry with a paper towel. Melt 1 tablespoon (14 g) of the butter in a sauté pan over medium heat. Add the potato cubes and cook until brown on all sides, about 4 to 5 minutes. Add the chicken stock, the remaining 1 tablespoon (14 g) butter, 1 tablespoon (20 g) caramelized onion (reserve the remainder for another use), garlic, salt, and pepper. Cook until the liquid is gone and the mixture is dry, about 3 to 4 minutes.

Evenly place a mound of the potato hash in the center of 2 plates. Lean 1 slice of egg bread against each mound of hash, then lean a plain toasted bread round and a sausage patty against each egg bread. Garnish with the chives and serve immediately.

LINTON HOPKINS

Atlanta, Georgia

Chef/owner of Restaurant Eugene, Holeman and Finch Public House, H&F Bottle Shop, H&F Burger, Linton's, Hop's Chicken, and Eugene Kitchen

CHEF SAYS

Items I always keep on hand for unexpected guests are . . .

Rice, chicken stock, Champagne, Parmigiano-Reggiano, and dry cured sausage.

When hosting a quick get-together, never overlook . . .

Having plenty of ice.

My secret tip for successful last-minute entertaining is . . .

Stick to the basics. Guests desire simplicity and goodness of food with minimal fuss.

One fun fact few people know about me is that . . .

I took a semester off from college to follow the Grateful Dead on tour.

MENU

Braised Chicken Thighs with Long-Grain Rice, Saffron, Cipollini Onions & San Marzano Tomatoes

Arugula with Olive Oil, Lemon & Parmigiano

CHEF'S PAIRING

A nice fruity Pinot Noir or Sangiovese

CHEF'S PLAYLIST

Django Reinhardt (acoustic jazz guitar in the gypsy style)

MAJOR KUDOS

James Beard award for "Best Chef: Southeast"; multiple-time semifinalist for James Beard awards; named by *Food & Wine* as one of their "Best New Chefs," "Best New Chef All-Stars," and inaugural team members for the magazine's Chefs Club Manhattan restaurant

HIS STORY

Spoiler alert: Linton didn't always want to be a chef.

During his younger days, Linton made extra money by working at a small catering joint and later at Mellow Mushroom Pizza. Then he graduated from Emory University with a degree in pre-med.

To make a long story short, before he could do anything with his degree, he ended up reading a book called *The Guide to Cooking Schools*. And suddenly it hit him. He could—and would actually rather—make a living doing what he loved best: cooking.

So, he headed out to the Culinary Institute of America. He eventually made it back to Atlanta and opened his own place. Then another. And another. And a few more. Oh, yeah, he also won a coveted opportunity to work with Delta Airlines and develop their in-flight meals, too.

But Linton takes all this experience in stride and applies it to home entertaining so seamlessly.

"I've made this meal many times before," he explains. "It's easy, requires very little clean-up, and is very delicious. A natural delicious quality is the true essence of hospitality."

We couldn't have said it better ourselves.

Braised Chicken Thighs with Long-Grain Rice, Saffron, Cipollini Onions & San Marzano Tomatoes

SERVES 4

"The method of cooking one-pot meals with cast-iron skillets," explains Linton, "is both old-fashioned and modern at the same time. Another name for this dish is perloo (or pilau), which evokes the story of the journey of rice from the Mediterranean to the American south."

1 (28-oz [794-g]) can whole San Marzano tomatoes (preferably Cento brand)

4 skin-on boneless chicken thighs

Salt, to taste

Freshly ground black pepper, to taste

2 tbsp (30 ml) peanut oil

8 cipollini onions, peeled (can substitute shallots)

1 cup (240 ml) dry white wine

Pinch of saffron

2 bay leaves

½ cup (120 ml) chicken stock

1 cup (185 g) uncooked long-grain white rice (preferably Carolina Gold)

Preheat the oven to 375°F (191°C).

Drain the tomatoes, reserving ½ cup (120 ml) juice. Crush the tomatoes by hand, then set aside.

Season the chicken thighs with salt and pepper. Heat the oil in a large cast-iron skillet on medium-high heat. Add the chicken thighs, skin side down, being careful not to crowd the pan. Sauté until golden brown on the skin side, about 5 minutes. Remove from the pan and set aside.

Add the onions to the pan. Cook about 2 minutes, stirring occasionally, until a little colored. Add the tomatoes, reserved juice, wine, saffron, and bay leaves. Add 1 teaspoon salt and the stock. Bring to a boil, then reduce the heat and simmer for 5 minutes.

Stir in the rice and bring back to a boil, then remove from the heat. Lay the thighs, skin side up, on top of the rice. Place the pan in the oven and bake for 15 to 20 minutes. Remove the bay leaves. Serve hot.

Arugula with Olive Oil, Lemon & Parmigiano

SERVES 4

This enticing salad may very well win the prize for the easiest recipe in this book. But make no mistake, it's all in what you buy that makes all the difference. "The ingredients should be of the highest quality for this very simple salad to impress," says Linton. Lesson learned: Don't dare skimp.

4 cups (120 g) baby arugula

6 tbsp (90 ml) extra virgin olive oil

4 tsp (20 ml) fresh lemon juice

Sea salt, to taste

Freshly cracked black pepper, to taste

4 oz (112 g) aged Parmigiano-Reggiano cheese

Evenly pile the arugula on 4 plates. Drizzle with the oil and lemon juice and season with salt and pepper. Just before serving, grate the cheese with a microplane and cover each serving of greens generously with a white snow of cheese.

*See photo on page 322.

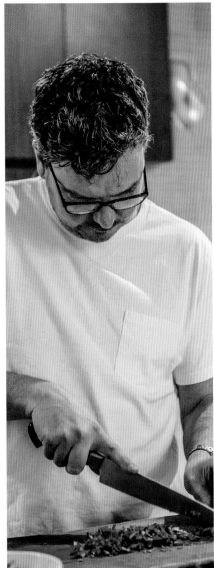

MATT HOYLE

New York, New York

Executive chef of Nobu 57

CHEF SAYS

Items I always keep on hand for unexpected guests are . . .

Jars of homemade pickles (beets, sauerkraut, or kimchee), whatever cheese we have (from cheddar to burrata), some salad leaves with an oil/vinegar dressing, carrots and celery chopped up, and tomatoes with salt and pepper. Simple stuff. And always with a baguette.

When hosting a quick get-together, never overlook . . .

Remembering to enjoy yourself and to spend time with your guests.

My secret tip for successful last-minute entertaining is . . .

Make it tasty and everything will be fine.

One fun fact few people know about me is that . . .

I started cooking in fish and chips shops for a few years in my hometown before moving into more high-end cuisine.

MENU
Kedgeree

CHEF'S PAIRING

For the kids, juice and maybe iced tea

For the adults, first a gin and tonic

Then white Châteauneuf-du-Pape or an Alsatian white (Pinot Gris/Riesling)

CHEF'S PLAYLIST
"After Laughter Comes Tears" by Wendy Rene

This Is Marijata by Marijata

The Magical Light of Saba by Cedric Brooks

Black Ark in Dub by Lee Perry

Black Mahogani by Moodymann

Universal Sounds of America with Sun Ra, Pharoah Sanders, and Art Ensemble of Chicago

Ege Bamyasi by Can

Moa Anbessa by Getatchew Mekurya & The Ex

Daxaar by Steve Reid Ensemble

Jukebox Jam! by Jazzman Records

MAJOR KUDOS
Three-star rating from the *New York Times*

HIS STORY

As a kid growing up in Lancashire, England, Matt enjoyed helping both his mother and grandmother cook. So after he finished with school, he went on to work in two local fish and chips shops. He fell in love with the whole experience . . . and that's where it all began.

Today, Matt continues to work with world-renowned chef, Nobu Matsuhisa, who owns thirty-two restaurants around the globe. Matt started out with him in London, then Mykonos, St. Moritz, and finally New York City, where he still heads the kitchen on West 57th Street more than a decade later.

"Serving a one-bowl meal that everyone can dig into, like this English rice dish of Indian descent, is great when friends or family are visiting," says Matt. "It has a wonderful variety of both flavors and textures. Plus, it tastes great.

"I added lentils, too," he explains, "which isn't normal in Britain, but I like the earthiness. And the spices are ones I feel balance it well. However, if you like more heat, just use extra cayenne pepper, jalapeños, or even some turmeric or curry powder, depending on your taste."

Kedgeree

SERVES 4

Kedgeree (also called "kidgeree" or "kitcherie") is a delicious traditional English breakfast that features smoked fish, rice, and eggs. It was actually inspired by the South Asian dish, *khichdi*, which hails from the days of the Raj. Rest assured, this meal will not only wow your guests, it'll also be a fascinating topic of conversation.

2 tbsp (7 g) cumin seeds

2 tbsp (16 g) coriander seeds

2 cardamom pods

2 tsp (3 g) curry powder

½ tsp cayenne pepper

2½ cups (600 ml) water

8 oz (224 g) uncooked brown Japanese rice (can substitute regular brown rice)

4 oz (112 g) lentils

2 bay leaves

Salt, to taste

Freshly ground black pepper, to taste

6–8 kale leaves, chopped

10 oz (280 g) smoked sablefish (also called "black cod," can substitute any smoked whitefish)

2 tbsp (28 g) butter

2 large eggs, hard-boiled (page 456), cooled, peeled, and quartered

Furikake or smoked seaweed powder, optional

In a dry pan, toast the cumin, coriander, and cardamom until they just start to turn color and you can smell their fragrance being released. Take off the heat. After they have cooled, grind in a clean coffee or spice grinder. Add the curry powder and cayenne pepper to this mix.

Place the water, rice, lentils, and bay leaves in a covered pan. Bring to a boil, then reduce to a gentle simmer. Cook until tender, about 30 minutes. There should be no water left in the pan. Season lightly with salt and pepper, then stir in 2 teaspoons (3 g) of the spice mixture (see Chef's Tip). Transfer to a large serving bowl, remove the bay leaves, and set aside.

Place the chopped kale leaves in a shallow saucepan and top with the smoked sablefish. Pour in 1 inch (2.5 cm) of water and add the butter. Cover and simmer for 6 minutes. Most of the water should be evaporated, leaving the fish and leaves lightly covered in the smoky, buttery sauce.

With a large fork or pair of chopsticks, gently turn the sablefish and kale into the rice mixture.

Arrange the egg quarters around the bowl, letting the heat and steam of the rice warm them up.

If using, sprinkle furikake liberally over the dish.

> **CHEF'S TIP**
> The spice mix will yield more than you need for this dish. The remaining spice mix will keep for a few weeks and has many uses, such as for seasoning stews, salsas, and plain egg dishes.

MIKE ISABELLA

Washington, D.C.

Chef/owner of G, Kapnos, and Arroz (Washington, D.C.); Grafiatto (Washington, D.C., and Richmond, Virginia); Yona, Pepita, and Kapnos Taverna (Arlington, Virginia); Kapnos Kouzina (Bethesda, Maryland); and Requin and Isabella Eatery (Fairfax, Virginia)

CHEF SAYS

Items I always keep on hand for unexpected guests are . . .

Rosemary (which can be used in main dishes and as décor accents), cured meats and cheese for an easy charcuterie board, sparkling water in glass bottles for a touch of elegance, vanilla ice cream (easy to serve with coffee, cookies, or berries, or to prepare a mini sundae bar), and mixers and wine, of course.

When hosting a quick get-together, never overlook . . .

Presentation. It matters. Keep a small collection of good-quality platters, bowls, cheese boards, and napkins (either cloth or paper). You can even order takeout and serve it on nice platters, and make it a night.

My secret tip for successful last-minute entertaining is . . .

Get a game plan. You still need a compressed timeline, even for last-minute gatherings. Start planning as soon as you know, and enlist help. Have friends bring wine, a dessert, or salad.

One fun fact few people know about me is that . . .

I was a wild kid, and my grandmother gave me things to do in the kitchen that kept me busy and out of trouble. When we went out to eat, I was always the kid trying the "weird" things on the menu. While my sister usually stuck to pasta with butter and cheese, I always wanted to order something new or different and then try to figure out how they made it.

MENU

Veal Cutlets with Asparagus, Basil & Lemon

CHEF'S PAIRING

A white wine that's light in flavor, tannins, and acidity, like a good Chardonnay or Pinot Blanc

CHEF'S PLAYLIST

The Pandora station "Cozy Night at Home"

MAJOR KUDOS

"Restaurateur of the Year" award from the Restaurant Association of Metropolitan Washington; *Food & Wine*'s "The People's Best New Chef: Mid-Atlantic" award; judge on FYI Network's *Man vs. Child: Chef Showdown*; runner-up on Bravo's *Top Chef All-Stars*; contestant on *Top Chef* and *Top Chef Duels*; member of the American Chef Corps

HIS STORY

To start with, just in case you were wondering, dear reader, no, Mike and I are not related. (Well, at least not that we know of.) So now that that's out of the way, let's get on with HIS STORY!

Mike grew up in northern New Jersey. In a boisterous Italian household. With a loving *nonna* who taught him to roll meatballs in her kitchen when he was only six.

Fast forward a dozen years later, when he left home to attend the Restaurant School in New York City. He worked his way through the finest restaurants in Manhattan. Then the finest restaurants in Philadelphia, Atlanta, and Washington, D.C., where he finally decided to stay put and open his own place or two or three or . . .

"This dish reminds me of home, cooking with my grandmother," says Mike. "This is a dish that could easily have been on our table for Sunday night dinner. It's simple, straightforward, and doesn't take long to prepare, yet presents as sophisticated and thoughtful."

Yes, please!

Veal Cutlets with Asparagus, Basil & Lemon

SERVES 4

"When I was growing up," explains Mike, "veal piccata was a popular dish in my hometown. But I like my veal dishes to have a little more depth and breadth of flavor and texture. This lightly breaded and pan-fried veal is light and creamy, and the basil and lemon brighten the asparagus salad."

FOR THE VEAL CUTLETS

½ cup (63 g) all-purpose flour

3 large eggs, beaten

2 cups (240 g) panko bread crumbs

½ cup (90 g) grated Parmigiano-Reggiano cheese

1 tbsp (3 g) dried oregano

1 tbsp (3 g) finely chopped fresh parsley

1 tbsp (5 g) lemon zest

1 tbsp (16 g) kosher salt

2 tsp (3 g) red chili flakes (crushed red pepper), finely ground

8 (2½-oz [70-g]) veal cutlets (scallops; 1¼ lb [562 g] total)

1 cup (240 ml) extra virgin olive oil

3 cloves garlic

FOR THE ASPARAGUS SALAD

Kosher salt, to taste

8 asparagus spears, woody ends removed

1 cup (149 g) halved cherry or grape tomatoes

3 tbsp (45 ml) extra virgin olive oil

2 tbsp (30 ml) fresh lemon juice

1 tsp (7 g) honey

Pinch of freshly ground white pepper

1 cup (30 g) baby arugula, loosely packed

¼ cup (10 g) torn fresh basil leaves

1 lemon, cut into 4 wedges, for serving

To prepare the veal, set up a breading station using three separate shallow bowls. Place the flour in the first bowl, the eggs in the second bowl, and in the third bowl, whisk together the panko, Parmigiano-Reggiano, oregano, parsley, lemon zest, salt, and chili flakes.

Dredge the veal in the flour, then the eggs, then the bread crumb mixture. Set aside.

Heat the olive oil and garlic in a large sauté pan over medium heat. Sauté the garlic for 8 minutes, or until golden brown, stirring frequently. Remove from the heat, discard the garlic, and set the pan with the garlic oil aside.

To make the asparagus salad, bring a medium-size saucepan of water to a boil, and have ready a bowl of ice water. Add 1 to 2 tablespoons (16 to 32 g) salt to the boiling water, drop in the asparagus, and blanch for 2 minutes. Drain the asparagus, then shock the spears in the ice water until chilled. Drain again and dry completely with paper towels. Slice on the bias into bite-size pieces and place in a serving bowl along with the tomatoes.

In a small bowl, whisk the oil, lemon juice, honey, ½ teaspoon salt, and white pepper. Toss with the asparagus and tomatoes until nicely coated, then set aside.

Set the pan with the garlic oil over medium-high heat, and when it is hot, add the veal cutlets, in batches if necessary (do not crowd the pan). Sauté for 1½ minutes on each side, or until golden brown. Remove the veal from the pan and place on a wire rack.

At serving time, toss the arugula and basil with the asparagus-tomato mixture. Arrange 2 of the veal cutlets on each of 4 plates. Top with the salad and place a lemon wedge on the side.

JENNIFER JASINSKI

Denver, Colorado

Chef/co-owner of Rioja, Bistro Vendôme, Euclid Hall Bar & Kitchen, and Stoic & Genuine

CHEF SAYS

Items I always keep on hand for unexpected guests are . . .

Some great cheese and preserves, usually some salumi or guanciale, good wine, and tequila.

When hosting a quick get-together, never overlook . . .

Having enough wine!

My secret tip for successful last-minute entertaining is . . .

Make sure you get your prep done ahead of time.

One fun fact few people know about me is that . . .

I love dogs. They are always part of every party. They love guests and getting attention!

MENU

Brioche-Crusted Skate Wing with Brussels Sprouts, Crisp Prosciutto, Pistachio Pistou & Lemon Crème Fraîche

Colorado Peaches with PX Sherry, Whipped Mascarpone Cream & Lavender Oat Crumble

CHEF'S PAIRING

2013 Tiefenbrunner Müller-Thurgau from Alto Adige

For the dessert, more of PX sherry!

CHEF'S PLAYLIST

Rodrigo y Gabriela

MAJOR KUDOS

Winner of James Beard award for "Best Chef: Southwest"; semifinalist for the James Beard "Outstanding Chef" award; "Best Chef" award from *Denver Magazine*; "Best Female Chefs in America" award from Thrillist; finalist on season 5 of Bravo's *Top Chef Masters*

HER STORY

Jennifer grew up in a single-parent household, which made helping out in the kitchen a necessity. This necessity eventually turned into fun, then joy, then passion as she slowly realized it was what she wanted to do as a living.

After getting the necessary training and experience, Jennifer finally found herself helping her mentor, Wolfgang Puck, open restaurants nationwide. Ten fast-paced years later, Jennifer decided to trade it all in for a quieter life in Denver. Or so she thought.

Now with four successful restaurants to her name, Jennifer is still quite busy, yet continues to find time to spend with family and friends—which takes us to her meal.

"It has a great wow factor," says Jennifer. "It looks like you made it in a restaurant, yet it's really quite simple. I don't think many people understand how easy it is to prepare skate."

If you've ever been tempted to try it, this is the recipe you want to make. Trust us.

Brioche-Crusted Skate Wing with Brussels Sprouts, Crisp Prosciutto, Pistachio Pistou & Lemon Crème Fraîche

SERVES 4 TO 6

Skate, one of Jennifer's favorite fish, has such delicate, tender "wings" that it's hard to believe they're actually the pectoral fins of edible rays. But with proper skinning and filleting (ideally performed by your fishmonger) and the right recipe (this one), you'll enjoy how really sweet they are—quite literally. As a bonus, Jennifer makes full use of a lot of textures here. The light crunch of the skate, the silkiness of the crème fraîche, and the bite of the Brussels sprouts all combine together to make this dish one you won't soon forget. Both the lemon crème fraîche and the pistachio pistou can be made a day ahead. (The crème fraîche should be kept refrigerated.) And prepare the Brussels sprouts garnish as close to the time of serving as possible. As for the lightly toasted pistachios called for in both the pistachio pistou and brussels sprouts recipes, it makes most sense to prepare them at the same time. Jennifer acknowledges that the yuzu juice in the lemon crème fraîche is an expensive item—and that while it can be found online, it may not be that readily available—and says that lemon juice can be substituted for it, but she also says that the results just won't be the same.

FOR THE LEMON CRÈME FRAÎCHE

1 cup (240 g) crème fraîche

Zest of 1 lemon

1 tbsp (15 ml) yuzu juice

Kosher salt, to taste

Freshly ground black pepper, to taste

FOR THE PISTACHIO PISTOU

½ cup (75 g) pistachios, lightly toasted (page 457)

1 clove garlic

¼ cup (60 ml) extra virgin olive oil

2 tbsp (5 g) lightly packed fresh parsley leaves

10 large spinach leaves

Kosher salt

Freshly ground black pepper

FOR THE BRUSSELS SPROUTS

8 cups (704 g) Brussels sprouts

1 cup (225 g) julienned prosciutto

¼ cup (60 ml) pure olive oil

½ cup (75 g) chopped shallots

½ cup (75 g) pistachios, lightly toasted (page 457)

Kosher salt, to taste

Freshly ground black pepper, to taste

FOR THE BRIOCHE-CRUSTED SKATE

4 cups (180 g) fresh bread crumbs (page 456), from a 1-lb (450-g) loaf of bread, preferably brioche

1 cup (120 g) panko bread crumbs

4 large egg whites

Kosher salt, to taste

Freshly ground black pepper, to taste

2 lb (907 g) fresh skate wing, bones and silver skin removed, cut into 4 or 6 pieces (can substitute halibut or scallops)

Canola oil, as needed

To make the lemon crème fraîche, place the crème fraîche, lemon zest, and yuzu juice in a bowl and stir to mix. Whisk by hand to thicken slightly. Season with salt and pepper.

(continued)

Brioche-Crusted Skate Wing with Brussels Sprouts, Crisp Prosciutto, Pistachio Pistou & Lemon Crème Fraîche (Cont.)

To make the pistachio pistou, combine the toasted pistachios, garlic, oil, parsley, and spinach in a blender and process until smooth. Remove to a bowl and season to taste with salt and pepper. Refrigerate until ready to serve.

To prepare the Brussels sprouts, use a paring knife to halve each Brussels sprout through the core. Make a little "V" along the outside of the core to cut it out. Separate the leaves and reserve; discard the cores.

In a large sauté pan on medium heat, sauté the prosciutto in the oil until crisp. Add the shallots, lower the heat, and sweat gently until they are translucent.

Add the Brussels sprouts and toasted pistachios. Allow the Brussels sprouts to heat through but not wilt completely; you still want a bit of texture. Once they are hot, season with salt and pepper and remove from the heat. Keep warm until time to serve.

To prepare the skate, combine the ground brioche with the panko. Beat the egg whites in a shallow bowl until frothy.

Season the skate portions with salt and pepper on both sides. Lightly dredge each first in the egg whites, then in the brioche/panko mix, making sure they are evenly and completely coated. As each is coated, lay it in a single layer on a baking sheet.

Set a large sauté pan over medium-high heat and add ¼ inch (6 mm) of canola oil. When the oil is hot, and working in batches, fry the skate wings gently until they are golden brown on the first side. Flip and cook until the skate wants to barely flake, about another 1 to 2 minutes. Remove the fish from the pan and reserve on the baking sheet, now covered with paper towels. As you work, replenish the oil in the pan as needed.

Work quickly through this as the breading on the fish is best eaten within the first few minutes of being cooked. Also, be sure not to crowd the pan to ensure you get a nice crunchy texture. If the pan is crowded, the bread coating will absorb the oil.

To assemble, on each of 4 large entrée plates, place a portion of the Brussels sprouts on the left side. Rest a skate wing on the sprouts but not completely covering them. Spoon a line of the pistachio pistou alongside the skate wing, then spoon a nice dollop (about 2 tablespoons [30 g]) of the lemon crème fraîche on top of the pistou. Serve immediately.

Colorado Peaches with PX Sherry, Whipped Mascarpone Cream & Lavender Oat Crumble

SERVES 4

This simple-yet-mouthwatering dessert boasts one star ingredient: the famous Colorado peach. And with good reason. Because of its unique growing environment (300 days of sunshine a year plus rich volcanic soil), it's widely considered one of the juiciest, best-tasting tree-ripe peaches in the country. One bite of its rich, sweet, and tangy flavor and you'll quickly see why Jennifer chose this great dessert.

FOR THE LAVENDER OAT CRUMBLE

4 tbsp (115 g) unsalted butter

½ cup (40 g) rolled oats (not instant)

2 tbsp (42 g) honey

¼ tsp dried lavender buds (available in specialty shops or online)

FOR THE WHIPPED MASCARPONE CREAM

1 cup (240 ml) heavy cream, chilled

3 tbsp (39 g) sugar, divided

¼ tsp pure vanilla extract

1 cup (227 g) mascarpone cheese

FOR THE PEACHES

4 ripe Colorado peaches (can substitute other peaches or ripe pears)

¾ cup (180 ml) 1971 Pedro Ximénez sherry (can substitute any good-quality sherry, preferably aged)

To make the lavender oat crumble, preheat the oven to 300°F (149°C).

Add the butter to a saucepan and swirl the pan while the butter melts to a light brown color. The butter solids go to the bottom of the pan, so swirling keeps them coloring without burning.

Immediately add the oats and stir well. Add the honey and lavender, then stir until well coated and mixed. Remove from the heat.

Spread the oat mixture on a sheet tray. Bake until golden, about 20 minutes, stirring occasionally so it browns evenly. Let cool.

To make the whipped mascarpone cream, add the cream, 1 tablespoon (13 g) of the sugar, and vanilla to the chilled bowl of a stand mixer. Whip the cream to stiff peaks. Remove to a separate bowl and set aside.

Clean out the mixer bowl, then add the mascarpone and the remaining 2 tablespoons (26 g) sugar. Whip on medium-high speed only until the sugar has dissolved, about 2 to 3 minutes. Do not overbeat or the mascarpone might break down.

Fold the whipped cream mixture into the mascarpone in 4 batches, folding only gently to combine. Make sure that the bottom of the bowl is well scraped in between additions as the heavier mascarpone will sink because of its weight. Keep chilled until ready to serve.

To prepare the peaches, first have ready a bowl of ice water and set near the stove.

Bring a pot of water to a boil, and after making a small *X* on the bottom of each peach with a knife, drop the peaches gently, one at a time, into the boiling water for just 5 seconds. Immediately, using a slotted spoon, transfer the peaches to the ice water to chill.

Remove the peaches from the water and peel the skin off each with a paring knife. Cut in half and remove the pit. Cut into slices or wedges, whichever you prefer.

To assemble, evenly divide the peach slices among 4 ice cream bowls or on 4 small plates, then place a dollop of the whipped mascarpone cream on top. Drizzle on 3 tablespoons (45 ml) of the sherry per serving, then finally sprinkle on the oat crumble. Serve immediately.

*See photo on page 334.

JOSEPH "JJ" JOHNSON

New York, New York

Executive chef of Minton's

CHEF SAYS

Items I always keep on hand for unexpected guests are . . .

A bottle of bourbon, good bottle of red wine, couple pounds of rib eye, amazing veggies from the farmers' market I shop at daily, and a wide range of good music.

When hosting a quick get-together, never overlook . . .

The beverage.

My secret tip for successful last-minute entertaining is . . .

A great chef's playlist, good conversation, and if there's no food in the fridge, order the best New York City pizza.

One fun fact few people know about me is that . . .

I have a passion for teaching children.

MENU

Roasted Niman Ranch Pork Chops with Black Garlic Marinade

Coriander Roasted Carrots

CHEF'S PAIRING

Classic Penicillin Cocktail

CHEF'S PLAYLIST

The Life of Pablo by Kanye West

MAJOR KUDOS

Named "Best New Restaurant in America" by *Esquire*; nominated for a James Beard "Rising Star Chef" award; won the Star Chefs' "Rising Star Community Chef" award; named one of *Forbes*'s "30 Under 30" and Zagat's "30 Under 30"; named one of "20 Under 40" of extraordinary philanthropists by the *Observer*; named "Chef of the Year" by New York African Restaurant Week; winner of Bravo's *Rocco's Dinner Party*

HIS STORY

When JJ was only seven, he happened to see a commercial on TV for the Culinary Institute of America. He immediately turned to his mother and said, "I want to be a chef!" She paused, then said, "You should be a doctor or politician. Why would you want to be a chef?"

But he was determined—and realized his dream many years later after making good on his promise and graduating from the CIA.

JJ went on to work at some of New York City's most esteemed restaurants. Then he won a reality-show cooking competition. And that brought him to the attention of a respected restauranteur, who invited JJ to travel to Ghana with him. Together they cooked alongside native chefs who taught them flavor profiles they'd never even heard of.

Back in the States, first The Cecil, then Minton's, was born. And now New Yorkers are enjoying a dining experience—dubbed Afro-Asian—unlike any other in the city.

"I chose this meal because it's something fun to make together as a family," says JJ. "It's also easy and offers a burst of flavors."

And he's absolutely correct.

Roasted Niman Ranch Pork Chops with Black Garlic Marinade

SERVES 4

This super quick and easy dish is sure to fool some people. Why? It features a top-secret, sought-after ingredient that adds a unique "what-in-the-world-is-that?!" kind of flavor: black garlic. Because it's aged, black garlic takes on a sticky, date-like texture with a sweet, earthy flavor that brings out so many rich subtleties. (Think aged balsamic, prune, licorice, molasses, caramel, and tamarind.) Find it at specialty spice shops, some upscale markets, and online, or easily make your own (assuming you have weeks to spare).

1 cup (240 ml) chicken stock

½ cup (120 ml) grapeseed or blended oil (can substitute ¼ cup [60 ml] olive oil plus ¼ cup [60 ml] vegetable oil)

1 lemon, zested and juiced

4 large shallots, sliced

1 small bunch fresh cilantro

1 whole clove black garlic, peeled

Salt, to taste

Freshly ground black pepper, to taste

4 (8-oz [224-g]) bone-in Niman Ranch pork rib chops (can substitute other brand of all-natural certified humane pork chops)

Preheat the oven to 400°F (204°C).

Place everything but the pork chops into a blender and process to a purée. Pour into an extra-large resealable plastic bag. Add the chops to the bag and seal the top, releasing the excess air. Turn the bag to coat the chops, then refrigerate for at least 30 minutes, turning the bag occasionally.

Remove the chops from the marinade, then transfer to a baking sheet. Bake for 15 to 25 minutes, or until an instant-read thermometer inserted at the thickest point registers 145°F (63°C).

Remove from the oven, transfer to a platter, and serve.

Coriander Roasted Carrots

SERVES 4

The humble carrot is now served in a much more exciting way! Coriander and cumin provide the extra bit of zest it deserves. To make this dish even more vibrant and give it an added wow factor, try using assorted colored carrots.

1½ lb (680 g) whole baby carrots

1 tbsp (15 ml) grapeseed oil (can substitute olive oil)

¼ cup (60 ml) olive oil

1 clove garlic

1½ tsp (3 g) ground cumin

1 tsp ground coriander

½ tsp kosher salt

Preheat the oven to 500°F (260°C). Line a baking sheet with parchment paper.

Place the carrots on the baking sheet and drizzle on the grapeseed oil. Roast for 6 minutes.

While the carrots roast, place the olive oil, garlic, cumin, coriander, and salt in a blender or food processor. Process to a smooth purée.

Remove the carrots from the oven and evenly coat with the coriander mixture, using a pastry brush.

Return the coated carrots to the oven and roast for an additional 5 minutes, or until the carrots are just tender enough to be pierced with a fork. Serve warm.

JEAN JOHO

Chicago, Illinois

Chef/proprietor of Everest and Studio Paris (Chicago), Eiffel Tower Restaurant (Las Vegas), and Brasserie JO (Boston); partner in M Burger, Nacional 27, Intro, and Naoki (Chicago); co-founder of Corner Bakery (Chicago); managing partner of Lettuce Entertain You Enterprises

CHEF SAYS

Items I always keep on hand for unexpected guests are . . .

Frozen steaks and chops, fresh fruits, vegetables and salad, domestic cheeses, and ice cream.

When hosting a quick get-together, never overlook . . .

Attention to details. Also, be careful with the temperature of your food. You don't want it to be too hot or too cold.

My secret tip for successful last-minute entertaining is . . .

Sit down, plan your meal, get organized, delegate what you can, and stay calm.

One fun fact few people know about me is that . . .

I love to fish.

MENU

Leeks with Mustard Vinaigrette, Double-Smoked Bacon, Walnuts & Eggs

Chicken Crapaudine

Pommes Paillasson

Caramelized Apple Tarte Flambée

CHEF'S PAIRING

With the appetizer: Pinot Blanc from Alsace

With the entrée: Pinot Noir Grand Cru from Alsace

With the dessert: Alsace Gewürztraminer

CHEF'S PLAYLIST

Classic, old-world jazz

MAJOR KUDOS

One Michelin star; James Beard awards for "Best Chef: Great Lakes" and "Best New Restaurant"; James Beard Foundation inductee to "Who's Who of Food & Beverage in America"; "Restaurateur of the Year" award from Gayot; "Best Chef of the Year" award from *Bon Appétit*; Robert Mondavi "Culinary Award of Excellence"; 4 stars by *Chicago Tribune, Chicago Sun Times,* and *Chicago Magazine*; five-diamond rating from AAA; awards from Relais & Chateaux/Relais Gourmand, Les Grande Table du Monde Traditions & Qualité, Maître Cuisiniers de France, and Académie Culinaire

HIS STORY

Joho (as everyone affectionately calls him) still manages to summit Everest daily. Okay, so maybe he takes the elevator. And maybe it's "only" forty stories high. And maybe it's actually the name of his restaurant on the top floor of the historic Chicago Stock Exchange building. Regardless, after thirty years of culinary excellence at this premier, world-class dining room, it really is a feat in itself.

Yet when you speak with Joho, he's got his feet firmly planted on the ground. He's humble, convivial, and direct.

"When I entertain friends, I like to prepare something unique. They expect it, after all," he says with a laugh.

Which is why he chose this meal for this book.

"The beauty of this menu is that you can get the ingredients all year long," says Joho. "Just be sure every ingredient is the best it can be. Your meal can only be as good as your ingredients."

Sage words of wisdom from on high.

Leeks with Mustard Vinaigrette, Double-Smoked Bacon, Walnuts & Eggs

SERVES 4

"This is one of my favorite summer appetizers," says Joho. "Even though leeks seem to be more novel now, people still don't know how to use them. It's actually quite simple." Which begs the question, why don't we cook with leeks more often? Luckily, leeks are in season all year long. Just be sure to buy them absolutely fresh, which will make this delicious starter even more so.

1 tbsp (16 g) kosher salt

8 small leeks, light green and white parts, cleaned and trimmed (page 456)

4 thick-cut strips double-smoked bacon, cut into ⅜-inch (10-mm) strips

FOR THE MUSTARD VINAIGRETTE

¼ cup (60 ml) extra virgin olive oil

2 tbsp (30 ml) sunflower oil

2 tbsp (30 ml) melfor vinegar (can substitute red wine vinegar)

1 tbsp (16 g) Dijon mustard

Fine sea salt, to taste

Freshly ground black pepper, to taste

Small bunch fresh chives, minced

2 eggs, hard-boiled (page 456), cooled, peeled, and chopped, for garnish

½ cup (58 g) roughly chopped walnuts, toasted (page 457), for garnish

Fill a large pot with water. Bring to a boil and add the salt.

Tie the leeks together in a bundle with kitchen twine. Submerge in the boiling water and cook until tender and well done, about 20 minutes. To check for doneness, pierce the leeks with a sharp paring knife. There should be no resistance.

Drain the leeks, then remove the twine and let the leeks cool on a baking sheet lined with paper towels.

Cut the cooled leeks in half lengthwise. Divide the pieces evenly among 4 serving plates, alternating head to tail, and set aside.

Cook the bacon in a sauté pan until nearly crispy. Transfer to a paper towel to drain.

To make the mustard vinaigrette, whisk together the olive and sunflower oils, vinegar, mustard, salt, and pepper. Stir in the minced chives at the end.

Drizzle each portion of leeks with the vinaigrette and garnish with the chopped eggs, bacon, and toasted walnuts.

Chicken Crapaudine

SERVES 4

"I make this dish for guests when I'm at my country home in Michigan," says Joho. "I only use one hundred percent natural organic chicken I buy from a local farmer. It's very important to only buy the best chicken you can. *Never skimp!*" Got that? Good.

1 whole organic, free-range chicken
(3–3½ lb [1.4–1.6 kg])

1 tsp sea salt

¼ tsp Espelette pepper (can substitute regular ground black)

2 tbsp (30 ml) grapeseed oil

2 cloves garlic, unpeeled

1 fresh thyme sprig

1 tbsp (15 ml) extra virgin olive oil, for drizzling

1 lemon

Watercress, for garnish

Preheat the oven to 400°F (204°C).

Remove the backbone of the chicken by cutting down along both sides between the backbone and the breast with poultry shears. Open out the chicken, skin side toward you, and push the breast down with your hands so that the chicken lays flat. You can ask your favorite butcher shop to do this task for you! Season with the salt and pepper.

Set a large cast-iron skillet over medium-high heat. Add the grapeseed oil. Gently place the chicken in the hot oil, breast side down. It is important to keep the chicken flat, so wrap something heavy, such as a brick, in aluminum foil and then place on the chicken. Cook until the skin is golden brown, about 35 minutes.

Remove the skillet from the heat and place in the oven. Bake the chicken for 10 minutes with the brick still on top. Remove the brick, lift the chicken, and turn carefully upside down. Replace the brick on top and bake for 15 minutes longer. Remove from the oven, take away the brick, and add the garlic and thyme to the skillet. No more weight is necessary at this point.

Return the skillet to the oven and bake for another 15 minutes. By now the chicken should be nice and golden brown. Remove from the oven and set the chicken on a platter, reserving the cooked garlic cloves.

To serve this dish in the traditional French style, cut the chicken into 8 pieces: 2 legs, 2 thighs, and each breast cut in half. Be sure to leave the wings attached. Drizzle the chicken with the oil, then zest the lemon with 5 or 6 pulls off a zester or the coarse side of a grater and sprinkle over the chicken. Garnish with the cooked garlic cloves and the watercress.

Pommes Paillasson

As chichi as this dish sounds, it's basically a shredded potato pancake. Or, better yet, a version of the classic tater tot. Either way, with its crispy exterior and soft interior, it's a delicious side dish worthy of your most elegant meal. (Fun fact: The French whimsically named it this because it resembles a woven straw doormat. It actually does, doesn't it?)

2 tbsp (30 ml) olive oil

4 tbsp (58 g) butter, divided

1 medium-size carrot, peeled and julienned

1 small zucchini, julienned

1 small celeriac, peeled and julienned

Fine sea salt, to taste

Freshly ground black pepper, to taste

½ cup (20 g) chopped fresh parsley

3 large russet potatoes, peeled

Smoked sea salt, for garnish, optional

Crème fraîche, for garnish, optional

Heat the oil and 2 tablespoons (28 g) of the butter in a cast-iron skillet over medium heat. Add the carrot, zucchini, and celeriac. Season with salt and pepper. Sweat the vegetables over low heat a few minutes until al dente, then add the parsley. Remove from the heat and set aside to cool.

Finely julienne the potatoes with a mandolin or in a food processor. After cutting, do not rinse. The potatoes will need their natural starches to help hold the dish together.

Transfer the potatoes to an ungreased baking sheet and season well with salt and pepper. Let sit for a few minutes.

Heat the remaining 2 tablespoons (28 g) of butter in a 9-inch (23-cm) nonstick skillet over medium heat. While the skillet is heating, press the potatoes between your hands to squeeze out excess water. Place a layer of half the potatoes in the skillet, followed by all of the vegetables, then finish with the rest of the potatoes. Make sure all the layers are flat.

Cook over medium heat until golden brown on the bottom, about 10 minutes, then, using a wide spatula, carefully flip the potato cake and cook for another 10 minutes.

Remove the potato cake from the pan to a cutting board. Cut into 8 wedges and place on a serving dish. If desired, sprinkle each wedge with smoked sea salt and add a dollop of crème fraîche to serve.

*See photo on page 344.

Caramelized Apple Tarte Flambée

SERVES 4

The trick to making this tart, which always reminds Joho of Alsace, is to use heirloom apples, if you can, and top-quality ingredients. You can also change it up a bit by substituting plums or pears. But whatever fruit you use, remember that serving it à la mode with rich vanilla ice cream tops all!

4 large tart apples

Fresh lemon juice

1 cup (240 g) fromage blanc (can substitute crème fraîche)

2 tbsp (26 g) sugar

½ oz (14 ml) Kirsch d'Alsace (can substitute cherry brandy)

8 oz (224 g) store-bought pizza dough or bread dough

4 tbsp (58 g) butter, melted, plus additional if needed

1 tsp ground cinnamon

Preheat the oven to 475°F (246°C). Line a baking sheet or baking stone with parchment paper.

Peel and core the apples. Cut into quarters, then slice crosswise. Toss the apples with a small amount of lemon juice to prevent browning. Set aside.

Combine the fromage blanc, sugar, and Kirsch in a bowl and stir to blend.

Roll the dough out on a floured surface into a 20 x 14–inch (51 x 36–cm) rectangular shape about ⅛-inch (3-mm) thick, or almost transparent. Roll the dough up loosely on the rolling pin and place carefully on the baking sheet. Spread the fromage blanc mixture over the dough, leaving a 1-inch (2.5-cm) border around the edges.

Arrange the sliced apples in a nice pattern over the cream. Drizzle with the melted butter and sprinkle with the cinnamon.

Bake until the crust and cream have browned and the apples are caramelized, about 7 minutes. If necessary, run the baking sheet under a hot broiler to attain caramelization.

*See photo on page 344.

DOUGLAS KATZ

Cleveland, Ohio

Chef/owner of Fire Food and Drink; chef/partner of Provenance, Provenance Cafe, and Catering By Provenance at the Cleveland Museum of Art; owner of Fire Spice Company

CHEF SAYS

Items I always keep on hand for unexpected guests are . . .

Wine, artisan crackers, cheese, nuts/dried fruit, and Dijon mustard. Plus local eggs and locally roasted coffee.

When hosting a quick get-together, never overlook . . .

Setting a nice table! Flowers from the garden and beautiful plateware, linen, and glassware. No matter how quick and simple the dinner, these touches make everything look well planned and delicious.

My secret tip for successful last-minute entertaining is . . .

Even though it's last minute, stay organized and don't rush through the techniques. Make lists! Ask your guests for help and stay calm. Have a glass of wine, and it'll all seem much easier.

One fun fact few people know about me is that . . .

I was born in Minot, North Dakota. And if that's not interesting enough, I love Indian and ethnic cooking. In fact, it enticed me to start my own spice and recipe company.

MENU

Longburgers with Sautéed Onions, Cheddar & Maple-Glazed Bacon

Smashed Baby Red Potatoes with Sautéed Onions

Baby Tomato Salad with Crumbled Goat Feta & Basil

CHEF'S PAIRING

A great local beer (such as Great Lakes Dortmunder) or an Oregon Pinot Noir

CHEF'S PLAYLIST

Steely Dan, The Police, or Sting

MAJOR KUDOS

James Beard award semifinalist for "Best Chef: Great Lakes"; named a "Rising Star of American Cuisine" by *Reader's Digest*; named one of the "Best New Restaurants" by *Esquire*; appearances on the *Rachael Ray Show* and Cooking Channel's *Unique Eats*; chef ambassador for the Monterey Bay Aquarium's "Cooking for Solutions" events

HIS STORY

Both his mother and grandmother were great cooks. Matzo balls, matzo brei, brisket, and bagels were childhood favorites. In fact, family trips were always planned around food first.

So it comes as no surprise that when Douglas was only seven years old, he had already set his sights on becoming a chef. And that desire never waned. In fact, he ran his own catering business all throughout high school and college at the University of Denver.

Armed with a degree in hotel and restaurant management, Douglas then decided to pursue what he considers to be his graduate school: the Culinary Institute of America.

After stints in Boston, Portland, and Aspen, Douglas returned home to put down roots—and begin on the road to becoming an international advocate for a food system that is sustainable, healthful, and local.

"This meal is a fun family favorite in our house," says Douglas. "It's really easy and delicious, too. Plus, the techniques are simple, and your guests can even help with the preparations."

Gotta love it!

Longburgers with Sautéed Onions, Cheddar & Maple-Glazed Bacon

SERVES 4

"I created this longburger one weeknight when my son was craving burgers," explains Douglas. "We already had local, freshly ground, grass-fed beef chuck in the fridge, but we didn't have any hamburger buns. Only long challah rolls. So I shaped the beef to fit, and I've been making them this way ever since!"

6 tbsp (90 ml) canola oil, divided

1 medium-size yellow onion, peeled, cored, and julienned

Kosher salt, to taste

8 thick slices bacon

Pure maple syrup, for brushing

1¼ lb (562 g) ground beef, preferably local, grass-fed beef, not too lean

Freshly cracked black pepper, to taste

4 slices Cheddar cheese, preferably local sharp

4 brioche, potato, or challah hot dog buns

Sliced pickles, ketchup, and mustard, for serving, optional

In a 10-inch (25-cm) skillet over medium-high heat, heat 3 tablespoons (45 ml) of the oil. Stir in the onion and season with salt. Cook, stirring occasionally, until browned, about 3 minutes. Remove from the pan, drain, and set aside.

Wipe out the skillet and cook the bacon until crispy. Remove to paper towels to drain, then brush lightly with the syrup and set aside.

Divide the ground beef into 4 parts, then form each into a patty the length of the hot dog bun. Season with salt and pepper on both sides.

In a large skillet or on a flat griddle, heat the remaining 3 tablespoons (45 ml) of canola oil until hot over medium-high heat. Place the burgers in the skillet and allow to brown on one side, about 1 to 2 minutes.

Flip the burgers. When they begin to brown on the second side, top with the sautéed onions, cheese, and bacon. Continue to cook for 1 more minute, or until the cheese melts.

Remove from the heat, then place each burger and its toppings on a bun. Serve warm, accompanied by the pickles, ketchup, and mustard, if desired.

Smashed Baby Red Potatoes with Sautéed Onions

This fabulous side dish gives you the crispy goodness of French fries on the outside and the soft flakiness of mashed potatoes on the inside. In other words, the best of both worlds—and an absolute must-try.

12 baby red potatoes the size of golf balls, unpeeled

Kosher salt, to taste

2 tbsp (28 g) butter

1 small yellow onion, peeled, cored, and diced

¼ cup (60 ml) canola oil

Freshly cracked black pepper, to taste

Place the potatoes in a small stockpot. Cover with cold water seasoned with lots of kosher salt. Bring to a boil, then reduce the heat to low and simmer until the potatoes are fork tender, 20 to 30 minutes.

Drain the potatoes and allow to cool. Once cooled, cut each potato in half and smash each half flat with the palm of your hand. Then cut in half again.

Melt the butter in a sauté pan over medium heat. Add the diced onion and season with salt. Cook for 2 to 3 minutes, or until soft and translucent. Remove from the pan and allow to cool.

Meanwhile, in a large 12-inch (30-cm) skillet over medium-high heat, heat the oil until hot. Gently add the potatoes and season with salt and pepper. Do not stir.

When the potatoes just start to brown, about 3 to 4 minutes, add the sautéed onions and cook for 1 minute. Flip the potatoes and continue cooking until golden brown, about 3 to 5 minutes. Season with more salt and pepper if needed.

Transfer to a serving dish, draining off any excess oil, and serve warm.

*See photo on page 354.

Baby Tomato Salad with Crumbled Goat Feta & Basil

SERVES 4

This lovely garden-fresh salad will literally take you mere minutes to prepare—but the compliments will be never ending. Again, literally.

2 cups (300 g) red baby tomatoes (preferably from the garden), halved

2 cups (300 g) yellow baby tomatoes (preferably from the garden), halved

1 head romaine, cut across the leaves into ½-inch (12-mm) strips

6 fresh basil leaves, torn

6 oz (168 g) goat feta, preferably local, drained and crumbled into large chunks

Juice of ½ lemon

2 tbsp (30 ml) extra virgin olive oil

Kosher salt, to taste

Freshly cracked black pepper, to taste

Combine the red tomatoes, yellow tomatoes, romaine, basil, and feta in a large serving bowl. Dress with the lemon juice and olive oil.

Season liberally with salt and pepper, then toss gently to combine the flavors.

*See photo on page 354.

TONY MAWS

Cambridge, Massachusetts

Chef/owner of Craigie on Main and The Kirkland Tap & Trotter

CHEF SAYS

Items I always keep on hand for unexpected guests are . . .

Hummus, yogurt that I can turn into a dip, small nub of cheese, a bunch of my own spice mixes, and olive oil.

When hosting a quick get-together, never overlook . . .

Making sure you're cooking food that you can actually serve in a timely fashion.

My secret tip for successful last-minute entertaining is . . .

Don't resort to bad pizza. Always have a good bottle, or four, on hand.

One fun fact few people know about me is that . . .

I'm a baseball and hockey coach.

MENU

Grilled Eggplant with Charred Rapini, Spiced Pumpkin Purée & Country Toast

CHEF'S PAIRING

Sour ale or a dry Riesling

CHEF'S PLAYLIST

Wilco

MAJOR KUDOS

James Beard award for "Best Chef: Northeast"; named one of *Food & Wine*'s "Best New Chefs"; multi-year designations as "Best Chef" by *Boston Magazine*

HIS STORY

Even though he grew up in Newton, Massachusetts, Tony loved watching his beloved Baba Hannah, from Tennessee, cook. In fact, he called it an "honor." That love would eventually materialize into a successful career, but not until much later. Let the story continue.

After Tony graduated from the University of Michigan with a degree in psychology, he took off for Europe. A year later he returned and ended up waiting tables on Martha's Vineyard. His boss at the time encouraged him to become a chef. So he sent out his resume, and chef Chris Schlesinger at the East Coast Grill hired him. Others did the same as he began earning his culinary chops at restaurants across the country (from Boston to San Francisco and Santa Fe) as well as in France.

Finally, he felt ready to open his own place. And the results have been nothing short of spectacular.

"I chose this meal because it's very tasty for a meal that comes together in only an hour," says Tony. "It's healthy, packed with color and flavor, and pretty unique."

Actually, we'd expect nothing less.

Grilled Eggplant with Charred Rapini, Spiced Pumpkin Purée & Country Toast

SERVES 4

What a fabulous vegetarian dish that incorporates a variety of marvelous ingredients, from farm-fresh vegetables to aromatic spices and deep-flavored sweeteners! Just fire up that grill and get ready to make some magic. "The leftovers are also amazing the next day," says Tony. "Just fry up an egg!" Hah, right. As if.

Good-quality extra virgin olive oil

1 Spanish onion, diced

1 tbsp (7 g) grated fresh ginger

1 small Long Island cheese pumpkin (can substitute another pumpkin or butternut squash), peeled, seeded, and cubed

Salt, to taste

Freshly ground black pepper, to taste

1 tsp curry powder

⅛ tsp grated nutmeg

⅛ tsp ground mace

2 tbsp (28 g) muscovado sugar (can substitute dark brown sugar)

2 Japanese eggplants (can substitute regular eggplant, about 1 lb [450 g]), unpeeled

2 tbsp (30 ml) Pedro Ximénez sherry vinegar (can substitute regular sherry vinegar or red wine vinegar)

1 lb (450 g) fresh rapini (broccoli rabe)

Country bread, thickly sliced and grilled, for serving, optional

Preheat a charcoal grill, first moving the coals off to the side for more indirect heat.

Heat 2 tablespoons (30 ml) oil in a heavy casserole on medium-high heat. Add the onion, ginger, and pumpkin, then reduce the heat to low and sweat for 5 minutes.

Add salt and pepper, then stir in the curry powder, nutmeg, and mace. Sweat for 10 more minutes, or until the pumpkin is soft.

Stir in the sugar and continue cooking for 5 more minutes. Add water to cover, bring to a simmer, and cook for another 5 minutes. Remove from the heat, then transfer to a blender and purée until smooth. Set aside.

Cut the eggplants on the bias into slices ½-inch (12-mm) thick. Season with salt and pepper and toss in a bowl with ½ cup (120 ml) more oil and the sherry vinegar.

Drain the eggplant, leaving the oil mixture in the bowl. Place the eggplant slices on the grill and cook until well colored and cooked through, about 5 to 7 minutes, making sure to turn so the color is even.

Add the rapini to the oil mixture in the bowl. Toss, then drain and place directly on the grill. Cook until crispy and slightly charred, about 3 to 5 minutes. Remove from the grill.

Slather oil on the bread slices. Place on the grill and turn to toast. You'll know the pieces are done when grill marks appear and the bread appears toasted.

Arrange the eggplant, rapini, and pumpkin purée together on each of 4 plates. Drizzle with more oil and serve with the grilled country toast, if desired.

RYAN McCASKEY

Chicago, Illinois

Chef/owner of Acadia

CHEF SAYS

Items I always keep on hand for unexpected guests are . . .

Champagne, cheese, port wine, salumi, and water crackers.

When hosting a quick get-together, never overlook . . .

Serving utensils and alcohol! You definitely need both. Not much of a party if you don't have any booze.

My secret tip for successful last-minute entertaining is . . .

Just be ready for anything. I have an arsenal of ingredients in my fridge. I can whip up almost anything quickly if need be.

One fun fact few people know about me is that . . .

I actually eat very simply at home. I rarely cook. I probably only cook about once a week. Most of my dining is ethnic carry-out or delivery. I love Mexican and Thai food.

MENU

Clam Chowder

Smoked Cheddar Mac & Cheese

Fried Chicken Thighs with Asian Glaze

CHEF'S PAIRING

Hamm's, Pabst Blue Ribbon, or Natural Light (natty light!) beer

CHEF'S PLAYLIST

Grateful Dead

MAJOR KUDOS

Two Michelin stars; five-star AAA rating; winner of the Jean Banchet "Best New Restaurant" award; several James Beard award nominations; four stars by the *Chicago Tribune*

HIS STORY

Born in Saigon, Vietnam, back in the early '70s, Ryan was one of the last orphans to be put on a special flight to the U.S. called Operation Babylift.

Adopted and raised by a loving family in suburban Chicago, Ryan spent many hours watching and helping his grandmother cook. And he became hooked. Actually, so much so that by the time he was a junior in high school, he was chosen as one of only nine pilot students to attend the Harper College Culinary Arts program.

That started him on the path to one day realizing his ultimate dream—that of working his magic in his own restaurant. Which he did, to immediate rave reviews.

"I chose this meal simply because it's easy, good, and hearty food that both my cooks and I like to make," says Ryan. "Most of the ingredients are cheap and easy to find at your local grocery store. What I think really shines through, though, is that these are classic dishes made well using techniques a chef would use. Even so, at the end of the day, it's just good food I'd serve to my own grandmother!"

Clam Chowder

SERVES 4

Whether or not it's cold outside, it's always a treat to start a meal with a piping hot bowl of soup. Chowder, which is basically a thick soup variety usually associated with seafood, also fits the bill quite nicely. Ryan knows this and offers up his version of clam chowder (sans clams, believe it or not) as a real treat indeed!

2 tbsp (28 g) butter, divided

1 tbsp (8 g) all-purpose flour

1⅓ cups (150 g) chopped onion

⅔ cup (60 g) chopped celery

1¾ cups (175 g) chopped leeks

¼ cup (36 g) chopped garlic

1 bay leaf

1 tsp chopped fresh thyme

1¼ cups (300 ml) half-and-half

5 cups (1.2 L) clam juice

Salt, to taste

Pepper, to taste

Prepare the roux by melting 1 tablespoon (14 g) of the butter in a small sauté pan over medium heat. Whisk in the flour. Continue to cook for 5 minutes, continuously stirring with a wooden spoon. Take off the heat, set aside, and let cool.

In a large saucepan, heat the remaining 1 tablespoon (14 g) butter over medium heat. Add the onion, celery, leeks, garlic, bay leaf, and thyme. Sweat until tender, about 5 minutes. Add the half-and-half. Continue to cook until reduced by half, about 5 minutes, then add the clam juice. Cook for 15 to 20 minutes, then stir in the roux. Cook at a gentle simmer (medium to medium-low heat) for 15 more minutes.

Remove the bay leaf and season with salt and pepper. Serve immediately.

Smoked Cheddar Mac & Cheese

SERVES 4

This ain't your mamma's macaroni and cheese. It's Ryan's unique twist on a classic American comfort-food recipe. For instance, cavatelli instead of elbows. Smoked cheddar instead of Velveeta, American cheese, or even plain old cheddar. And a sprinkling of minced chives on top for just a bit of pizzazz. Yes, please!

1 lb (450 g) cavatappi pasta (can substitute rotini)

3 cups (720 ml) heavy cream

1 cup (115 g) grated smoked cheddar cheese

½ tsp dry mustard

Salt, to taste

Minced fresh chives, for garnish, optional

Prepare the pasta according to package directions.

In the meantime, set a medium-size pan with some surface area, such as a Dutch oven, over medium-high heat. Add the heavy cream, which should bubble and start reducing right away. After it is reduced halfway, about 5 minutes, add the cheese, mustard, and salt. Stir to melt and incorporate, then continue to reduce until thick and creamy.

Remove from the heat and add the cooked pasta. Toss and serve warm, garnished with chives if desired.

Fried Chicken Thighs with Asian Glaze

SERVES 4

Little nuggets of moist, tender, juicy chicken thigh meat. Enrobed in a deeply flavorful and rich mahogany sheen of a glaze. Perfectly, quickly, and so easily prepared. All we can say is, "Bring it on!"

FOR THE BRINE

1 cup (200 g) sugar

½ cup (124 g) salt

4 cups (946 ml) water

2 lb (900 g) boneless, skinless chicken thigh meat, cubed

FOR THE GLAZE

2¼ cups (756 g) honey

½ cup (56 g) minced fresh ginger

¼ cup (12 g) chopped scallions

2 tbsp (10 g) minced garlic

1 tbsp (15 ml) toasted sesame oil

1 tbsp (3 g) chopped fresh cilantro

1 tsp Sriracha hot sauce

FOR THE DREDGE

1 cup (125 g) all-purpose flour

2¼ tsp (12 g) MSG, optional

1½ tsp (5 g) garlic powder

1 tbsp (5 g) smoked paprika

2¼ tsp (11 g) salt

½ tsp freshly ground black pepper

Canola oil, for deep frying

Prepared coleslaw, to serve, optional

Prepare the brine by combining the sugar, salt, and cold water in a large bowl. Add the chicken and soak for 30 minutes.

Meanwhile, prepare the glaze by combining all the ingredients in a bowl and mixing together well. Set aside.

In a separate bowl, make the dredge by mixing together the flour, optional MSG, garlic powder, smoked paprika, salt, and pepper in a bowl.

When the chicken is done soaking, drain and rinse. Pat thoroughly dry with paper towels, then toss the pieces in the dredging mixture to coat completely.

Heat the canola oil in an electric deep fryer, according to the fryer's instructions, to 365°F (185°C). If not using a fryer, pour just enough oil into a deep, heavy pot so the chicken pieces will be submerged and heat to 365°F (185°C) on a deep-frying thermometer.

Carefully drop in the chicken pieces, a handful at a time, and fry for 5 to 6 minutes, turning the chicken halfway through. As soon as the chicken pieces are done, remove with a slotted spoon or skimmer. Let drain briefly on paper towels, then toss lightly in the glaze. Draining off the glaze as necessary, remove the chicken pieces to a platter while you fry the remainder.

Serve warm with coleslaw, if desired.

TORY MILLER

Madison, Wisconsin

Chef/owner of L'Etoile, Graze, Estrellón, and Sujeo

CHEF SAYS

Items I always keep on hand for unexpected guests are . . .

Salumi or some kind of cured meat, olives, cheese, bread or crackers, and bourbon.

When hosting a quick get-together, never overlook . . .

Thinking about whether or not it makes sense to plate individual meals or serve family style/buffet style. It's important to think about how people are going to be eating what you're serving.

My secret tip for successful last-minute entertaining is . . .

Put your guests to work! Everyone wants to be in the kitchen, so have them help out with easy tasks like picking herbs, peeling potatoes, grating cheese, etc.

One fun fact few people know about me is that . . .

I grew up in my grandparents' diner and cooking there instilled in me the ability to think on my feet. That training always helps me prepare something fun for last-minute guests.

MENU

Roasted Olives with Chili & Orange

Roasted Asparagus with Sunny-Side-Up Eggs, Parmesan & Whole-Grain Mustard Vinaigrette

Pan-Seared Scallops with Heirloom Tomatoes & Spicy Caper Herb Oil

Red Wine Torrijas with Vanilla Sour Cream & Fresh Berries

CHEF'S PAIRING

Sangria (using existing ingredients from my recipes—orange slices, cinnamon stick, red wine—plus lemon San Pellegrino over ice)

CHEF'S PLAYLIST

Gypsy Kings

MAJOR KUDOS

James Beard award for "Best Chef: Midwest"; named one of "America's Top 50 Restaurants" by *Gourmet*; named one of "Top 100" by *Saveur*; named "Chef of the Year" by *Madison Magazine*; given *Sante*'s Culinary Hospitality of the Year Grand Award

HIS STORY

Once upon a time there was a little boy from South Korea. He was adopted by a loving family in rural Wisconsin. He grew up helping his grandparents in their diner. He eventually left for New York to attend the prestigious French Culinary Institute. He worked in some of the best kitchens, first in this country, and then—the world. Then he moved back home to Wisconsin . . . and lived happily ever after.

This fairytale ending is the life Tory is living today. Yet even with multiple award-winning restaurants and countless accolades, he's still a very humble guy who loves family and friends.

"I picked these recipes because they're fast and easy," says Tory, "yet also elegant and impressive. They come together very quickly, and because we're using fresh vegetables and scallops, there isn't any need for very long cooking times. You can also multitask to bring everything together at once. You don't need to spend hours slaving away in the kitchen to provide your guests with a restaurant-quality meal."

Roasted Olives with Chili & Orange

SERVES 4 TO 6

This is one of Tory's favorite appetizers. "Having something quick like these olives is a great thing to get your guests eating and drinking right away," he says. "Plus dipping the bread into the oil is interactive and communal!"

12 oz (336 g) mixed cured olives, plus 2–3 tbsp (30–45 ml) olive brine or juice

6 tbsp (90 ml) extra virgin olive oil

2 cloves garlic

2 dried Thai chiles

1 fresh rosemary sprig

1 bay leaf

1 small orange, with peel, halved and thinly sliced

Crusty bread or French baguette

Place the olives and brine in a heatproof bowl. Set aside.

Heat the oil in a sauté pan on medium-high heat. Add the garlic and cook for 30 seconds, then add the chiles and cook for 10 seconds. Add the rosemary, bay leaf, and orange slices and cook for 30 seconds more.

Pour the mixture immediately over the olives and brine. Remove the bay leaf. Stir to mix and warm through, then serve with the bread for dipping.

Roasted Asparagus with Sunny-Side-Up Eggs, Parmesan & Whole-Grain Mustard Vinaigrette

SERVES 4

This vibrant dish, also a great brunch addition, takes its cue from fresh asparagus, in season from February through June (with April being the peak). Roasting it brings out its inherent sweetness. And for a helpful hint, Tory suggests using a microplane to grate the shallots. "It's faster and makes a fine pulp that's great for vinaigrettes," he says.

1 lb (450 g) asparagus spears, trimmed

⅓ cup plus 7 tbsp (85 ml) extra virgin olive oil, plus additional for drizzling, divided

Sea salt, to taste

Freshly ground black pepper, to taste

2 tbsp (32 g) whole-grain mustard

1 tbsp (10 g) grated shallots

2 tbsp (30 ml) sherry vinegar (can substitute red wine vinegar)

4 large eggs

¼ cup (45 g) grated or shaved Parmigiano-Reggiano cheese

1 tbsp (3 g) minced fresh chives, for garnish, optional

Preheat the oven to 425°F (218°C).

Line a sheet pan with aluminum foil and add the asparagus in a single layer. Drizzle with ⅓ cup (80 ml) olive oil. Season with salt and pepper. Roast for 10 to 15 minutes, turning halfway through.

Meanwhile, mix the mustard, grated shallots, and vinegar in a bowl. Whisk in 6 tablespoons (90 ml) of the olive oil. Set aside.

Set a large nonstick sauté pan over medium-high heat and add the remaining 1 tablespoon (15 ml) olive oil. Crack the eggs in carefully and turn down the heat to just below medium. Cook the eggs until the whites are just set.

Remove the asparagus to a serving platter. Drizzle with the vinaigrette, sprinkle with the cheese, and top with the sunny-side-up eggs. Season with salt and pepper. If desired, garnish with chives. Serve immediately.

Pan-Seared Scallops with Heirloom Tomatoes & Spicy Caper Herb Oil

SERVES 4

Tory explains that the herb oil for this scallops dish has an Asian influence coming from the soy sauce and fish sauce. "It provides a kick to the dish," he adds, "that brings out the natural MSG flavor and umami in the tomatoes. Also, be sure to pick tomatoes with nice color and size variety."

8 jumbo scallops

Salt, to taste

Freshly ground black pepper, to taste

2–4 tbsp (30–60 ml) canola oil

2 tbsp (28 g) butter

FOR THE HERB OIL

1 tbsp (3 g) chopped fresh flat-leaf parsley

1 tbsp (3 g) chopped fresh chives

1 tbsp (3 g) chopped fresh mint

1 tbsp (3 g) chopped fresh cilantro

1 tbsp (3 g) chopped fresh Thai basil (can substitute regular basil)

1 tbsp (15 g) capers

1 tbsp (8 g) minced shallot

1 tbsp (9 g) minced garlic

¼ cup (60 ml) extra virgin olive oil

1 tbsp (15 ml) light soy sauce

1 tbsp (15 ml) fish sauce

1 fresh Thai chile, thinly sliced

About 2 lb (900 g) mixed fresh, ripe heirloom cherry tomatoes

1 lime, halved

Pat the scallops dry with a paper towel. Season with salt and pepper.

Heat the oil in a skillet over medium-high heat. Add the scallops and cook without turning or moving until they start to turn brown around the edges. Add the butter to the pan. When melted, use the butter to baste the scallops to complete the cooking. Do not turn the scallops. This whole process should take around 5 minutes.

Remove from the heat and set the scallops on a paper towel–lined plate, seared side up.

To make the herb oil, mix all the ingredients in a bowl and stir well.

Arrange the tomatoes on a serving platter. Season with salt and pepper. Add the cooked scallops and drizzle with the herb oil. Squeeze the lime juice over to serve.

Red Wine Torrijas with Vanilla Sour Cream & Fresh Berries

SERVES 4

Think of *torrijas*, created by nuns and traditionally eaten in Spain during Lent, as a variation of French toast. Only maybe better. Especially with vanilla sour cream. And fresh berries. Lots and lots of fresh, sweet, sun-kissed berries. Ooooh!

4 cups (946 ml) whole milk

½ cup plus 1 tbsp (113 g) granulated sugar, divided

1 tbsp (5 g) orange zest

1 cinnamon stick

1 cup (240 ml) red wine

4 thick slices of French baguette (can substitute any bread you would normally make French toast with)

1 cup (240 ml) sour cream

3 tbsp (21 g) powdered sugar, plus additonal for dusting

1 tsp pure vanilla extract

4 large eggs

Olive oil, for frying

½ tsp ground cinnamon

Fresh berries

Heat the milk, ½ cup (120 g) granulated sugar, orange zest, and cinnamon stick in a medium-size saucepan over medium heat. Reduce the heat to low and simmer for 15 minutes. Remove from the heat and stir in the wine.

Soak the bread slices in the milk mixture for at least 10 minutes. The bread should not fall apart but should be close to it.

In the meantime, whisk the sour cream, powdered sugar, and vanilla in a small bowl until blended. Place in the refrigerator to chill.

Once the bread is soaked, remove carefully from the milk mixture with a slotted spoon or skimmer and set aside on a plate to cool.

Beat the eggs in a bowl and set near the stove.

Heat ½ inch (12 mm) oil in a skillet over medium-high heat until it reaches about 350°F (177°C). Working in batches as necessary, dip each slice of bread in the eggs to coat both sides. Add the bread to the hot oil and fry for no more than 1 minute on each side. Remove carefully to a rack or paper towels to cool.

Mix the remaining 1 tablespoon (13 g) granulated sugar with the cinnamon. Sprinkle over the bread.

Arrange the bread slices on a serving platter. Serve topped with the vanilla sour cream and the berries. Dust with powdered sugar.

BRUCE MOFFETT

Charlotte, North Carolina

Chef/owner of Moffett Restaurant Group, which includes Barrington's Restaurant, Good Food on Montford, and Stagioni

CHEF SAYS

Items I always keep on hand for unexpected guests are . . .

Good cheese, artisan salami, crusty bread, fragrant olive oil, and an assortment of seasonal fruit.

When hosting a quick get-together, never overlook . . .

Just having fun. You don't need to impress.

My secret tip for successful last-minute entertaining is . . .

Don't overwhelm yourself. Remember, last-minute guests are happy just to eat and drink, and are more interested in socializing and catching up than a complex meal.

One fun fact few people know about me is that . . .

Cooking is my second career. I worked for a U.S. senator after graduating from college. But the pace of the political circuit in Washington, D.C., didn't suit me, so I enrolled in culinary school.

MENU

Swordfish with Succotash, Basil Pesto Cream & Citrus Compote

Craig's Summer Salad

Roasted Peaches with Brown Sugar Sauce & Sour Cream

CHEF'S PAIRING

A white Burgundy, specifically a 2013 Louis Latour Macon-Lugny (This light wine with citrus flavors pairs perfectly with the light meal and a summer night.)

CHEF'S PLAYLIST

Classical music, probably Bach

MAJOR KUDOS

Semifinalist for James Beard "Best Chef: Southeast" award; "Restauranteur of the Year" award by *Charlotte Magazine*; Zagat's award for "Top for Food in Charlotte"; listed as one of "10 Chefs to Know in Charlotte" by *Braiser*; "Distinguishing Visiting Chef" award from Johnson and Wales University; "Pegasus" award from Public Relations Society of America, Charlotte chapter

HIS STORY

He's got degrees from the University of Rhode Island plus the Culinary Institute of America. He worked the political circuit in D.C., plus some pretty impressive kitchens throughout Atlanta and Boston. And he finally landed in Charlotte, where he opened his first restaurant plus two more subsequent ones.

But when asked to choose a meal for this book, Bruce was immediately transported back to his childhood.

"This meal reminds me of summers at my grandmother's house on the shore in Rhode Island," reminisces Bruce. "We would use her garden to gather our ingredients and then go to the local fish market to get our swordfish. Now I realize cooking is as much about the preparation as it is about the eating. That's what makes it an experience. And since this meal doesn't require a great deal of preparation, it's easy to socialize with your guests at the same time."

We'd say it's a win-win for everyone!

Swordfish with Succotash, Basil Pesto Cream & Citrus Compote

SERVES 4

There is actually a trifecta of very impressive components to this elegant entrée. A creamy pesto-infused succotash mixture punctuated with white wine. Simply prepared swordfish that's exceptionally moist and succulent, highlighting its natural sea flavor. And a caper-capped citrus compote that's as colorful as it is delicious. Seriously, what's not to love?

FOR THE CITRUS COMPOTE

2 oranges

2 lemons

2 limes

2 tbsp (30 ml) olive oil

2 tbsp (30 g) capers

FOR THE SUCCOTASH

2–4 tbsp (30–60 ml) grapeseed oil (can substitute vegetable oil but not olive oil)

2 cups (300 g) fresh sweet corn kernels

½ cup (120 ml) white wine (like Chardonnay)

4 tsp (20 ml) fresh lemon juice

1 cup (240 ml) heavy cream

2 cups (300 g) lima beans, preferably fresh

1 cup (240 g) diced fresh tomatoes

¼ cup (60 g) pesto, homemade or prepared

4 (6-oz [168-g]) portions swordfish

Salt, to taste

Freshly ground black pepper, to taste

2–4 tbsp (30–60 ml) grapeseed oil

Fresh basil leaves, for garnish, optional

Preheat the oven to 450°F (232°C).

Using a sharp paring knife, peel the skin and white pith from each orange, lemon, and lime, then hold each over a medium-size bowl and cut into segments between the membranes, letting them fall into the bowl. After the segments are in the bowl, squeeze the membranes over them to extract the juice, then discard. When all the segments are cut and in the bowl, toss them gently with the olive oil and capers and set aside at room temperature.

To make the succotash, set a skillet over medium-high heat and add enough grapeseed oil to coat the bottom of the pan (about 2 to 4 tablespoons [30 to 60 ml]). Watch carefully. When the oil is smoking, add the corn and roast until it browns slightly, about 2 to 3 minutes. Slowly add the white wine and lemon juice. Bring to a boil and allow the alcohol to cook off, about 1 minute, or until reduced by half. Add the heavy cream and reduce to a sauce consistency, about 4 to 5 minutes, or until the mixture nicely coats the back of a spoon. Stir in the lima beans and tomatoes, then heat just to a boil. Immediately add the pesto and stir to combine. Remove from the heat and set aside to keep warm.

Season the swordfish with salt and pepper. Place a cast-iron skillet over medium-high heat. Add enough oil to coat the bottom of the pan (about 2 to 4 tablespoons [30 to 60 ml]). Heat until the oil smokes. Place the swordfish in the pan. It should sizzle when it hits the pan, otherwise it will stick. Cook until it browns on one side, about 4 to 5 minutes. Carefully flip and immediately place the pan in the oven until the fish is cooked through, another 7 to 8 minutes, or until firm to the touch. When the swordfish is done cooking, take it out of the pan and transfer it to a paper towel.

Spoon the succotash onto a serving platter and place the fish on top. Garnish with the citrus salad and basil, if desired. Serve immediately.

Craig's Summer Salad

SERVES 4

This refreshing salad is named after Bruce's grandmother, Craig. (Craig was Grandma Betty Perkins's nickname, which came from a radio show she loved!) The vegetables called for here, which she would have had in her garden, are particularly fresh, sweet, and tender during summer months, especially the French beans. What differentiates them from common green beans is their smaller size and delicate, velvety pods, which contain only the tiniest seeds.

4 medium-size ripe tomatoes, preferably Red Slicers

2 tsp (10 g) sea salt, plus more to season

24 French beans, cut in half

2 cloves garlic, crushed

2 tbsp (30 ml) white wine vinegar

¼ cup (60 ml) plus 2 tbsp (30 ml) extra virgin olive oil

8 fresh basil leaves, thinly sliced

1 tsp chopped fresh tarragon

4 small heads of lettuce, roughly torn

Bring a large pot of water to a rolling boil. Meanwhile, fill a medium-size bowl with water and plenty of ice. Set by the stove.

Gently place the tomatoes in the boiling water for 20 seconds. Spoon the tomatoes out of the water and plunge into the ice bath. When chilled, remove from the ice bath (saving it), gently peel off the skin and dice the flesh. Place the flesh in a colander to drain off the extra liquid. Set aside.

In the same pot of boiling water, generously add salt to season. Add the green beans and check for tenderness after 3 to 4 minutes. You should be able to bite through the green bean with the slightest resistance, but it should still have structure similar to al dente pasta. Remove from the pot and plunge into the ice bath. When chilled, remove from the water and pat dry. Set aside.

Place 2 teaspoons (10 g) sea salt in a large wooden salad bowl. Add the garlic and crush into the salt, using the back of a wooden spoon. Circle the bowl with the spoon and the garlic until most of the cloves disappear into the salt. Remove any remaining chunks of garlic.

Add the vinegar to the bowl. Slowly add the oil, using a wire whisk to emulsify it into the vinegar. Add the basil, tarragon, green beans, and tomatoes. Mix together and let marinate, covered, for 30 minutes to 1 hour.

When ready to serve, add the lettuce and toss well.

Roasted Peaches with Brown Sugar Sauce & Sour Cream

SERVES 4

This delicious summertime dessert takes full advantage of the sweetness imparted by ripe orchard peaches in season. Bathed in a rich brown sugar sauce accentuated by white wine and peach Schnapps, it's also quite an impressive showstopper at the end of any meal.

1 cup (8 oz) flavorful white wine (like oaked Chardonnay)

1 cup (8 oz) peach Schnapps

1 cup (220 g) brown sugar, firmly packed, plus additional for sprinkling, divided

2 tbsp (30 ml) fresh lemon juice

4 ripe peaches, halved and pitted

4 tbsp (115 g) unsalted butter, cut into pieces

Sour cream, for garnish

1 pint (288 g) blackberries, for garnish

Preheat the oven to 350°F (177°C).

Combine the wine, Schnapps, brown sugar, and lemon juice in a sauté pan with a heatproof handle. Stir, bring to a boil, and cook for about 1 minute, or until the sugar has dissolved and the alcohol has cooked off. Add the peaches, flat side down. Place in the oven and bake for 15 minutes.

Carefully remove the peaches from the liquid and set aside to keep warm.

Set the pan over medium-high heat and continue to cook until the liquid is reduced by half, about 4 to 5 minutes. Whisk in the butter, a piece at a time, until dissolved. Remove from the heat.

Place 1 warm peach in each of 4 bowls. Spoon the sauce over each. Place a dollop of the sour cream on top. Garnish with the blackberries. Lightly sprinkle brown sugar over the top and serve.

MATT MOLINA

Los Angeles, California

Chef/co-owner of Everson Royce Bar (E.R.B.)

CHEF SAYS

Items I always keep on hand for unexpected guests are . . .

Canned black beans, garlic, lime, tortillas, and extra virgin olive oil. What I love is that if I combine these five ingredients (plus a little help from their friend, fresh cilantro), you can have a snack or party waiting to break out!

When hosting a quick get-together, never overlook . . .

Dessert! Even though I may not have time to make something sweet to finish the meal, I always have my favorite ice cream and cookies ready to go!

My secret tip for successful last-minute entertaining is . . .

Present the food family style for the table. It may not sound like a secret, but it makes your guests interact with the food and they get to serve each other lovingly, which makes the table warm 'n' fuzzy. Trust me, all your guests will be asking you when the next dinner is.

One fun fact few people know about me is that . . .

I'm a sucker for "Drumsticks." Yes, that chocolate-dipped ice cream cone they sell in every gas station/grocery store/ice cream truck everywhere. Can't get enough of them!

MENU

Skirt Steak with Black Beans in Green Chile Salsa Verde

CHEF'S PAIRING

Beer, white wine, red wine, tequila, Coca-Cola, or sparkling water

CHEF'S PLAYLIST

Louis Armstrong, Sam Cooke, Tears for Fears, The Meters, Chuck Berry, Tame Impala, The Pharcyde, and Elvis Costello

MAJOR KUDOS

James Beard award for "Best Chef: Pacific"; multiple James Beard award nominations; three stars from the *LA Times*

HIS STORY

Matt grew up in LA (in the San Gabriel Valley, specifically) in a lively Latino household with four siblings. He played the drums. And was in a band. But his one true passion was watching Emeril, Mario, and Bobby on TV. So Matt made two life-changing decisions.

Number 1. When he was tall enough to reach the stove, he cooked his first solo meal: manicotti with tomato sauce. ("It required one or two more steps than opening up a can of vegetables," says Matt, "so I thought it was incredibly labor intensive.") He was hooked.

And number 2. Only three weeks after graduating from high school, almost on a whim, he took off for the Los Angeles Culinary Institute.

He eventually went on to work under renowned chefs Nancy Silverton and Mario Batali at their white-hot Osteria Mozza and Pizzeria Mozza before eventually leaving for new horizons.

"I entertain at my apartment a lot," says Matt. "I'm lucky to say I live in a complex that houses three of my best friends, so I'm well versed in impromptu meals that I prepare for us."

That's perfectly perfect, Matt.

Skirt Steak with Black Beans in Green Chile Salsa Verde

SERVES 4

"The black beans are the star here," says Matt. "Most conversations with my guests begin with them being appreciative that I took the time to slave away all day to make them. But the kicker is that I actually didn't slave; they're deliciously spiked *canned* beans! Add seared skirt steak and the rest of the accompaniments, and you've got a near-perfect impromptu taco party." (P.S. Throw in a mixed green salad simply dressed with oil, lemon juice, and salt, and you're all good to go!)

2 tbsp (30 ml) extra virgin olive oil

8–10 large cloves garlic, sliced

½ tsp kosher salt, plus additional for seasoning, divided

1 cup (240 g) green chile salsa verde, preferably Herdez (can substitute any other Hispanic-style salsa)

1 (15-oz [420-g]) can black beans, drained but not rinsed

½ cup (20 g) roughly chopped fresh cilantro, plus additional for garnish

1 tbsp (15 ml) fresh lime juice

1½ lb (680 g) skirt steak

Freshly ground black pepper, to taste

½ cup (120 ml) canola oil, divided

FOR SERVING

Flour or corn tortillas, warmed

Fresh lime wedges

Hass avocado quarters, optional

Fresh radishes, quartered or sliced, optional

Fresh cilantro leaves, optional

Heat the oil in a medium-size saucepan over medium-high heat. Add the garlic and salt and sauté for about 1½ minutes, or until the garlic is toasted and fragrant. Stir in the salsa verde and bring to a simmer, stirring constantly to blend the sauce. Simmer for 3 to 4 minutes, or until the sauce has thickened slightly. Stir in the beans, then simmer for 3 to 4 minutes. Remove from the heat, stir in the cilantro and lime juice, and set aside.

Cut the skirt steak so it will fit comfortably in a large skillet. Season both sides of each steak piece with the kosher salt and pepper.

Heat 2 tablespoons (30 ml) of the canola oil in the skillet over medium-high heat for 2 to 3 minutes, or until almost smoking. Remove from the heat briefly, then gently add half the steaks. Return to medium-high heat and sear for 3 minutes, or until nicely browned on both sides (see Chef's Tip).

Remove from the heat again and gently flip the steaks. Set back on medium-high heat and sear for 3 more minutes, or until the steaks are nicely browned and reach an internal temperature of 130°F to 135°F (54°C to 57°C) for medium-rare. If working with thinner-sliced steaks, sear for only about 2 minutes on each side. Transfer to a resting platter.

Repeat, heating the remaining oil and cooking the remaining steaks the same way.

To serve, spoon the black beans evenly onto 4 plates. Slice each steak against the grain at an angle ¼-inch (6-mm) thick. Lay the slices on top of the beans.

Serve with the tortillas and lime wedges. However, feel free to riff on this dish by adding quartered avocado, radishes, and cilantro leaves to your plates!

CHEF'S TIP
Turning off the heat before you add the steaks to a sizzling hot pan will prevent the oil from flaring up along the sides of the pan.

KEVIN SBRAGA

Philadelphia, Pennsylvania

Chef/owner of Fat Ham Restaurants

CHEF SAYS

Items I always keep on hand for unexpected guests are . . .

Dried pasta, gravy in the freezer, thin cutlets, onions, and garlic.

When hosting a quick get-together, never overlook . . .

Knowing if anyone has a dietary restriction. The most inhospitable thing you can do is invite someone over, cook for them, and then find out they can't eat it because they have a dairy or peanut allergy.

My secret tip for successful last-minute entertaining is . . .

Have fun with it. It can't be too serious. And you can't be stuck in the kitchen slaving away. You need to be able to entertain your guests.

One fun fact few people know about me is that . . .

I have a great sense of humor and I can be pretty sarcastic.

MENU

Roasted Onion Rigatoni

Eggplant Agrodolce

CHEF'S PAIRING

A medium-bodied red wine with the Canaiolo Nero grape from the Lazio region in Italy

CHEF'S PLAYLIST

Lionel Richie

MAJOR KUDOS

Winner of Bravo's *Top Chef*, season seven; judge on Fox's *MasterChef*; winner of "Best Meat Presentation" at Bocuse d'Or USA competition; *Esquire*'s "Best New Restaurant" award; named one of "Top 10 Chefs" by *Philadelphia Style*

HIS STORY

He simply couldn't help it. He grew up making meatballs with his Italian-American mom and bread with his African-American dad, who owned a bakery. How could he *not* follow a predestined culinary path?!

Which is exactly what Kevin did . . . first going to Johnson and Wales University in Miami. Next, working at various A-list establishments under esteemed chefs. Then, appearing on TV as a food show contestant, winner, *and* judge! And now as the successful chef/owner of not one, not two, but three award-winning restaurants!

Yet, when it comes to entertaining, Kevin knows how to keep it real.

"Besides being a chef and restaurateur," he admits, "I'm also the father of two kids. So, I know the importance of quality food with limited time."

He adds, "These dishes are delicious, fulfilling, and simple. Growing up, eating pasta two or three times a week was the norm. I now crave pasta, and so do my children. The interesting thing is how much they enjoy making it from scratch!"

Roasted Onion Rigatoni

SERVES 4

As they say, "This ain't your mamma's rigatoni!" Kevin ups the ante here with the addition and unexpected twist of a roasted onion. Soft, sweet, and bursting with lush, rich brown flavors. Give it a try, and you'll never go back to plain old rigatoni again. No disrespect, Mom.

1 white onion, peeled

1 tbsp (15 ml) olive oil

Kosher salt

2 tbsp (28 g) butter

4 oz (112 g) bacon

3 cloves garlic, minced

2 cups fresh baby spinach

1 lb (450 g) rigatoni

Pecorino Romano cheese, grated, to taste

Freshly cracked black pepper, to taste

Preheat the oven to 350°F (177°C). Place the onion on a large piece of aluminum foil. Drizzle with the oil and season with the salt. Wrap the foil around the onion and roast in the oven until tender, about 40 minutes. Remove from the foil and allow to cool to room temperature, about 10 minutes. Then cut into small dice.

Bring 6 quarts (5.7 L) of water to a boil in a large pot.

Meanwhile, melt the butter in a sauté pan over medium heat. Add the bacon and cook until the fat is rendered out and the bacon is crispy, about 3 minutes. Stir in the garlic, diced roasted onion, and spinach and cook until the spinach is lightly wilted, about 2 minutes. Remove from the heat.

Add the salt and pasta to the boiling water. Cook according to the package directions until al dente, about 8 minutes. Drain, reserving 1 cup (240 ml) of the cooking water. Return the pasta to the pot. Add the spinach mixture and the cooking water to create a very light sauce. The pasta should not be "swimming," rather just lightly coated. Serve in individual pasta bowls, garnished with the cheese and seasoned with the pepper.

Eggplant Agrodolce

SERVES 4

This rich, full-bodied sauce that envelops the eggplant perfectly balances both sourness (from the vinegar) and sweetness (from the sugar). The result is nothing short of *delizioso*! As great in a sandwich or salad as on an antipasto platter.

2 eggplants (1 lb [450 g] total), peeled and cut into large dice

Salt

2 tbsp (30 ml) olive oil

½ cup (50 g) small-diced white onion

2 cloves garlic, minced

1 jalapeño chile, seeded and minced

½ cup (50 g) minced fennel

1 cup (240 ml) white balsamic vinegar

½ cup (100 g) sugar

Freshly ground black pepper, to taste

¼ cup (10 g) loosely packed fresh mint leaves, very thinly sliced

Season the diced eggplant generously with salt. Allow to drain in a colander for 10 minutes. Rinse under running water and pat dry. Set aside.

Meanwhile, heat the oil in a large sauté pan over medium-low heat. Add the onion, garlic, jalapeño, and fennel. Sweat until tender, about 4 minutes. Add the diced eggplant, then stir the balsamic vinegar and sugar in well, scraping the bottom of the pan, until the vinegar bubbles, the sugar dissolves, and the eggplant is well mixed in. Cover and cook over low heat for 10 minutes, or until the eggplant is tender.

Once the eggplant is tender, remove from the heat and season with salt and pepper. Turn into a bowl to cool to room temperature, or chill in the refrigerator.

At serving time, fold in the mint.

BARTON SEAVER

South Freeport, Maine

Director of the Sustainable Seafood and Health Initiative at the Center for Health and the Global Environment at the Harvard T. H. Chan School of Public Health; senior adviser in Sustainable Seafood Innovations at the University of New England; explorer for the National Geographic Society

CHEF SAYS

Items I always keep on hand for unexpected guests are . . .

Champagne, good-quality anchovies for hors d'oeuvres, smoked fish, and a liquor cabinet as well-stocked as a good cocktail bar. I also like to send my guests home with a little something. For the past five years I've been making and aging my own vinegars, so I always keep little bottles on hand to give as a parting gift.

When hosting a quick get-together, never overlook . . .

Taking a moment to acknowledge each other's company when you all finally sit down to the table. Say thank you, take a deep breath, and ease into the meal because you never want the frantic pace of preparation to influence the enjoyment of the meal.

My secret tip for successful last-minute entertaining is . . .

Realize that it's absolutely no different from preplanned entertaining. You know how to cook, and you know how to have fun with your friends. Have a drink and enjoy their company.

One fun fact few people know about me is that . . .

I'm a passionate fan of old jazz and blues. I collect and almost exclusively listen to old vinyl records and even have an old Victrola to play my 78s.

MENU

Salmon Fillet with Blistered Cherry Tomatoes in Garlic-Herb Olive Oil

Seared Smashed Potatoes

Broccolini with Pecan Bagna Cauda

CHEF'S PAIRING

Vouvray

CHEF'S PLAYLIST

Warm, up-tempo, dirty blues like Sonny Boy Williamson

MAJOR KUDOS

"Chef of the Year" award by *Esquire*; named one of "Top 10 Eco-Friendly Restaurants" by *Bon Appétit*; honored as a "Seafood Champion" by the Seafood Choices Alliance; named the first Sustainability Fellow in Residence at the New England Aquarium; named to the United States Culinary Ambassador Corps; TED Talk presenter aboard the *National Geographic Endeavour*

HIS STORY

There's really nothing fishy (excuse the pun!) about Barton's rise to prominence in the world of seafood sustainability. But let's start from the beginning.

He grew up in Washington, D.C. Went to the Culinary Institute of America (graduating with honors). Worked in Chicago, New York, Spain, Morocco, then back in Washington, D.C., again, where he opened seven restaurants, including award-winning Hook in Georgetown, which served seventy-eight species of fish in a single year!

Eventually, Barton chose to leave restaurants so he could instead travel with National Geographic to, quite simply, use dinner as a means to promote both healthy humans and healthy environments.

"Together, the ingredients in these recipes make a colorful, textured, and nutritious meal," says Barton. "Each of the components can be made separately and served at different temperatures, thus a lot of pressure is taken off the cook."

Salmon Fillet with Blistered Cherry Tomatoes in Garlic-Herb Olive Oil

SERVES 4

"The ease of cooking the fish over the cherry tomatoes," says Barton, "is an epiphany for a lot of people I make this for. Being that you're making a sauce, charring the tomatoes, and crisping the skin, all while keeping the fish moist using a technique that's very simple, has made this a go-to dish for a lot of my friends when they cook at home."

1¼ lb (562 g) salmon fillet, skin on

Salt, to taste

¼ cup (60 ml) olive oil

4 cloves garlic, thickly sliced

2 pints (600 g) cherry tomatoes

1 fresh rosemary sprig

Preheat the broiler on high.

Season the salmon fillet generously on both sides with the salt. Set aside.

Set a large ovenproof skillet on medium-high heat until it's smoking hot. Add the oil, then the garlic, and cook until the garlic is just golden brown. Carefully add the tomatoes and rosemary, using a splatter screen as needed. As soon as the tomatoes begin to blister, about 3 minutes, season with the salt and remove from the heat.

Place the salmon, skin side up, on top of the tomatoes, then, wearing oven mitts, transfer the skillet to the oven. Broil for 10 minutes per inch (2.5 cm) of thickness on the fish. The skin on the salmon should be blistered and bubbling.

Remove from the oven and serve from the skillet.

Seared Smashed Potatoes

SERVES 4

Only three ingredients. And just two steps. But the result is one fabulous side dish featuring potatoes that are tender on the bottom and crispy on top. It just doesn't get any better—or easier—than this! You're welcome.

1 lb (450 g) very small red-skinned potatoes

⅓ cup (85 g) kosher salt

⅓ cup (80 ml) olive oil

Combine the potatoes and salt in a medium-size pot. Add enough cold water to just cover. Bring to a boil and cook for 15 minutes, or just until right before the potatoes begin falling apart. Remove from the heat and drain, then allow the potatoes to air dry for a few minutes.

Add the oil to a 8- to 10-inch (20- to 25-cm) cast-iron skillet over medium heat. Add the potatoes, crushing each with a potato masher or a smaller pan until they form a loose cake. Give the skillet a shake to prevent the potatoes from sticking, then increase the heat to medium high. Allow the potatoes to sit, undisturbed, over the heat for 15 minutes, or until crispy on the bottom, adjusting the heat if necessary so the potatoes don't burn.

To serve, flip the potatoes onto a serving platter, using a spatula if any of the potatoes stick to the skillet.

*See photo on page 392.

Broccolini with Pecan Bagna Càuda

SERVES 4

Bagna càuda (pronounced BAHN-yah COW-dah) is a simmered Piedmontese "hot bath" full of umami and full-bodied heat compliments of garlic, anchovies, red chili flakes, and olive oil. But then throw in a surprise ingredient—the pecans—and you've suddenly got yourself a veggie side with some crunch and a really deep, layered flavor profile. Wowza!

2 bunches broccolini or broccoli rabe (broccoli raab, broccoli rape, or rapini)

1 (2-oz [28-g]) can anchovies in oil

⅓ cup (40 g) pecan pieces

4 cloves garlic, sliced

¼ cup (60 ml) olive oil

Juice of 1 lemon

2 tsp (3 g) red chili flakes (crushed red pepper)

Bring a pot of salted water to a boil. Add the broccolini and blanch for 3 minutes, or until the stems are tender when pierced with a knife. Drain and arrange on a platter.

In a small saucepan, combine the anchovies and their oil, pecans, garlic, and olive oil and set over medium heat. Allow the anchovies and garlic to melt into the oil, and the pecans and garlic to become fragrant and nutty, about 7 minutes. Once the pecans have reached a toasty golden brown, finish with the lemon juice and chili flakes and remove from the heat.

Pour the sauce over the broccolini and serve at room temperature.

ALON SHAYA

New Orleans, Louisiana

Chef/partner of Shaya, Domenica, and Pizza Domenica

CHEF SAYS

Items I always keep on hand for unexpected guests are . . .

Rosé wine, a good bourbon, bread (which we always keep in the freezer, then defrost it in the microwave, slice it, toast it, and top it with anything from garlic and olive oil, to tomatoes and balsamic), and vegetables from the market. Plus anchovies (which make a quick and easy appetizer).

When hosting a quick get-together, never overlook . . .

Making sure you have some good music to play. Too often you get caught up in the food and setting the table. You have to set the mood first so people feel relaxed when they get to your house. Put on some music, light some candles, and get some flowers on display. It will make the food taste better, and you'll look like a pro.

My secret tip for successful last-minute entertaining is . . .

Prepare food that can be made ahead of time, and just set out or rewarm when people show up. You want to be part of the party, so make sure you're not still deboning fish when your friends get there.

One fun fact few people know about me is that . . .

I love nothing more than cold rotisserie chicken with pickles and Sriracha as a late-night snack at home. It takes me about twenty seconds to prepare.

MENU

Ricotta Crostini with Date & Pecan Pesto

Spicy Rigatoni

Cast Iron–Seared Rib Eyes with Blood Orange Chimichurri

CHEF'S PAIRING

Billecart-Salmon Brut Rosé

MAJOR KUDOS

James Beard awards for "Best Chef: South" and "Best New Restaurant"; "Chef of the Year" award from *New Orleans Magazine*; "Restaurant of the Year" award from *Esquire*; "One of America's 50 Best New Restaurants" award from *Bon Appétit*; "Best Restaurant in America" and "Best Restaurant in New Orleans" awards from Eater; one of *Southern Living*'s "30 Best Restaurants in the South"

HIS STORY

So, what does an award-winning chef who was born in Israel, grew up in Philadelphia, trained in Hyde Park, worked in Italy, and now lives in New Orleans fix for his own last-minute guests?

Simple. A little of everything he loves! "My most comforting and enjoyable meals are the ones I eat with my family," says Alon. "It's a moment of reflection for me as a chef, which reminds me that simplicity and good technique will always be the most important things to remember while cooking and eating."

He adds, "These particular recipes are no-brainers and always crowd pleasers. They're simple to prepare and many of the ingredients can be stored in the pantry."

As for what his friends think of this menu? "It's like handing someone a basket of cute puppies," answers Alon with a sly smile. "They will be so happy and thank you for making their day. And if, by chance, your guests don't quite like it, well, then they don't deserve to be your friends in the first place!"

Seriously, who doesn't love cute puppies?

Ricotta Crostini with Date & Pecan Pesto

SERVES 4

Yes, we all know what goes into a traditional pesto recipe. But dates and pecans instead of basil and pine nuts? If Alon has anything to do with it, all we can say is, "Bring it on!" This batch makes 2 cups (480 g) and is particularly great for dishes that include wild game, duck, or pork.

½ cup (60 g) chopped pecans

½ cup (20 g) fresh parsley leaves, lightly packed

¼ cup (45 g) grated Parmigiano-Reggiano cheese

½ cup (120 ml) pecan oil (can substitute canola oil)

1 tsp kosher salt

4 dates, seeded and finely chopped

2 tsp (10 ml) balsamic vinegar

8 slices ciabatta bread (can substitute other country-style bread), sliced 1-inch (2.5-cm) thick

3 tbsp (45 ml) extra virgin olive oil

2 cups (454 g) good-quality ricotta

To make the pesto, place the pecans, parsley, Parmigiano-Reggiano, pecan oil, and salt in the bowl of a food processor. Lightly pulse until well combined but not totally puréed. Watch closely, since the mixture will come together pretty quickly.

Transfer the mixture to a bowl. Fold in the chopped dates and balsamic vinegar and set aside (see Chef's Tip).

Preheat the broiler.

Brush the bread with the olive oil and toast under the broiler until golden. Spread the ricotta evenly over the toasted bread, then spoon the pesto on top and serve right away.

CHEF'S TIP
The pesto will keep for one day if not using right away. Store, covered, in the refrigerator.

Spicy Rigatoni

SERVES 4

This recipe has a special place in Alon's heart. "When I worked at Pizzeria Gabbiano in Parma, Italy," explains Alon, "my pizza mentor's sister would prepare this simple rigatoni pasta for us. I remember how light and fragrant the sauce was. I'd drizzle a little spicy chili oil over it and think that Italian food just doesn't get any better than this." He adds, "I use this as a go-to dish a lot because of that moment."

2 tbsp plus 1 tsp (37 g) salt, divided

1 lb (450 g) rigatoni

1½ cups (360 g) canned San Marzano tomatoes, with their juices

¼ cup (60 ml) extra virgin olive oil

1 clove garlic, thinly sliced

Zest of 1 lemon

8 fresh basil leaves, torn

2 hot fresh chiles, seeded and minced (tabasco, Thai, or cayenne are good varieties)

6 tbsp (68 g) grated Parmigiano-Reggiano cheese

½ cup (20 g) fresh basil leaves, torn into pieces, loosely packed

Place 1 gallon (3.8 L) of water in a large pot and bring to a rolling boil. Add the 2 tablespoons (32 g) salt and stir to dissolve. Add the rigatoni and cook according to package directions. Alon typically likes to cook it for 1 minute less than the time indicated to keep it a little more al dente. Drain the pasta in a colander and set aside.

Finely chop the tomatoes, then set aside in a small bowl with their juices.

In a large skillet over medium heat, heat the oil until very hot but not yet smoking. Add the garlic, lemon zest, basil, and chiles. Allow to cook for 30 seconds to 1 minute, or until the garlic just begins to brown.

Add the chopped tomatoes with their juices and cook until the sauce lightly thickens. Add the cooked pasta, and cook for another 2 minutes, stirring constantly until the sauce coats the pasta and becomes shiny. Season with the remaining 1 teaspoon salt and remove from the heat.

Stir in the grated cheese and basil. Serve immediately.

Cast Iron–Seared Rib Eyes
with Blood Orange Chimichurri

SERVES 4

The beauty of this simple-but-super-delicious recipe is that (a) it doesn't require thinking too far ahead, and (b) you can easily substitute ingredients you already have in your fridge for the ones listed here. For instance, in the summer, use fresh blueberries instead of blood oranges. You can't go wrong . . . and it'll always be a nice surprise.

FOR THE RIB EYES

2 (14-oz [392-g]) rib eye steaks, choice or prime, 1-inch (2.5-cm) thick

2 tsp (10 g) salt

FOR THE BLOOD ORANGE CHIMICHURRI

1 blood orange

2 cups (80 g) loosely packed fresh parsley leaves, chopped

1½ cups (60 g) loosely packed fresh cilantro leaves, chopped

1½ cups (360 ml) extra virgin olive oil

3 tbsp (45 ml) fresh lemon juice

1 clove garlic, grated

1 tsp salt

½ tsp red chili flakes (crushed red pepper)

¼ cup (60 ml) canola oil

To prepare the rib eyes, use a paper towel to pat the steaks on both sides until very dry. Sprinkle ½ teaspoon salt on each side of each steak and give it a pat to make sure it sticks. Refrigerate the steaks, uncovered, for about 30 minutes, although the longer the better (up to 12 hours). Remove from the refrigerator and let come to room temperature for 20 to 30 minutes before cooking.

Meanwhile, to make the blood orange chimichurri, use a sharp paring knife to peel the skin and white pith from the orange; discard the skin and pith. Hold the orange over a medium-size bowl and cut into segments between the membranes, letting them fall into the bowl. After all the segments are in the bowl, squeeze the membranes over them to extract the juice, then discard the membranes; there should be about 2 tablespoons (30 ml) juice in the bowl.

To the orange segments and juice in the bowl add the remaining chimichurri ingredients and toss to combine. Set aside (see Chef's Tip).

Set a large cast-iron skillet over medium-high heat until it's blazing hot. Add the canola oil and let it get so hot it smokes. Carefully lay the steaks in the skillet side by side. If this crowds them too much, cook them one at a time.

Decrease the heat to medium and let the steaks cook for 3 minutes, then flip and let cook for another 5 minutes for medium rare. Remove from the heat and set the steaks on a carving board or platter to rest for 3 minutes to let the juices settle and keep the meat moist. If you're worried about them getting cold, you can reheat under the broiler, 1 minute per side, before slicing.

When ready to serve, carve each steak on the bias into ½-inch (12-mm) slices and divide among 4 plates. Spoon some chimichurri over each portion of meat and serve.

CHEF'S TIP
This is best served when it's fresh, since the leaves will eventually start to lose their vibrant color, but you can refrigerate for up to 4 hours.

BRYCE SHUMAN

New York, New York

Executive chef of Betony

CHEF SAYS

Items I always keep on hand for unexpected guests are . . .

Hummus and pretzels, a good firm cheese like a clothbound cheddar and fresh fruit, a six pack of my favorite beer, a good vanilla ice cream and walnuts, and a few homemade soups that I keep stocked in the freezer.

When hosting a quick get-together, never overlook . . .

The ambiance and the feel of the room. Imagine yourself entering the space as a guest. Make sure the setting is right for the occasion. A great dinner is about all of the senses: sights, sounds, smells, feel, and taste.

My secret tip for successful last-minute entertaining is . . .

Be prepared by having the right glasses, silverware, napkins, and plateware so when people arrive, it's easy to pull out and prepare to set the table and make a beautiful setting. Then you can enjoy the party yourself. I also usually keep fresh flowers in the house—it adds that extra touch. This is easy to do with a little bit of planning ahead, and it really goes a long way.

One fun fact few people know about me is that . . .

I collect analog synthesizers and classic guitar pedals.

MENU

Crown Rib Roast with Sautéed Tuscan Kale, Pan-Roasted Crosnes & Brown Butter Sauce with Capers

CHEF'S PAIRING

2006 Viúva Gomes Collares

CHEF'S PLAYLIST

Leo Kottke or Taj Mahal

MAJOR KUDOS

One Michelin star; three stars from the *New York Times*; named one of the "Best New Chefs" by *Food & Wine*; "Restaurant of the Year" award from *Esquire*; named one of "America's 100 Best Wine Restaurants" by *Wine Enthusiast*; James Beard award nominee

HIS STORY

Imagine eating foods as exotic as raw caribou and seal—while living in the Arctic. Or smashing an orange in your hands and sticking a straw in it—while in the rain forests of Costa Rica. Or learning how to make traditional *tzatziki*—while in Crete. All as a young kid.

Yep, that was Bryce's life as he traveled all around the globe with his mother, a cultural anthropologist. But even with all these awesome culinary experiences, after graduating from high school in North Carolina, all he wanted to do was become an actor.

As fate would have it, he didn't get into the schools he wanted, so he took a job washing dishes at a local restaurant. And that's where the magic started.

After working his way up at a number of top-echelon kitchens, he ended up at Eleven Madison Park, one of the top restaurants in the world. Six years later he opened Betony (named after an herb in the mint family), eventually earning a rare Michelin star.

"The components in this meal, if cooked well, can create a really substantial and impressive meal," says Bryce. "It's a luxurious way to treat yourself, family, and friends."

Of that, we don't doubt.

Crown Rib Roast with Sautéed Tuscan Kale, Pan-Roasted Crosnes & Brown Butter Sauce with Capers

SERVES 8

"Caramelization is definitely happening on this roast," says Bryce. "Some people think caramelization is to seal in the juices, but it's more about creating intense, more concentrated and complex flavors. It also creates intense aromas and fills your kitchen with the sweet smell of cooking at home." The roast is accompanied by Bryce's riff on sautéed Tuscan kale (a.k.a. lacinato kale, dinosaur kale, or *cavalo nero*), which is decidedly sweet and tender, savory and delicious, all at the same time—and by crosnes (aka Chinese artichokes or *chorogi*, and pronounced "crones"), which are actually crisp, juicy little tubers about the size of chess pieces and a member of the mint family. Eat them raw, pickled, or simply pan-roasted like Bryce likes them. To top it all, he adds a tasty tart sauce to "offset the richness of the meat." Delish!

FOR THE CROWN RIB ROAST

10 lb (4.5 kg) bone-in rib eye, frenched and tied by your butcher

2 tsp (10 g) kosher salt

1 tsp freshly ground black pepper

¼ cup (60 ml) grapeseed oil (can substitute vegetable oil)

8 oz (230 g, 2 sticks) butter

4 fresh thyme sprigs

2 cloves garlic

FOR THE SAUTÉED TUSCAN KALE

Extra virgin olive oil, as needed

3 cups (90 g) Tuscan kale leaves

½ tsp kosher salt

½ tsp red chili flakes (crushed red pepper), plus additional if desired

FOR THE PAN-ROASTED CROSNES

¼ cup (58 g) butter and pan drippings reserved from roast

2 cups (250 g) crosnes (can substitute baby sunchokes)

3 fresh thyme sprigs

1 clove garlic, peeled

½ tsp kosher salt

¾ cup (168 g) butter and pan drippings
reserved from roast

2 tbsp (30 g) capers

½ tsp coarsely ground black pepper

1 tbsp (15 ml) fresh lemon juice

Kosher salt, to taste

To prepare the crown rib roast, preheat the oven to 425°F (218°C).

Season the beef well with salt and pepper. Wrap the rack around itself so that the ends meet and secure it with butcher's twine. Wrap the exposed bone ends with aluminum foil to preserve their whiteness.

Heat the oil in an extra-large cast-iron skillet over medium-high heat. Sear the crown roast, flesh side down. Rotate the roast constantly until evenly colored on all sides, about 12 minutes total, then remove to a large platter. Add the butter, still over medium-high heat, and let it brown. Add the thyme and garlic. Return the roast to the skillet and baste liberally, then remove it again, to a roasting pan this time. Take the skillet off the heat and pour the buttery pan drippings into a bowl to reserve for use in the preparation of the crosnes and brown butter sauce.

Place the roasting pan in the oven and cook the roast until the thickest part registers about 135°F (57°C) on a meat thermometer, approximately 15 minutes. Remove from the oven and allow the crown to rest for 10 to 15 minutes before carving, or until the internal temperature registers 145°F (63°C).

To make the sautéed Tuscan kale, in the same skillet that the roast was cooked in, over medium-high heat, add enough oil to cover the bottom of the pan, then toss in the kale and 1 teaspoon water. Immediately season with salt to draw out the moisture and start the wilting process. Cook until the kale is tender, about 2 minutes. Season with the chili flakes, then remove from the pan and place in a serving bowl.

To make the pan-roasted crosnes, preheat the oven to 375°F (191°C).

In an ovenproof skillet, preferably the same one used to cook the crown roast, add ¼ cup (56 g) of the reserved buttery pan drippings and the crosnes. Toss constantly until the crosnes are evenly colored, about 3 to 5 minutes. Add the thyme. Crush the garlic clove with the palm of your hand one time to release its aromas and open it up, then add to the skillet. Season with the salt.

Place in the oven and cook until just tender, about 3 minutes. Remove from the skillet to a serving bowl, discarding the garlic and thyme. Keep warm until ready to serve.

To make the brown butter sauce with capers, in the same pan used to roast the crosnes and the roast, add ¾ cup (168 g) of the reserved buttery pan drippings and capers. Sauté briefly, about 2 minutes, over medium heat, then remove from the heat and stir in the pepper, lemon juice, and salt to taste. Serve with the crown roast and sides.

ANA SORTUN

Cambridge, Massachusetts

Executive chef/co-owner of Oleana Restaurant and Sofra Bakery & Café (Cambridge); co-owner of Sarma Restaurant (Somerville, Massachusetts)

CHEF SAYS

Items I always keep on hand for unexpected guests are . . .

Anson Mills Carolina rice, feta cheese, Greek-style yogurt, Turkish spice blends, and Turkish pine nuts.

When hosting a quick get-together, never overlook . . .

Setting the table first. Then you can get everyone involved in the kitchen.

My secret tip for successful last-minute entertaining is . . .

Be creative with your pantry!

One fun fact few people know about me is that . . .

My full name is Oleana.

MENU

Feta & Bread Dumplings with Garlicky Greens & Toum

CHEF'S PAIRING

A medium-bodied Mediterranean-style red wine, like COS from Sicily

CHEF'S PLAYLIST

Taj Mahal

MAJOR KUDOS

James Beard award for "Best Chef: Northeast"; semifinalist for James Beard "Outstanding Chef" award; Zagat award for "Best Farm-to-Table Restaurant"; one of *Food & Wine*'s "Chef Superstars"; appearance on Bravo's *Top Chef Masters*

HER STORY

She was raised in Seattle. Trained in Paris. Studied in Turkey. And settled in Massachusetts.

To say Ana has been around the world and back again is no exaggeration. And her dish in this book, which is something she'd make from what she normally has in her pantry and fridge for guests who showed up spontaneously, reflects precisely that.

"This recipe is from a trip to Puglia, where dumplings are traditionally made with ricotta," says Ana. "I did a spin on it with Middle Eastern flavors because that is what my pantry is full of."

Since Ana's husband owns a farm in the Sudbury River Valley, just outside Boston, there is never any shortage of fresh produce in their home, either.

"We are always loaded with dark leafy greens," explains Ana. "And since our daughter, Siena, puts feta on her salad every night, we always have that on hand, too."

This dish is something Ana will make for her family if she's in a hurry.

"I love the comfort of this meal," she admits. "It's quick to make and perfect for last minute."

Feta & Bread Dumplings with Garlicky Greens & Toum

SERVES 4

"If you don't have any homemade bread crumbs," explains Ana, "you can easily just use bread with the crust removed and soak it in the yogurt and milk. After it sits for a while, squeeze it dry of any liquid. Then pack in a measuring cup to make it somewhat equal to the bread crumbs." As for the garlicky greens, imagine healthy, dark greens . . . wilted . . . and blended with a rich, creamy, garlicky white sauce called, in Lebanese, *toum*, which is a staple of Lebanese cuisine—and vegan, to boot!

FOR THE GARLICKY GREENS & TOUM

6 cloves garlic

1 tsp salt, divided, plus additional if needed

1½ tbsp (25 ml) fresh lemon juice

½ cup (120 ml) grapeseed oil (can substitute vegetable oil)

2 tbsp (30 ml) olive oil

2 bunches Swiss chard leaves (reserve stems for another use), roughly chopped (can substitute kale, spinach, or other dark leafy greens)

Freshly ground black pepper, to taste

FOR THE FETA & BREAD DUMPLINGS

2 cups (240 g) bread crumbs, preferably homemade (can substitute panko but not other store-bought brands)

½ cup (125 g) unflavored whole-milk Greek yogurt

½ cup (120 ml) milk, plus additional if needed

1 whole egg plus 1 yolk

4 oz (112 g) crumbled feta

1 cup (180 g) grated Kasseri cheese (can substitute Parmigiano-Reggiano)

1–2 tsp (2–5 g) nigella seeds, optional

¾ tsp kosher salt

½ tsp Maras pepper (can substitute freshly ground black pepper)

4 tbsp (60 ml) extra virgin olive oil (can substitute butter), divided

2 cups (490 g) puréed tomato sauce, preferably homemade

1 tsp dried mint, for garnish

To make the garlicky greens and toum, first prepare the toum. Place the garlic in a blender with ½ teaspoon of the salt and the lemon juice. Blend for 2 to 3 minutes, until as smooth as possible.

With the blender on low speed, add the grapeseed oil very slowly, as if making a mayonnaise. Make sure each amount of oil is fully absorbed before adding more. Add 1 tablespoon (15 ml) of water and finish blending. Set aside.

To prepare the garlicky greens, preheat the oven to 400°F (204°C).

Add the olive oil to a very large, ovenproof sauté pan fitted with a lid and heat on medium heat. Add the Swiss chard to the pan. Season with the remaining ½ teaspoon salt. Cover with the lid and cook for about 4 minutes, or until soft and wilted.

Uncover and stir in the toum, then continue to stir so the toum is incorporated throughout the greens. Cover and place in the oven for 15 minutes to bake in the garlic. Remove from the oven, keeping the oven set at 400°F (204°C), season with pepper and more salt if needed, and set aside.

To make the feta and bread dumplings, combine the bread crumbs with the yogurt and milk in a medium-size bowl. Let stand for 5 minutes to allow the bread crumbs to soak up the liquid. Add the eggs, feta, grated cheese, nigella seeds (if using), salt, and Maras pepper. Mix until a soft dough is formed. If the mixture is very stiff, add more milk until it sticks together and is shapeable but soft, like room temperature chocolate chip cookie dough.

Divide the mixture into 4 equal parts. Divide each part into 4 dumplings so that you have a total of 16 dumplings. Use a small ice cream scoop to shape them or roll them into balls by hand and flatten slightly.

Heat 2 tablespoons (30 ml) of the oil in a medium-size sauté pan, preferably nonstick, over medium-low heat. Pan fry 8 dumplings at a time until they are golden on one side, about 3 minutes. The heat should be gentle, as they will be dry if they fry too hard. Turn them and brown the other side. Transfer them to a baking sheet.

Wipe out the sauté pan and pan fry the other 8 dumplings with the remaining 2 tablespoons (30 ml) oil.

Add these dumplings to the baking sheet with the others and pop into the oven. Bake for 6 minutes, or until the dumplings are hot and sizzling. The oven will not only get them hot all the way through, it will also puff them a little bit, too.

Meanwhile, warm the tomato sauce in a small saucepan over low heat.

Spoon ½ cup (125 g) tomato sauce onto each of 4 plates. Arrange 4 dumplings over the sauce and spoon some greens next to each portion. Garnish with the dried mint.

ANGELO SOSA

New York, New York

Chef/partner of Añejo Hell's Kitchen, Añejo Tribeca, and ABAJO Cocktail Bar; founder of AOSbysosa Couture Chef Line

CHEF SAYS

Items I always keep on hand for unexpected guests are . . .

Sriracha, pickles, green hot sauce, fruit, and dog food (though not for me . . . for our eight dogs).

When hosting a quick get-together, never overlook . . .

Timing. It's everything. Don't wait until the last minute to prepare everything. When your guests come, you want to enjoy yourself, too.

My secret tip for successful last-minute entertaining is . . .

Candles, diffusers, and music, and fill the room with love.

One fun fact few people know about me is that . . .

I have a special needs son who is beautiful and inspiring to me. His name is Jacob Elias, and he's my true inspiration of happiness.

MENU

Sunny-Side-Up Eggs with Chinese Sausage & "Takeout" Fried Rice

CHEF'S PAIRING

Stella Artois beer

CHEF'S PLAYLIST

Andrea Bocelli

MAJOR KUDOS

StarChef's New York's Rising Star award for "Best New Restaurant Concept"; contestant on Bravo's *Top Chef DC* and *Top Chef All Stars*

HIS STORY

With an Italian mother, Dominican father, and six older siblings, Angelo enjoyed a lively childhood growing up in Connecticut as the baby of the family. Food was naturally a central part of their everyday lives.

So, no one was really surprised when Angelo decided to attend the Culinary Institute of America. After graduating with high honors, he stayed on to teach and also run the school's most highly acclaimed on-campus restaurant, the Escoffier Room.

Eventually, he left to attain his life goal of working with not only some of the best chefs in the world (Jean-Georges Vongerichten and Alain Ducasse), but also an A-list restaurateur (Stephen Starr). Now he's working his magic at his own popular spots in New York.

"This recipe is super simple with a burst of flavor and a great way to utilize leftover rice from Chinese takeout," says Angelo. "I personally freeze my rice so it becomes hard and crumbles well. This dish is the best way to clear out your fridge by using whatever ingredients are in there. That way you don't have to run out and go shopping!"

Sunny-Side-Up Eggs with Chinese Sausage & "Takeout" Fried Rice

SERVES 4

This fun and vibrantly colorful breakfast dish could easily double as a lunch or dinner entrée, too. The trick is to save the rice from your last Chinese takeout and freeze it. That will make putting this meal together a real snap.

5 large eggs, divided

Pinch of kosher salt

1 cup (225 g) minced Chinese sausage, cured chorizo, or cooked breakfast sausage

3 tbsp (45 ml) grapeseed oil (can substitute vegetable oil)

2 tbsp (18 g) minced garlic

2 tbsp (14 g) grated fresh ginger

2 cups (500 g) leftover cooked rice

¼ cup (60 ml) light soy sauce

1 tbsp (15 ml) toasted sesame oil

3 tbsp (9 g) finely chopped scallions

Place a large nonstick sauté pan over medium heat. When it's hot, crack 4 of the eggs into the pan side by side, and cook them sunny side up until the whites are just beginning to set. Lightly salt the whites of the eggs. Add the sausage to the whites alone and continue cooking until the whites are just set. Using a spatula, remove the eggs separately to a platter and set aside to keep warm.

Meanwhile, set a wok or large saucepan over medium-high heat. When the pan is really hot, add the oil, garlic, and ginger. Cook for about 1 minute, or until aromatic.

Crack the remaining egg into the wok and, using a wooden spoon, scramble it quickly. Add the rice, stirring to separate it. Continue cooking and stirring the mixture for another 5 minutes, then season with the soy sauce. To retain its nutty flavor, drizzle the sesame oil on the rice at the very end of the cooking. Remove from the heat.

Divide the rice among 4 bowls, then place 1 fried egg on top of each serving of rice. Garnish with the scallions and serve immediately.

SUSAN SPICER

New Orleans, Louisiana

Chef/co-owner of Bayona, Mondo, and WildFlour Bread

CHEF SAYS

Items I always keep on hand for unexpected guests are . . .

Cheese, sausage or cured meat, pepper jelly or mostarda, ciabatta or other bread for crostini in the freezer, and ice cream (well, maybe that's for me!).

When hosting a quick get-together, never overlook . . .

Sitting outside, if possible, or at least having some greenery or flowers on the table and an open window.

My secret tip for successful last-minute entertaining is . . .

Always keep a bottle or two of wine chilling.

One fun fact few people know about me is that . . .

I'd love to be a singer.

MENU

Lemongrass Grilled Shrimp with Thai Fried Rice & Pineapple Nuoc Cham

CHEF'S PAIRING

Beer, a Riesling, or a Thai variation on a margarita

CHEF'S PLAYLIST

Soul, R&B, or old-time country (My husband also has some fun cocktail music from around the world!)

MAJOR KUDOS

James Beard "Best Chef: Southeast" award; induction into James Beard's "Who's Who of Food and Beverage in America"; named one of *Food & Wine*'s "10 Best New Chefs"; guest chef for both Cunard and Crystal cruise lines; judge on Bravo's *Top Chef*

HER STORY

When Susan was a toddler, she lived for a time in Holland (her father was a navy officer). And to this day, she still has fond memories of the food she tasted there, particularly Indonesian food.

"There was a wonderful noodle dish called *bami goreng* that had all kinds of spices in it," she says. "That's probably where I first developed an interest in global cuisine."

That interest led her to eventually pursue a career in the culinary arts, first as a catering assistant, then as an apprentice in Paris, and finally as the owner of her own successful restaurant.

Today, Susan makes guest appearances all over the world based on her vast knowledge of other cultures and foods. Which is why her meal choice for this book comes as no surprise.

"I almost always have shrimp and rice on hand," says Susan. "I can make so many different kinds of dishes with those two ingredients. But this particular dish is exceptionally light and bright. And besides, everyone loves shrimp!"

You're so right, Susan. So absolutely right.

Lemongrass Grilled Shrimp with Thai Fried Rice & Pineapple Nuoc Cham

SERVES 4

A little bit of spiciness and a little bit of sweetness. It all comes together so beautifully in this delicious, Asian-inspired dish. "These ingredients, which I love to keep on hand, may seem very exotic," says Susan, "but you can find most of them in grocery stores nowadays."

3 tbsp (45 ml) canola or mild vegetable oil

2 tbsp (5 g) fresh or frozen lemongrass, grated

2 tsp (5 g) minced fresh ginger

1 tsp minced garlic

1 tsp fish sauce

24 peeled and deveined (21 to 25 count) shrimp, tails left on

FOR THE PINEAPPLE NUOC CHAM

½ fresh pineapple, peeled and diced

Juice of 2 limes, plus additional as needed

2 tbsp (30 ml) fish sauce

3 tbsp (39 g) sugar, plus additional as needed

1 tsp red chili paste or sambal oelek

1 tbsp (2 g) very thinly sliced fresh kaffir lime leaves, optional

FOR THE THAI FRIED RICE

2 large eggs

1 tsp soy sauce

1 tbsp (15 ml) canola oil, divided

1 cup (150 g) thinly sliced shallots

½ cup (75 g) diced or sliced onion

½ cup (50 g) diced or sliced carrot

½ cup (75 g) green peas, snow peas, or chopped bok choy

2 cups (500 g) cooked rice

1 tsp fish sauce

¼ cup (12 g) thinly sliced scallions

2 tbsp (5 g) chopped fresh cilantro

Salt, to taste, if needed

Fresh mint leaves (can substitute Thai basil or regular basil), to garnish

Preheat the broiler or grill. Have ready 4 bamboo or metal skewers. If using bamboo skewers, soak them in warm water.

Mix the oil, lemongrass, ginger, garlic, and fish sauce in a bowl. Add the shrimp, toss well to coat, and marinate for at least 10 minutes.

Meanwhile, to make the pineapple nuoc cham, mix all the ingredients in a small bowl until the sugar is dissolved. If using pineapple juice, you can purée in a blender. Adjust the sugar and lime juice as needed to reflect your taste. Set aside.

To make the Thai fried rice, whisk the eggs and soy sauce in a small bowl. Heat 1 teaspoon of the oil in a small sauté pan over medium heat. Add the egg mixture and scramble until just set, then remove from the heat. Once cool, chop. Set aside.

Heat the remaining 2 teaspoons (10 ml) of oil in a 10-inch (25-cm) sauté pan over medium-low heat. Add the shallots and fry until light golden brown and crisp, about 5 minutes. The shallots will continue to crisp up as they cool. Remove the shallots from the pan and drain on paper towels. Strain off the oil, then pour it back into the pan.

Heat the oil in the pan over medium-high heat until hot, then stir in the onion and carrot. Cook about 3 minutes, or until the onion is wilted and just starting to color. Add the peas, toss, and cook for 1 more minute. Stir in the rice. Cook without disturbing for about 2 to 3 minutes, or until the rice starts to crisp a little. Stir with a spoon or a rubber spatula, and let the rice cook 2 to 3 more minutes. Add the fish sauce, scrambled eggs, scallions, and cilantro. Stir and just heat through. Taste for seasoning and add salt if needed. Set aside and keep warm.

Thread 6 marinated shrimp on each skewer. Broil or grill until the shrimp start to brown just a little and are cooked through.

Divide the rice among 4 plates. Top each serving with one skewer, then garnish with the mint. Top with the fried shallots and serve, accompanied by the pineapple nuoc cham.

ETHAN STOWELL

Seattle, Washington

Chef/owner of Anchovies & Olives, Ballard Pizza Co. (three locations), Bar Cotto, Bramling Cross, Frelard Pizza Co., How to Cook a Wolf, Marine Hardware, Mkt., Red Cow, Rione XIII, Staple & Fancy, and Tavolàta (two locations); chef/partner of Goldfinch Tavern at Four Seasons Hotel Seattle

CHEF SAYS

Items I always keep on hand for unexpected guests are . . .

Oil-packed anchovies, hard cheese, prosciutto di Parma, rustic crackers, and dry pasta.

When hosting a quick get-together, never overlook . . .

Inviting your friends to hang out in the kitchen with you.

My secret tip for successful last-minute entertaining is . . .

Always start with a refreshing aperitif.

One fun fact few people know about me is that . . .

I'm a huge pop music fan.

MENU

Panzanella

Spaghetti with Garlic, Chili & Anchovies

Vanilla Bean Ice Cream with Roasted Figs & Aged Balsamic

CHEF'S PAIRING

2013 Occhipinti Il Frappato

CHEF'S PLAYLIST

Taylor Swift, Justin Timberlake, Nick Jonas, Justin Bieber, Shawn Mendes, Miley Cyrus, Scissor Sisters, DNCE, and Kenny Loggins

MAJOR KUDOS

"Best New Chef" award from *Food & Wine*; "Top 10 Best New Restaurants" award from *Bon Appétit*; "10 Best New Restaurants in America" award from *GQ*; listing as one of "50 Best New U.S. Restaurants" by *Travel + Leisure*; multiple "Best New Restaurant" awards from *Seattle Magazine*; Richard Melman Innovator of the Year Award

HIS STORY

You would think that a kid whose parents famously ran the prestigious Pacific Northwest Ballet Company would somehow follow in their *grands jetés*. Errr, footsteps.

Yet young Ethan quickly realized he wasn't cut out for dancing. So he took up food instead. First at a local drive-in (making shakes!). Then with a family friend's catering company. Then at an upscale restaurant in Atlanta and back in Seattle again. But all the while, he kept dreaming about opening his own place. Which he did, again and again and again.

Today, Ethan owns more than a dozen award-winning eateries that all focus on freshness and simplicity. So, when it comes to his own at-home entertaining, it's no different.

"This spaghetti dish is one of my most favorite things ever," admits Ethan. "It has simple flavors and comes together quickly. It might even be my last meal! It's both easy and delicious."

His guests enjoy it just as much. And to that, we say encore!

Panzanella

SERVES 4

By definition, panzanella is a Tuscan salad of bread and tomatoes that's especially popular in the summer. Here, Ethan utilizes gorgeous seasonal tomatoes that you can easily get from your own garden or at a local farmers' market. This makes a beautiful and colorful side dish. But double the recipe, and suddenly you've got yourself a marvelous main dish instead!

½ French baguette, cubed

7 tbsp (105 ml) extra virgin olive oil, divided

Kosher salt, to taste

Freshly ground black pepper, to taste

8 oil-packed anchovy fillets, drained and chopped

1 clove garlic, thinly sliced crosswise

8 oz (224 g) ripe heirloom tomatoes, cut into large chunks

½ small bunch fresh basil, leaves torn

Juice of 1 lemon

¼ red onion, shaved, preferably on a mandolin

4 oz (112 g) Pecorino Romano cheese, shaved, for garnish

Preheat the oven to 350°F (177°C).

Place bread cubes on a baking sheet and toss with 3 tablespoons (45 ml) of the olive oil. Season with salt and pepper. Bake in the oven until slightly dry but still chewy in the center, about 15 minutes.

Combine the anchovies and garlic in a large bowl with the remaining 4 tablespoons (60 ml) of olive oil and a pinch of salt and pepper. Add the tomatoes, basil, lemon juice, and shaved onion and toss to combine. Add the bread cubes and allow to sit for 10 to 15 minutes, stirring occasionally.

Divide the panzanella among 4 shallow bowls. Garnish with shaved Pecorino and serve.

Spaghetti with Garlic, Chili & Anchovies

SERVES 4

This is a fabulous recipe for a light, flavorful pasta dish that takes full advantage of your pantry staples (minus the parsley). And if you dare think for even a second that you might want to omit the anchovies, don't. They punctuate the sauce to give it a rich, salty, umami flavor that will completely surprise—and delight—both you and your guests! For a milder version, just use less anchovies.

1 lb (450 g) dry spaghetti or 1½ lb (680 g) fresh spaghetti

¾ cup (180 ml) olive oil

3 cloves garlic, sliced

2 tsp (10 g) red chili flakes (crushed red pepper)

6–12 oil-packed anchovy fillets (depending on your taste), drained and chopped

¼ cup (10 g) chopped fresh parsley, packed

Freshly grated Parmigiano-Reggiano cheese, to taste

Bring a large pot of salted water to a boil. Add the pasta and cook according to package directions less 1 minute.

While the pasta is cooking, heat the olive oil over medium-low heat in a large, deep sauté pan. Add the garlic, chili flakes, and anchovies. Cook gently, stirring occasionally, until the garlic is soft and the anchovies melt into the oil, about 2 to 3 minutes.

When the pasta is done, drain in a colander, then add to the sauté pan. Add the parsley and toss well. Remove from the heat.

Divide the pasta among 4 deep bowls and top each with a generous serving of the cheese. Serve immediately.

Vanilla Bean Ice Cream with Roasted Figs & Aged Balsamic

SERVES 4

There's nothing more satisfying than a dessert as simple as this. But what makes it truly stand out, rather than just plopping ice cream in front of your guests, is the extra dimension of layered flavors. Ripe, luscious, sweet figs (in season during early summer and again during early fall) add a unique seedy texture, while aged balsamic (don't skimp on the quality!) imbues an intensely complex and elegantly smooth essence. Together, they're a marriage made in heaven.

8 fresh figs, preferably Kadota, cut in half

4 scoops premium vanilla bean ice cream

¼ cup (60 ml) aged balsamic vinegar (or see page 456), preferably 25 years old

Preheat the oven to 350°F (177°C).

Place the halved figs, skin side down, on a baking sheet. Roast for 10 minutes, then remove from the oven.

Arrange 4 fig halves in each of 4 serving bowls. Add 1 scoop of ice cream to each bowl, then drizzle the balsamic vinegar evenly over the top.

BILL TELEPAN

New York, New York

Executive chef of Oceana; chef/partner of Wellness in the Schools

CHEF SAYS

Items I always keep on hand for unexpected guests are . . .

Extra wine, pasta, lots of vegetables, good bread, and cheese.

When hosting a quick get-together, never overlook . . .

The importance of straightening up the house, no matter how quickly, and closing your bedroom doors.

My secret tip for successful last-minute entertaining is . . .

Always have a bottle of Champagne, white wine, and some cocktail mixers waiting in the fridge. From that point, if you don't have any food, you can always serve drinks and order delivery.

One fun fact few people know about me is that . . .

I am a mean karaoke machine!

MENU

Chicken Milanese

Arugula Salad with Balsamic Vinaigrette

Roasted New Potatoes

Broccoli & Broccoli Rabe with Lemon Oil

CHEF'S PAIRING

A good white Burgundy, beer (like a light Pilsner), or a light red wine like Pinot Noir

CHEF'S PLAYLIST

Cool alternative rock if having friends over. Classical music if having family over.

MAJOR KUDOS

One Michelin star; named one of top ten chefs in *Food & Wine*'s Chefs Make Change coalition; invitation to join First Lady Michelle Obama's Chefs Move to School task force; keynote speaker at the Culinary Institute of America's 2014 commencement ceremony

HIS STORY

Bill's food focus is firmly, passionately—and some might even say stubbornly—on only the highest-quality, farm-fresh, locally sourced ingredients available in season. Period.

Frankly, this Greenmarket devotee has been like that for decades, well before today's farm-to-table movement became vogue.

"You probably can't imagine him cooking anything that's been out of the earth for more than a few hours," boasts one recent article.

With a daughter of his own, it's no wonder Bill's so dedicated to the cause of WITS, a national nonprofit that inspires healthy eating, environmental awareness, and fitness as a way of life for kids in public schools.

For his one-hour meal, Bill's choice is quite unfussy yet sophisticated (and seriously delicious). "There are different components to this meal that appeal to a variety of people," he explains. "Since there are so many dietary restrictions and different taste buds, this is an easy and delicious choice that most can appreciate."

What else makes this the perfect meal for last-minute entertaining? "It can sit for a while," says Bill. "You can prep everything in advance, have drinks with your guests, and serve at room temperature. It's just as good!"

He's quick to point out that it's also a very kid-friendly meal and can be helpful in introducing children to healthy ingredients like broccoli and real roasted potatoes. So long, French fries!

Chicken Milanese

"I used to serve a similar dish using pasture-raised veal from Upstate New York when I was a chef at Judson Grill," says Bill. "The dish was offered on the lunch menu and was super popular. I always thought it would be a great option to make for dinner at home."

1 cup (125 g) all-purpose flour

2 cups (90 g) fresh bread crumbs (page 456)

3 large eggs

2 tbsp (30 ml) water

Salt, to taste

Freshly ground black pepper, to taste

4 (4–6-oz [112–168-g]) chicken cutlets, lightly pounded, not too thin

¼ cup (60 ml) olive oil, or as needed

Place the flour and bread crumbs in two separate bowls. Lightly beat the eggs in a third bowl and thin with 2 tablespoons (30 ml) water. Season the flour with salt and pepper.

Dredge each piece of chicken in the flour, then dip in the egg mixture, then dredge in the bread crumbs. Place each piece after it is finished onto a sheet of wax paper.

Heat oil in a large skillet over medium-high heat. Pan fry the chicken, in batches as necessary, until golden brown, about 2 to 3 minutes per side (see Chef's Tip). As each piece of chicken is pan fried, remove to a platter and keep warm.

CHEF'S TIP

During the cooking, as soon as bread crumbs left in the pan from the previous batch begin to burn, pour off the remaining oil and wipe out the pan, then add fresh oil and continue pan frying the remaining chicken.

Arugula Salad with Balsamic Vinaigrette

When just a basic salad is what's called for, this is the one. The arugula, also known as rocket salad, adds a bit of a peppery punch. And the vinaigrette dressing boasts one surprising ingredient: red chili flakes. Together, they're simple, flavorful, powerful.

2 tbsp (30 ml) balsamic vinegar

2 tbsp (30 ml) red wine vinegar

½ clove garlic, mashed to a paste or grated on a microplane

¼ tsp red chili flakes (crushed red pepper)

Salt, to taste

½ cup (120 ml) extra virgin olive oil

4 oz (112 g) arugula

¼–½ red onion, thinly sliced

¼ cup (45 g) grated Parmigiano-Reggiano cheese

To make the vinaigrette, combine the balsamic vinegar, red wine vinegar, garlic, chili flakes, and a pinch of salt in a bowl. Stir to combine, then slowly whisk in the oil.

Place the arugula, onion, and grated Parmigiano-Reggiano in a bowl. Add some of the vinaigrette and toss to combine well. Season with more salt, if desired. Add more dressing as needed or serve on the side, if desired.

Roasted New Potatoes

SERVES 4

In season during spring and early summer, new potatoes are simply potatoes that are harvested when they're still very young (before their sugar content has converted to starch). They're small, with thin skins, and best when newly plucked from the soil. If you're not lucky enough to have your own garden, be sure to visit your nearest farmers' market for these gems.

1 lb (450 g) small new potatoes (can substitute fingerling potatoes)

2 tbsp (30 ml) water

1 tbsp (15 ml) extra virgin olive oil

4 fresh thyme sprigs

Pinch of salt

Preheat the oven to 425°F (218°C). Line a baking sheet with foil.

Toss the potatoes with the water, oil, thyme, and a good pinch of salt in a bowl, then turn into the center of the baking sheet. Fold up the foil and crimp on all sides to create a pouch.

Roast the potatoes in the oven until tender, about 20 to 30 minutes. Check for doneness by pushing into the foil to make sure the potatoes are tender.

Open the foil pouch carefully, to avoid escaping steam, and turn into a serving dish. Or, if not serving right away, let the potatoes sit in the opened foil pouch at room temperature. Then, close to serving time, close the pouch and place it in the oven to reheat briefly.

Broccoli & Broccoli Rabe with Lemon Oil

SERVES 4

Although available all year 'round, broccoli and its zestier (and totally unrelated) friend, broccoli rabe—also known as broccoli raab, broccoli rape, or rapini—taste best during their peak season: early spring. Be sure to look for deep green coloring and compact bud clusters. And because they're both considered power foods, this vibrant combo vegetable dish is super packed with lots of nutrients. What's not to love or appreciate?

FOR THE LEMON OIL

2 lemons, zested and juiced

¼ cup (60 ml) extra virgin olive oil

½ tsp red chili flakes (crushed red pepper)

⅓ cup (60 g) grated Parmigiano-Reggiano cheese

1 tbsp (3 g) chopped fresh parsley

Salt, to taste

Freshly ground black pepper, to taste

FOR THE BROCCOLI AND BROCCOLI RABE

2 tbsp (30 ml) extra virgin olive oil

4 cloves garlic, minced

1 small bunch broccoli, cut into small florets

1 bunch broccoli rabe, thick stems removed, cut into 1- to 2-inch (2.5- to 5-cm) pieces

Salt, to taste

Freshly ground black pepper, to taste

To make the lemon oil, combine all the ingredients in a bowl and whisk together well. Set aside.

To make the broccoli and broccoli rabe, heat the oil in a large sauté pan with a cover over medium-high heat until hot but not smoking. Add the minced garlic and cook, stirring constantly, until lightly browned, about 1 minute.

Add the broccoli and broccoli rabe and stir, then cover and cook for about 30 seconds. Add a good pinch of salt and pepper, then re-cover and continue to cook for about 2 to 3 minutes, stirring occasionally. Remove from the heat.

Turn the vegetables into a serving bowl, toss well with the lemon oil, and serve.

BART VANDAELE

Washington, D.C.

Chef/owner of Belga Café, B Too, and Betsy

CHEF SAYS

Items I always keep on hand for unexpected guests are . . .

Real Irish butter, fresh eggs from my chickens, bacon, a good Iberico ham, and white wine. Plus, some cheese and baguettes or other bread.

When hosting a quick get-together, never overlook . . .

Timing. Be with your guests. Don't stay in the kitchen too long. And don't panic when a dish comes out slightly different than expected. Don't tell your guests, just let them enjoy.

My secret tip for successful last-minute entertaining is . . .

Don't overdo it. Make something you master really well so you don't have to stress.

One fun fact few people know about me is that . . .

I love being in my garden, seeding, planting, digging, and taking care of my chickens. (I have seven, and they're all named Betsy.) All that is Zen to me.

MENU

Baby Back Ribs with Mesquite Rub & Avocado Crème

Grilled Fingerling Potatoes with Thyme

Grilled Asparagus, Flemish Style

Warm Figs with Basil, Red Wine & Ice Cream

CHEF'S PAIRING

To start with, my favorite cocktail: gin and tonic.

Then a Pinot Blanc and a light Burgundy red or some Belgian beer.

CHEF'S PLAYLIST

Lounge music, a mix of European songs ('80s, '90s, or more recent), or stream of a Belgian radio station

MAJOR KUDOS

Winner of Starchef.com's "Rising Star Chef" award; contestant on Bravo's *Top Chef*; made a knight in the Order of Leopold II; won "Wine Excellence Award" from *Wine Spectator*; named "Beer Bar of the Year" by *Cheers*

HIS STORY

He's Belgian. Born and bred in Belgium. Which is probably why he was able, so effortlessly, to introduce authentic Belgian cuisine to the folks in D.C. But let's start at the beginning.

Bart grew up helping (or more accurately, playing) in his parents' restaurant. At only twelve he enrolled in a six-year program at the Culinary Institute for Restaurant and Hotel Management in Bruges. After graduating, he quickly worked his way up through the culinary ranks of various Michelin-starred restaurants throughout Europe.

Then Bart accepted a position that brought him to America's capital: executive chef for the European Union's head diplomat to the U.S. That was followed by an equally impressive stint as executive chef at the Dutch Embassy.

But eventually Bart decided to open his own wildly successful place, followed by a few more.

"My quick meal would be in my garden," says Bart. "I love entertaining outside. I designed my big backyard for the best dinner parties ever. Everybody feels much more relaxed when gathering around the grill. I want my guests to feel immediately at home and welcome. That is *the* most important element for a successful meal."

This special meal is an awesome combination of grilled ribs and potatoes, avocado crème, and a side of mayonnaise—a Belgian obsession—plus a sophisticated dessert in which ice cream collides (in the best possible way) with wine and basil.

Baby Back Ribs with Mesquite Rub & Avocado Crème

"Grilling means having fun for me," admits Bart. "And in return for my grilling, my guests will not mind providing me with drinks!"

FOR THE BABY BACK RIBS

6 racks of pork baby back ribs

1 tbsp (16 g) prepared mustard

Herbes de Provence, to taste

Grainy mesquite rub (not powder), for seasoning

Fleur de sel (can substitute sea salt), to taste

Freshly ground black pepper, to taste

FOR THE AVOCADO CRÈME

1 bunch fresh cilantro, stemmed and chopped

1 jalapeño chile, seeded and chopped

5 shallots, chopped

1 small green bell pepper, seeded and chopped

2 cloves garlic, chopped

Juice of ½ lemon

3 ripe avocados, peeled, pitted, and chopped

Salt, to taste

Freshly ground black pepper, to taste

FOR SERVING

Zest and juice of 2 limes

Olive oil, for drizzling

Mayonnaise

Preheat the grill to 400°F (204°C).

To prepare the baby back ribs, cut each rack in half. Break the membrane in the back by cutting it with a knife the long way. Brush the mustard on the ribs, then season with the herbes de Provence, mesquite rub, salt, and pepper. Wrap in plastic wrap and let rest for 10 minutes.

Place the ribs on the grill. Grill for 5 to 6 minutes on each side. Close the grill top, maintaining the heat on high, and let the ribs continue to cook undisturbed for 20 minutes, so they get a bit of a smoked taste. When the ribs are done, remove to a baking tray, cover with aluminum foil, and let rest for 10 minutes.

To make the avocado crème, combine the cilantro, jalapeño, shallots, green pepper, garlic, and lemon juice in a blender. Start to blend, adding water as you go until the mixture has a creamy texture. Add the avocados, season with salt and pepper as needed, and blend until smooth. Remove the mixture to a bowl.

Cut the ribs in pieces and arrange on a large serving platter. Drizzle with the lime juice and olive oil and sprinkle with the lime zest. Serve warm, accompanied by the avocado crème and mayonnaise.

Grilled Fingerling Potatoes with Thyme

SERVES 4

Super simple. Super easy. Super delicious. It just doesn't get any more enticing than this!

1 lb (450 g) fingerling potatoes, unpeeled, halved lengthwise

1 cup (240 ml) olive oil

4 cloves garlic, chopped

Salt, to taste

Freshly ground black pepper, to taste

Chopped fresh thyme, to taste

Preheat the grill.

Place the potatoes with the oil and garlic in a bowl. Season with the salt, pepper, and thyme and toss well.

Drain the potatoes and transfer to a grill basket. Grill until tender, about 10 minutes. Take off the heat and keep warm.

Grilled Asparagus, Flemish Style

SERVES 4

This traditional Flemish vegetarian dish calls for only a few ingredients, is really easy to make, and best of all, tastes divine.

4 large eggs, hard-boiled (page 456) and cooled

24 medium-size asparagus spears, trimmed

Regular olive oil, for brushing

Kosher salt, to taste

Freshly ground black pepper, to taste

Freshly grated nutmeg, to taste

1 lemon, halved

1 cup (240 ml) extra virgin olive oil

½ cup (120 ml) white wine vinegar, preferably chardonnay

1½ tsp (7 g) whole-grain mustard

½ bunch fresh chives, finely chopped

½ bunch fresh parsley, chopped, plus a few whole leaves for garnish

3½ oz (98 g) Parmigiano-Reggiano curls

Preheat the grill.

Peel and chop the hard-boiled eggs and set aside.

Brush the asparagus with the oil. Season with the salt, pepper, and nutmeg. Place on the grill, turning after a couple of minutes so they color evenly. They are ready when tender, about 5 minutes. Take off the grill and set aside.

To make the dressing, grill the lemon halves, flesh side down, for 3 to 5 minutes. Remove from the grill and squeeze the juice into a bowl. Add the oil, vinegar, and mustard and stir well. Add the chopped chives and parsley. Season with salt and pepper.

To serve, place the grilled asparagus on a serving platter and top with the chopped hard-boiled eggs. Drizzle with the dressing and garnish with the parsley leaves and Parmigiano-Reggiano curls to serve.

Warm Figs with Basil, Red Wine & Ice Cream

SERVES 4

A great meal deserves a great dessert. And this one's certainly it. Quartered fresh figs are simmered in a deeply sweet and richly bold sauce made with *vincotto* (a centuries-old condiment produced in Italy from unfermented grape must, literally meaning "cooked wine"). This mixture is then used to enrobe ice cream topped with crumbles of *speculoos*—a spiced shortbread biscuit that's a popular specialty of Belgium (and available online). Wow, oh wow, oh wow.

12 fresh ripe figs

8 tbsp unsalted butter (115 g, 1 stick), cut into 12 pieces

Leaves from 8 sprigs fresh basil, preferably both green and red, chopped (reserve some whole leaves for garnish)

2 cups (480 ml) red wine, preferably Malbec

¼ cup (84 g) honey, preferably lavender honey

1 tbsp (15 ml) vincotto (can substitute aged balsamic vinegar—or see page 456—mixed with 1 tsp sugar)

Freshly ground black pepper, to taste

1 pint (480 g) vanilla ice cream, for serving

Speculoos cookies (can substitute regular shortbread cookies, with a pinch of allspice), crumbled, for garnish

Preheat the grill to 400°F (204°C).

Snip the stems from the figs and open them into star shapes by cutting from the stem end in quarters, nearly to the other end of the fig. Arrange, cut sides up, in a large cast-iron skillet. Top each fig with one piece of butter, then sprinkle with the chopped basil. Pour the wine over the figs, then drizzle with the honey and vincotto. Season with pepper, then cover the skillet with a lid.

Place on the grill for 20 minutes, uncovering to stir every 5 minutes (see Chef's Tip). When the figs are cooked, remove them from the skillet and set aside.

Pour the cooking juices from the skillet into a blender along with 4 of the cooked figs and process to a smooth purée.

To serve, place 2 of the remaining cooked figs in each of 4 bowls. Add 1 or 2 scoops of ice cream to each bowl and ladle a couple of tablespoons of the fig and wine sauce over the ice cream and figs. Garnish with a couple of the basil leaves and the speculoos crumble.

CHEF'S TIP

Alternatively, you can cook the figs on the stovetop for 15 to 20 minutes over medium-high heat, stirring regularly. Or bake in the oven at 350°F (177°C) for 20 minutes.

Bonus Recipe: Gin & Tonic, My Way
SERVES 1

Combine 2 ounces (60 ml) of Copperhead Gin (a Belgian gin) with a small bottle of Fever-Tree Bitter, 1 to 2 violet flowers, 4 juniper berries, and either 2 or 3 fresh whole leaves of basil and/or mint, or 3 small rosemary sprigs. Finish with a big ice cube. (I keep special big ice cube molds in the freezer.)

JOANNE WEIR

San Francisco, California

Chef/managing partner of Copita; Host of award-winning PBS series Joanne Weir's Cooking Class *and* Joanne Weir Gets Fresh*; consulting editor-at-large at* Fine Cooking

CHEF SAYS

Items I always keep on hand for unexpected guests are . . .

Marcona almonds, a wedge of fresh goat cheese, seeded crackers, Castelvetrano olives, and something with bubbles.

When hosting a quick get-together, never overlook . . .

Having everyone chip in, pour wine, set the table, and stir a pot. It makes for a much more fun and lively time.

My secret tip for successful last-minute entertaining is . . .

Place a glass of wine in hand immediately upon arrival.

One fun fact few people know about me is that . . .

I love potato chips so much that if they're in my house, they will call my name until they're gone. Hence, I don't buy them.

MENU

Spiced Hummus with Preserved Lemons

"Merguez" Lamb Burgers with Cucumber & Ginger Yogurt

Moscato & Honey-Poached Figs

CHEF'S PAIRING

A Pinot Noir from Santa Lucia Highlands, California

CHEF'S PLAYLIST

Cesária Évora

MAJOR KUDOS

James Beard award for "Best Cookbook: General Category"; numerous James Beard award nominations; "Julia Child Cooking Teacher Award of Excellence" and "Tour Operator of the Year Award" from the International Association of Culinary Professionals; Gourmand World Cookbook Award for "Best Mediterranean Cookbook"; appointment by the U.S. State Department to serve in the American Chef Corps

HER STORY

What are the chances you'd become a chef if your great-grandmother owned a restaurant, your grandfather was a U.S. Army cook, and your mother was a professional caterer? Probably pretty great. Yet it wasn't such a surefire path for Joanne—at least not at first.

After earning her degree in art education, Joanne went on to teach fine arts for a number of years. She liked it enough, but her heart kept returning to food—and cooking. So she left to study under Madeleine Kamman in France, was awarded the Master Chef Diploma (with honors!), worked with Alice Waters at Chez Panisse, and eventually started her own highly successful business as an international cooking teacher.

Which is why this meal is such an interesting choice. "I'm loving anything North African and Middle Eastern right now," admits Joanne. "The cuisine packs a punch from all the spices, and you can even make the preserved lemons yourself. This meal doesn't take long to prepare, and the end results are wow! Plus, the flavors are so exotic!"

Great-grandma Lettie would be so proud.

Spiced Hummus with Preserved Lemons

SERVES 6

If you think this is just like any other hummus you've had before, think again. Joanne's version incorporates a certain *je ne sais quoi* and depth of flavor that clearly sets it apart. Look for preserved lemons at any Middle Eastern grocery store. Or opt to make your own. But if you do, know that it will take about a month—so plan accordingly.

1 (15.5-oz [434-g]) can garbanzo beans, drained and rinsed

¼ cup (10 g) fresh flat-leaf parsley leaves, loosely packed

2 tbsp (10 g) preserved lemon rind

1 small clove garlic, coarsely chopped

3 tbsp (42 g) tahini paste

1 tbsp (15 ml) juice from a preserved lemon

2 tbsp (30 ml) fresh lemon juice

2 tbsp (30 ml) water

1 tsp kosher salt

Extra virgin olive oil, for drizzling

Chopped fresh parsley, for garnish

Black olives, for garnish, optional

2 pita breads, toasted (page 457) and cut into wedges

Place the garbanzo beans, parsley, preserved lemon rind, garlic, tahini paste, preserved lemon juice, fresh lemon juice, and 2 tablespoons (30 ml) water in a food processor. Process until smooth, about 2 to 4 minutes. Add additional water if the hummus is too thick. Season with salt.

Transfer the mixture to a serving plate. Make a well in the center of the hummus and drizzle the olive oil into the well. Garnish with the parsley and olives, if desired. Serve with the pita bread.

"Merguez" Lamb Burgers with Cucumber & Ginger Yogurt

SERVES 6

Merguez, a traditional and spicy North African sausage, is extremely popular in Morocco. In fact, it's gaining widespread popularity all throughout Europe now as well. Here, Joanne transforms it into burgers you can easily make at home. Add her cooling yogurt sauce, and you've got yourself one memorable meal.

FOR THE CUCUMBER & GINGER YOGURT

¾ cup (184 g) unflavored Greek yogurt

¼ English cucumber, peeled, seeded, and ¼-inch (6-mm) diced

2 tsp (5 g) grated fresh ginger

1 small clove garlic, minced

Salt, to taste

FOR THE "MERGUEZ" LAMB BURGERS

1 lb (450 g) lean grass-fed ground lamb

¾ lb (340 g) ground pork

4 cloves garlic, minced

1½ tbsp (7 g) paprika

1½ tsp (7 g) ground cumin

½ tsp ground cloves

½ tsp ground cinnamon

Large pinch of cayenne pepper

1½ tsp (7 g) kosher salt

¾ tsp freshly ground pepper

¼ cup (10 g) chopped fresh cilantro, leaves and stems

6 slices coarse-textured bread, toasted (page 457)

Fresh cilantro sprigs, for garnish

To make the cucumber and ginger yogurt, combine the yogurt, cucumber, ginger, and garlic in a bowl and stir to mix. Season with salt and set aside.

To make the "Merguez" lamb burgers, place approximately one-quarter of the ground lamb, one-quarter of the pork, and all the garlic in a food processor and process until smooth. Add the paprika, cumin, cloves, cinnamon, cayenne, salt, and pepper. Pulse several times, just until mixed, then transfer the mixture to a bowl and add the remaining lamb, pork, and the chopped cilantro. Mix well with a wooden spoon.

Preheat a cast-iron ridged grill pan for 10 minutes over medium heat.

Form the meat mixture into 6 patties approximately the same size as the toasted bread. Cook the lamb burgers, turning occasionally, until medium rare, about 4 to 5 minutes per side.

To serve, place a slice of the toasted bread on each of 6 plates and place a lamb burger on top. Top each burger with some cucumber and ginger yogurt. Garnish with the cilantro sprigs and serve.

Moscato & Honey-Poached Figs

SERVES 6

Ahhh, figs. Luxurious, luscious figs. If you love them, you're going to love this recipe. And if you've never tried them, you're still going to love this recipe. That's because poaching figs—in this case, dried figs, which are conveniently available year-round—imparts a whole new flavor. For the syrup, Joanne prefers using sweet Moscato wine, with its slight fizz and tones of nectarine, peach, and orange. Creamy, rum-laced mascarpone adds the finishing touch to this exciting, all-star dessert!

½ cup plus 1 tbsp (189 g) honey, divided

3 cups (720 ml) Moscato sparkling wine

1 cup (240 ml) water

1 (4-inch [10-cm]) strip orange zest

1¼ lb (562 g) dried Mission or Calimyrna figs, stems removed

⅔ cup (185 g) mascarpone

1 tbsp (15 ml) dark rum

⅓ cup (50 g) shelled and roasted pistachios, chopped, for garnish

Bring the ½ cup (170 g) of the honey, Moscato, water, and orange zest to a boil over high heat. Add the figs and simmer, covered, until the figs are tender, 25 to 30 minutes. Remove the figs with a slotted spoon and set aside. Increase the heat to high and simmer until the syrup has reduced by half and thickened slightly, 10 to 12 minutes. Return the figs to the pan. In a bowl, whisk the mascarpone, rum, and 1 tablespoon (21 g) of the remaining honey until well mixed, about 10 seconds.

To serve, warm the figs over medium heat for 3 to 4 minutes. Spoon the figs and syrup into serving bowls, dividing equally. Place a dollop of the mascarpone on top of the warm figs, dividing evenly between the bowls. Sprinkle with pistachios and serve immediately.

ERIC WILLIAMS

Cleveland, Ohio

Chef/owner of Momocho and Jack Flaps (Cleveland) and El Carcinero (Lakewood, Ohio); executive chef/ partner of Happy Dog (Cleveland)

CHEF SAYS

Items I always keep on hand for unexpected guests are . . .

Wine, good cheese, cured meats, a number of pasta options, and a nice assortment of fruits and vegetables.

When hosting a quick get-together, never overlook . . .

Being yourself. Don't be nervous or offended by being caught off guard. I'm sure your unexpected guests didn't stop in to just eat or drink. They want to visit with you.

My secret tip for successful last-minute entertaining is . . .

Just enjoy the time together with your friends or family. Tell stories, laugh, and have a cocktail!

One fun fact few people know about me is that . . .

At one point in my early career, I lost my job cooking. I was really nervous, anxious about what to do for money, where to apply next, or if I even should consider continuing in the kitchen. So, I started selling perfume door to door. That job only lasted one day!

MENU

Pasta Carbonara

CHEF'S PAIRING

Wine or cold beer, maybe a Pilsner

CHEF'S PLAYLIST

A bunch of different groups, styles, and generations, from '40s music to Metallica

MAJOR KUDOS

Multiple James Beard award nominations for "Best Chef: Great Lakes"; winner of Guy Fieri's "Grocery Games: Diners, Drive-Ins and Dives Tournament"; named one of "Top 10 Best Restaurants" by *Food & Wine*; spot on *Bon Appétit*'s "Hot 10 List"; featured on the Cooking Channel's *Unique Eats*; named "Best Chef" by *Cleveland Scene*

HIS STORY

As he tells it, Eric Williams never quite had an "aha!" moment when he simply knew he wanted to be a chef. With Eric, it happened gradually . . . unexpectedly . . . serendipitously.

"The restaurant business has a way of grabbing hold of you and never letting go," laughs Eric. "I love what I do for many reasons."

Raised in Garfield Heights, Ohio, Eric was only fifteen when he took a job as a cook at a local mom-and-pop pizzeria to earn some extra cash. After he graduated from high school, he took on a second job as a cook at a local sports bar. From there he just kept on learning, advancing, and rising as far as he could at a myriad of successful Cleveland eateries.

"All my training comes from on-the-job experience," explains Eric. "I developed my own style of cooking by combining techniques with flavor combinations I myself enjoy eating." He calls it Mod Mex.

"I chose this recipe because it's a family favorite," explains Eric. "It's simple. It's delicious. And it's a perfect last-minute dish that can be prepared in less than 40 minutes. Plus, the ingredients are always readily available."

As we would say, perfect.

Pasta Carbonara

SERVES 4

"This dish is always a quick dinner option for us," says Eric. "When my wife makes it, she sadly leaves out the pancetta. When I make it, I'll sneak in even more pancetta. I guess it all depends on what you like." Meat or no meat, this recipe is always a winner.

4 large eggs

2 tbsp (30 ml) olive oil

8 oz (224 g) pancetta, diced (can substitute prosciutto or good slab bacon)

2 tsp (3 g) freshly cracked black pepper, plus additional for serving, if needed

1 clove garlic, minced

1 lb (450 g) linguine

½ cup (90 g) grated Parmigiano-Reggiano cheese, plus additional for garnish

Crack open the eggs, one at a time, putting the white as it is separated in a bowl and leaving the yolk in one of the egg shell halves. Set all the egg yolks, in their shells, carefully aside and set the bowl with the whites aside as well.

Heat the oil in a sauté pan over medium heat. Add the pancetta and cook slowly to render out the fat. If desired, drain off excess fat. Season with pepper, then add the garlic and sauté for 5 to 7 minutes, or until the garlic becomes golden.

Cook the linguine according to package directions. Drain but reserve 2 to 3 cups (480 to 720 ml) of pasta water.

Add 2 cups (480 ml) of the reserved pasta water to the pan with the pancetta. Bring to a boil, then remove from the heat. Whisk in the reserved egg whites. Add the cooked pasta and the ½ cup (90 g) cheese and toss well. If needed, add more liquid from the remaining 1 cup (240 ml) reserved pasta water.

Divide the pasta among 4 bowls. Top each bowl with one of the raw egg yolks. Garnish with the cheese and more pepper, if desired. Stir well to coat the pasta with the light sauce and serve immediately.

SPECIAL PROCESSES

BLANCHING

A process by which a vegetable is cooked partially by one method and then cooled. To a saucepan of boiling water, salted or not, add vegetables and cook just briefly, according to the recipe, and then drain and cool, in either an ice bath or under cold running water, to stop the cooking.

CARAMELIZING

A method whereby foods, primarily vegetables, are cooked slowly until the natural sugar in the food causes browning.

CLARIFYING BUTTER

Set a sauté pan over low heat and add 4 ounces (115 g, 1 stick) butter. Let the butter sit over the heat, without stirring, just until melted. Remove immediately from the heat and let the butter sit for a short while until it separates. Use a spoon to skim off and discard any white foam on top, then slowly pour the pure butter into a glass measuring cup, being careful to leave the solids remaining at the bottom of the pan; you can also strain the butter through a cheesecloth-lined strainer. Use the clarified butter as needed now, refrigerating any unused in a tightly covered jar in the refrigerator, where it will last almost indefinitely.

CLEANING AND TRIMMING

Leeks: Just at the place where the light green starts on the leek, about an inch (2.5 cm) above the white part, cut off and discard the dark green leaves. Slice off the roots, then make a lengthwise cut from the top of the leek almost through the bottom. Rinse the leek thoroughly under cold water, separating the leaves to make sure to eliminate any dirt between them. Drain well before using.

Mushrooms: Wipe the mushrooms clean with a dampened paper towel (do not wash!), then slice off the ends of the stems and use mushrooms as directed.

HARD-BOILING EGGS

Place eggs in a saucepan, cover well with water, and bring to a boil over medium-high heat. When the water starts boiling, immediately turn off the heat and cover the pan. Let the eggs sit, covered, in the water for 11 to 14 minutes, according to their size (12 minutes for large). Then drain off the water and, with the eggs still in the pan, run cold water into the pan and let the eggs cool to the desired temperature. Peel and use as directed in the recipe.

JULIENNING

A method of cutting vegetables or other ingredients into matchstick strips. Slice your ingredient into lengthwise slices about ⅛-inch (3-mm) thick. Then stack the slices into ⅛-inch (3-mm) thick lengthwise strips. Finally, holding the strips together, cut into crosswise pieces of whatever length you desired. If the ingredient you are julienning is round, slice off a bit from the bottom so the ingredient will sit firmly on the work surface as you slice down.

MAKING AGED BALSAMIC VINEGAR

Since aged balsamic vinegar, such as the twenty-five- or thirty-year-old kind, is expensive and may be difficult to find, you can make a substitute. In a saucepan, add ½ cup (100 g) sugar to 2 cups (480 ml) of ordinary balsamic vinegar and set over low heat, stirring to dissolve the sugar. Then let cook for 20 to 40 minutes, until the mixture is reduced to about ¾ cup (180 ml) and is syrupy. Use as needed or store in the refrigerator for future use.

MAKING BREAD CRUMBS

Use slices of slightly stale bread, if possible. If only fresh bread is available, place a few slices on a baking sheet and lightly toast, for just a few minutes, in a 300°F (149°C) or 350°F (177°C) oven. Then pulse in a food processor until the desired size of bread crumb is reached. Unused bread crumbs may be frozen.

POACHING

A method in which an ingredient is simmered in liquid at just below the boiling point.

ROASTING GARLIC

Preheat the oven to 400°F (204°C). Leaving the skin on a whole head of garlic intact, slice off about ¼ inch (6 mm) across the top of the head, exposing the garlic cloves. Drizzle a few teaspoons of olive oil over the exposed cloves, then wrap the head in aluminum foil, place in a small baking dish, and bake for 30 to 35 minutes, or until the garlic feels soft when you press it. Let cool slightly, then use your fingers to press the flesh of the garlic out of the skin of each clove. Use as directed in a recipe or simply eat it. Delicious!

SWEATING

A technique by which ingredients are cooked in a small amount of fat over low heat, often covered, until they are tender but still hold their shape. With this method, the ingredients become tender without browning and they basically cook in their own juices.

TOASTING

Bread, Country, or French Baguette: Heat the oven to 350°F (177°C). Cut the bread into slices and place on a greased baking sheet, Bake for about 5 minutes, or until lightly golden brown. Cool on a rack.

Bread Cubes: Heat the oven to 300°F (149°C). Stack 4 slices of white bread on top of each other. Using a serrated knife, cut into large cubes; removing the crust is optional. Arrange the cubes in a single layer on a baking sheet and bake for 10 to 15 minutes, shaking once or twice, until lightly browned and crisp. Cool on a rack.

Nuts: Toasting nuts is a process that has to be done under a vigilant eye because the nuts can turn from toasted to burned in a split second. For that reason, a heavy skillet on top of the stove is the best way to go, since you can watch it all the way—and it's a method that works for all the nuts you could possibly want to toast.

Set a heavy skillet, preferably cast iron, over medium heat and let heat for about a minute, or until the surface feels hot when you hold your hand above it (do not touch!). Scatter in your nuts and let cook for about a minute, then start stirring the nuts as they continue to cook for another 2 minutes or so, until they smell toasty and are lightly colored (in the case of sliced or slivered almonds or hazelnuts) or slightly darker (like pecans or walnuts). Then remove immediately from the heat and turn out onto a plate to cool. Total cooking time: 2 to 3 minutes, 4 minutes tops.

A note on pistachios: Be sure you take care when toasting pistachios, as they can become very bitter. Because these nuts are darker when raw than most others, it is difficult to judge toasting by the color. For best results, taste them often while they are toasting.

Seeds (pumpkin or squash): Heat the oven to 375°F (191°C). Make sure the seeds are cleaned of all fibers and are dry. Toss the seeds with a small amount of olive oil in a bowl, just to barely coat the seeds. Scatter in a rimmed baking sheet and bake for 7 to 10 minutes, until lightly browned and crisp. Remove to a plate to cool.

Seeds (sesame, white, or black): Set a dry heavy skillet, preferably cast iron, over medium heat until hot, about 1 minute. If toasting white seeds, add to the skillet and cook and stir until lightly colored, 3 to 5 minutes; if toasting black seeds, add to the skillet and cook and stir until the seeds become lighter in color and smell "toasty," 3 to 5 minutes. In both cases, watch carefully so the seeds don't burn. Quickly turn out of the skillet to a plate to cool.

Unsweetened flaked coconut: Set a dry heavy skillet, preferably cast iron, over medium heat until hot, about 1 minute. Add the coconut and cook and stir until the coconut is golden, about 5 minutes; watch carefully so the coconut doesn't burn. Quickly turn out of the skillet to a plate or baking sheet to cool.

ACKNOWLEDGMENTS

Somehow, the two simple words "thank you" don't seem nearly strong enough to convey the depth of my gratitude to every single person who helped make this book a reality. In fact, you and I would not even be holding it in our hands right now had it not been for the following incredible individuals.

First and foremost, to my wonderful husband, Joe, and my beautiful children, Nina, Damien, Julia, Monica, and Andrea—along with their spouses, Shawn, Laura, and T.J., and all their children—who gave me the daily strength, support, and encouragement I needed to tackle this huge of a project. They did so with unwavering love and no complaints, literally. (Even when they were eating hot dogs while I was writing about grilled lobster.) I owe them big time—and maybe a lobster or two.

To my gifted agent, Jeanne Fredericks, who never once stopped believing in me or the worth of my book. From beginning to end, she represented me with total grace, diplomacy, and aplomb, all of which are her strengths (and my weaknesses).

To the dynamic A-team at Page Street Publishing: Will Kiester, Marissa Giambelluca, Meg Baskis, Meg Palmer, and Jill Browning. Their enthusiasm, which was undeniably contagious, never waned once, even throughout all the unexpected twists and turns of the process. In fact, they helped make the entire journey a real joy—and my dream a reality.

To (long drum roll with cymbal crash, please) all the fabulous, big-hearted, mega-talented super chefs who agreed to participate. They took a gamble on me, a virtual unknown nationally, but I hope I've done them proud. This magnificent book is a tribute to each and every one of them. Their hard work. Their incredible dedication. And their unbelievably generous nature. Even though they are all culinary gods in my eyes, I now consider them my newfound friends, too. Boy, am I lucky!

To all the chefs' dedicated assistants, coordinators, managers, marketers, publicists, and reps (too many to mention, really) who gently nudged their bosses and kindly helped facilitate this book's timely completion. As my go-betweens, I owe them all a huge debt of gratitude.

To the one and only Ken Goodman, photographer extraordinaire. He rocked it all! From his rapport with the chefs . . . to his professional demeanor . . . to his invaluable suggestions and contributions . . . to his breathtaking photographs, he surpassed all my expectations (which were high to begin with). And to his crackerjack assistant, Lisa McGilvray, who did double duty as scheduler/travel agent/calender updater/calmer of nerves. I'd also like to sneak in my appreciation here to Ken's wife, Jessica, and their kids, Sadie and Henry, who patiently held down the fort at home while he was jet-setting around the country on all my shoots.

To the incomparable Ted Allen, who so graciously agreed to write my foreword. (I had to pinch myself when he said yes!) He took time out of his own super-hectic schedule to do so, and I need him to know how appreciative I am. Greater eloquence could not have come from anyone else.

Many thanks to SieMatic for the use of their gorgeous kitchen showroom.

And last, but most certainly not least, to everyone who tested the recipes in this book. Their feedback (excuse the pun!) helped fine-tune every ingredient and instruction to make it a rewarding, foolproof experience for you. These wonderful individuals include Connor Benton, Schuyler Berdan, Mika Gedeon, Marissa Giambelluca, Dan Lipke, Sarah Monroe, Christina Mulé, Elizabeth Seise, Alison Taylor, and Natasha Taylor.

Thank you from the bottom of my heart, one and all.

ABOUT THE AUTHOR

Maria Isabella is both a bestselling cookbook author and an award-winning writer with more than 30 years' experience in the worlds of food, advertising, and marketing.

She began life as a first-generation daughter of newly arrived immigrant parents. Her father, from Serbia; her mother, from Italy. In fact, she only spoke Serbian and Italian until she started school. But she certainly knew how to eat well, as her parents had turned their entire backyard into a full-blown garden boasting a complete variety of vegetables, fruit trees, grapevines, and berry bushes. They believed in natural, organic, farm-to-table foods before the concept was ever considered trendy.

After Maria finally learned to speak English, she went on to graduate from college with honors and earn a degree in communications with a minor in international marketing. Pausing her budding career to get married and start a family, she reentered the workforce when the youngest of her five children, a set of identical twins, started third grade. Her new position as a senior copywriter for a global ad agency led to interesting freelance assignments that took full advantage of her growing passion: cooking and baking.

She eventually became an ad hoc cookbook editor for Vitamix, a focus group member for both America's Test Kitchen and *Bon Appétit*, a recurring judge for the International Association of Culinary Professionals (IACP) cookbook awards, a reviewer of new cookbooks released by Penguin Random House and the Crown Publishing Group, an invited judge for local recipe contests, a contributing writer for *Edible* magazine, a dessert examiner, a recipe tester, a cooking and baking instructor, a local chapter board member of Les Dames d'Escoffier, a member of the James Beard Foundation, and a blogger. Oh yeah, she also wrote a cookbook or two.

Today, Maria enjoys a somewhat slower pace as a part-time content marketing and social media editor for American Greetings, but she still likes to try new recipes from her extensive library of cookbooks (two hundred and counting!), mostly for her grandchildren.

Maria and her husband, an attorney-cum–master of spaghetti sauce and baseball-size meatballs, live in the great food mecca of Cleveland, Ohio. They enjoy traveling the world and (yep, you guessed it!) trying new cuisines.

For more fun facts and information, visit Maria's website at www.maria-isabella.com.

INDEX